1985

The Author

In spite of his world-wide reputation as one of the leading novelists of his day, many people do not realise quite how versatile Anthony Burgess is. His writings include criticism, scripts and translations, his book and lyrics were used in the Broadway musical, *Cyrano*, adapted by him from Edmond Rostand's *Cyrano de Bergerac*, and he has composed a Symphony which has been publicly performed in the USA. His books have been published all over the world and include *A Clockwork Orange*, *The Clockwork Testament*, *Inside Mr Enderby*, *One Hand Clapping* and *Beard's Roman Women*.

1985

Anthony Burgess

Arrow Books

Arrow Books Limited
17-21 Conway Street, London W1P 6JD

An imprint of the Hutchinson Publishing Group

London Melbourne Sydney Auckland
Johannesburg and agencies throughout
the world

First published by Hutchinson 1978
Arrow edition 1980
Reprinted 1980, 1981, 1983 and 1984

The author is grateful to Mrs Sonia Brownwell
Orwell, Martin Secker & Warburg Ltd, and
Harcourt Brace Jovanovich, Inc., for
permission to use lines from *1984* by George
Orwell

Printed and bound in Great Britain by
Anchor Brendon Limited, Tiptree, Essex

ISBN 0 09 921450 4

to Liana

Contents

$2 + 2 = 5$

a notice put up in Moscow during the first Five Year Plan, indicating the possibility of getting the job done in four years, if workers put their backs into it

Part One

1984

Catechism

When did the twentieth-century nightmare begin?

In 1945, when, for many people, it seemed to have ended.

How did it begin?

With the first use of atomic bombs, developed with urgency to finish speedily a war that had gone on too long. But with the end of the conflict between the fascist States and the free world (which was not all free, because a great part of it was totalitarian), the stage was cleared for the enactment of the basic encounter of the century. The communist powers faced the capitalist powers, and both sides had unlimited nuclear weapons.

So that – ?

So that what had been used to end one war was now employed to start another.

What was the outcome of the Great Nuclear War of the 1950s?

Countless atomic bombs were dropped on the industrial centres of western Europe, the Americas and the Soviet Empire. The devastation was so terrible that the ruling élites of the world came to realize that nuclear warfare, in destroying organized society, destroyed their own capacity for maintaining power.

So that – ?

By common consent the nuclear age was brought to an end. Wars henceforth would be waged with conventional weapons of the kind developed during the Second World War. That wars should continue to be fought, and on a global scale, was taken for granted.

What was the disposition of the nations at the end of the Great Nuclear War?

The end of that war saw the world divided into three large power-units or superstates. Nations did not exist any more. Oceania was the name given to the empire comprising the United States, Latin America and the former British Commonwealth. The centre of authority was probably, but not certainly, North America, though the ideology that united the territories of the superstate had been developed by British intellectuals and was known as English Socialism or Ingsoc. The old geographical nomenclatures had ceased to have much meaning: indeed, their association with small national loyalties and traditional cultures was regarded as harmful to the new orthodoxy.

What happened to Great Britain, for instance?

Britain was renamed Airstrip One – a neutral designation not intended to be contemptuous.

The other superstates?

The two other superstates were Eurasia and Eastasia. Eurasia had been formed by the absorption of the whole of continental Europe into the Soviet Union. Eastasia was made up of China, Japan and the south-east Asian mainland, together with portions of Manchuria, Mongolia and Tibet that, bordering on the territories of Eurasia, fluctuated in imposed loyalty according to the progress of the war.

War?

War between the superstates started in 1959, and it has been going on ever since.

War with conventional weapons, then?

True. Limited armament and professional troops. Armies are, by the standards of earlier modern wars, comparatively small. The combatants are unable to destroy each other: if they could, the war would end, and the war must not end.

Why must it not end?

War is peace, meaning war is a way of life to the new age as peace was a way of life to the old. A way of life and an aspect of political philosophy.

But what is the war about?

Let me say first what the war is *not* about. There is no material cause for fighting. There is no ideological incompatibility. Oceania, Eurasia and Eastasia all accept the common principle of a single ruling party and a total suppression of individual freedom. The war has nothing to do with opposed world-views or, strictly, with territorial expansion.

But it has to do with – ?

The ostensible reason for waging war is to gain possession of a rough quadrilateral of territory whose corners are Tangier, Brazzaville, Darwin and Hong Kong. Here there is a bottomless reserve of cheap coolie labour, with hundreds of millions of men and women inured to hard work and starvation wages. The contest for this prize is conducted in equatorial Africa, the Middle East, southern India, and the Malay archipelago, and it does not move much outside the area of dispute. There is also a measure of fighting around the northern icecap, where valuable mineral deposits are believed to lie.

Ostensible. The real aim?

To use up the products of the industrial machine, to keep the wheels turning but the standard of living low. For the well-fed, physically contented citizen, with a wide range of goods for consumption and the money to buy them, is a bad subject for an oligarchical state. A man filled with meat turns his back on the dry bones of political doctrine. Fanatical devotion to the ruling party comes more readily from the materially deprived. Moreover, loyalty and what used to be called patriotism are best sustained when the enemy seems to be at the gates.

What enemy?

A good question. I said perpetual war, but it is not, to be strictly accurate, always the same war. Oceania is sometimes in alliance with Eurasia against Eastasia, sometimes with Eastasia against Eurasia. Sometimes she faces an alliance of the other two. The shifts in alignment occur with great rapidity and require correspondingly rapid readjustments of policy. But it is essential that the war be officially presented as always the same war, and it follows that the enemy must always be one and the same. The enemy at any given point in time must be the eternal enemy, the enemy past and future.

Impossible.

Impossible? The ruling party has total control of the collective memory and, by the alteration, or strictly rectification, of records, can easily bring the past into line with the present. What is true now must always have been true. Truth is actuality. Actuality is now. There is another reason for requiring an eternal enemy, but consideration of that had best be deferred.

Until – ?

Until you properly understand the true aim of Ingsoc.

Describe Oceanian society.

It is very simply stratified. Eighty-five per cent of the population is proletarian. The proles, as they are officially called, are despicable, being uneducated, apolitical, grumbling but inert. They perform the most menial tasks and are satisfied with the most brutish diversions. The remaining fifteen per cent consists of the Party – Inner and Outer. The Inner Party is an elective aristocracy, dedicated to the implementation of the Ingsoc metaphysic. The Outer Party is made up of functionaries, a kind of lower civil service whose members are employed in the four main departments of government – the Ministries of Love, Plenty, Truth and Peace.

Peace?

Really war. But war is peace.

Who is the head of the Party?

A personage called Big Brother who, never having been born, can never die. Big Brother is God. He must be obeyed, but he must also be loved.

Is that possible?

It is essential.

But can one be made to love to order?

There are ways and means. The elimination of marital love, of love between parents and children, the destruction of joy in sex and in begetting help to direct what may be regarded as an emotional need towards its proper object. The existence of the traitor Emmanuel Goldstein, always in league with the enemy, who hates Big Brother and wishes to destroy Oceania, ensures a perpetual diffusion of fear and loathing among the population, with a compensatory devotion to him who alone can protect and save.

What is the Ingsoc metaphysic?

Ultimate reality, like the first cause or causes, has no existence outside the mind that observes it. Sense-data and ideas alike are mere subjective phantoms. The mind is not, however, an individual mind but a collective one. Big Brother's mind contains all others. His vision of reality is the true one, and all others are false, heretical, a danger to the State. The individual must learn to accept without question, without even hesitation, the vision of the Party, using a technique known as doublethink to reconcile what appear to be contradictions. Outward conformity of belief is not enough. There must be total and sincere allegiance. If the individual memory of the past conflicts with Party history, the device of instantaneous memory control must be employed. Any contradiction can be resolved, and must be. Doublethink – wholly instinctive, sincere, unqualified – is an essential instrument of orthodoxy.

What, apart from metaphysical idealism and the perfection of its diffusion through the body of the Party, is the true aim of Ingsoc?

If you expect demagogic hypocrisy, you will not get it. Rule is not directed towards the welfare of the ruled. Rule is for power. The Party desires total control of everything outside itself, ingesting all of exterior reality into its organism, but it is deliberately reluctant to absorb its enemies. The war with Eastasia or Eurasia or both will never end, the treacherous Goldstein will never die, because Ingsoc needs enemies as a nutcracker needs nuts. Only over an enemy can power be satisfactorily exercised. The future is a boot perpetually crushing the face of a victim. All other pleasures will in time be subordinated to the pleasure of power – food, art, nature and, above all, sex.

May nobody revolt against this monstrous denial of human freedom?

Nobody. Except, of course, the occasional madman. It is the loving concern of Big Brother to restore such a deviate to sanity. And then to vaporize him as a flaw in the pattern, to convert him into an unperson. Rebellion belongs to the old way. And what is this *human freedom*? Freedom from what? Freedom to do what? A man may be free of illness as a dog may be free of fleas, but freedom as an absolute is freedom in a void. The watchwords of old revolutions were always nonsense. Liberty. Equality. Fraternity. The pursuit of happiness. Virtue. Knowledge. Power is different. Power makes sense. God is power. Power is for ever . . . .

Intentions

There are many who, not knowing Orwell's novel *Nineteen Eighty-Four*, nevertheless know such terms as doublethink and Newspeak and Big Brother, and, above all, associate the cipher 1984 with a situation in which the individual has lost all his rights of moral choice (this is what *freedom* means) and is subject to the arbitrary power of some ruling body – not necessarily the State. That the year 1984 may come and go without the realization of the nightmare – with, indeed, an augmentation of personal freedom and a decay of corporate power – will not necessarily invalidate the horrible identification. Doublethink, which the art of fiction can abet, enables us to reconcile the most blatant disparities. In the film Stanley Kramer made of Nevil Shute's novel *On The Beach*, the world comes to an end in 1962. Seeing the film in a television old-movie slot, we in the seventies can still shudder at what is going to happen in the sixties. In an idyllic 1984, the 1984 of Orwell's vision will still serve as a symbol of humanity's worst fears.

1984 is used as a somewhat vague metaphor of social tyranny, and one has to regret the vagueness. American college students have said, 'Like 1984, man,' when asked not to smoke pot in the classroom or advised gently to do a little reading. By extension, the term Orwellian is made to apply to anything from a computer print-out to the functional coldness of a new airport. There are no computers on Airstrip One, and most of the buildings we hear of are decaying Victorian. Present-day Leningrad, with its façades in need of a lick of paint, its carious warehouses, is closer to the look of Big Brother's London than is, say, Dallas International. For Orwellian read Wellsian – specifically the décor of the 1936 film *Things to Come*. The whole point of the urban scene in *Nineteen Eighty-Four* is that it doesn't matter what it looks like, since reality is all in the mind. And there is nothing 'Orwellian' about particular deprivations – like a ban on copulation in trams: it is the total and absolute, planned, philosophically consistent subordination of the individual to the collective that Orwell is projecting into a future that, though it is set in 1984, could be any time between now and 1962, when Nevil Shute brings the world to an end.

We have the following tasks. To understand the waking origins of Orwell's bad dream – in himself and in the phase of history that helped to make him. To see where he went wrong and where he seems likely to have been right. To contrive an alternative picture – using his own fictional technique – of the condition to which the seventies seem to be moving and which may well subsist in a real 1984 – or, to avoid plagiarism, 1985. Orwell's story was set in England, and so will be mine. Americans may reflect, before deploring this author's inverted chauvinism, that Britain has usually, with the absent-mindedness that acquired her an empire, blazed the major trails of social change. Change for the worse, as well as the better.

The French are cleverer than the British. They are skilful at the intellectual work of getting new constitutions on to paper, but the forms of new order have to emerge in Britain first. Montesquieu's *The Spirit of the Laws*, which had such an influence on the American Constitution, could not have been written if there had not been an existing social contract in Britain – one that Montesquieu did not thoroughly understand. The British do not well understand their political systems either, but they make no claim to be clever. It was Walter Bagehot who described the British as stupid. They lack the collective intelligence on which the French pride themselves, but they do not noticeably suffer for this deficiency. French intellectuality may have had something to do with the French surrender of 1940; British stupidity counselled resistance to Nazi Germany. Out of stupidity, which may be glossed as intuition, came the seventeenth-century revolution and the settlement of 1688, complete with limitation of the power of the executive and Bill of Rights. Out of the muddle and mess of contemporary Britain the pattern of the future of the West may well be emerging. It is a pattern which many of us must deplore, but only Ingsoc and Big Brother will prove capable of breaking it.

1948: an old man interviewed

Orwell's book is essentially a comic book.

A WHAT?

Consider. My bookshelves are disorganized. Wishing to reread *Nineteen Eighty-Four*, I could find at first only the Italian edition. This, for the moment, would have to do. But there was something wrong with that first sentence. *'Era una bella e fredda mattina d'aprile e gli orologi batterono l'una.'* It was a bright cold day in April and the clocks struck one. It ought to be *'battevano tredici colpi'*: they were striking thirteen. Latin logic, you see. The translator couldn't believe that clocks would strike thirteen, even in 1984, since no reasonable ear could ever take in more than twelve. So Italian readers were forced to miss a signal of the comic. Here's the original: 'It was a bright cold day in April, and the clocks were striking thirteen.' You laugh, or smile.

Or shudder?

Or shudder pleasurably. As at the beginning of the best kind of ogre story – one in which strange and terrible and unbelievable things are imposed on a familiar world. The world of English April weather, to begin with. A liverish wind mocking the sun. Swirls of dust at street corners. Grit in your eye. A run-down weary city at the end of a long war. Apartment blocks collapsing, a smell of boiled cabbage and old rag mats in the hallway.

COMIC, *for God's sake?*

Comic in the way of the old music halls. The comedy of the all-too-recognizable. You have to remember what it was like in 1948 to appreciate *Nineteen Eighty-Four*. Somebody in 1949 told me – that was the year the book came out – that Orwell had wanted to call it *Nineteen Forty-Eight*. But they wouldn't let him.

You remember the first reviews?

Yes. For the most part, tepidly laudatory. Only Bertrand Russell saw that this was that rare thing, a philosophical novel. The others said that Mr Orwell was more convincing with his boiled cabbage and rag mats than with his totalitarianism. Some truth there. Orwell was known as a kind of comic poet of the run-down and seedy. *Down and Out in Paris and London. The Road to Wigan Pier.* Wigan Pier – that was always a great music-hall joke. Orwell was good at things like working-class kitchens, nice cups of tea so strong as to be mahogany coloured, the latest murder in the *News of the World*, fish and chips, stopped-up drains. He got the feel of 1948 all right. Physical grittiness. Weariness and privation. Those weren't tragic. All the tragedy then was reserved for the Nazi death-camps. And the Russian ones too, but you weren't supposed to think of those. Ergo, our own troubles were comic.

You mean: if a thing isn't tragic it has to be comic?

In art, if not in real life. Let me tell you more about 1949, when I was reading Orwell's book about 1948. The war had been over four years, and we missed the dangers – buzz-bombs, for instance. You can put up with privations when you have the luxury of danger. But now we had worse privations than during the war, and they seemed to get worse every week. The meat ration was down to a couple of slices of fatty corned beef. One egg a month, and the egg was usually bad. I seem to remember you could get cabbages easily enough. Boiled cabbage was a redolent staple of the British diet. You couldn't get cigarettes. Razor blades had disappeared from the market. I remember a short story that began, 'It was the fifty-fourth day of the new razor blade' – there's comedy for you. You saw the effects of German bombing everywhere, with London pride and loosestrife growing brilliantly in the craters. It's all in Orwell.

What you seem to be saying is that Nineteen Eighty-Four *is no more than a comic transcription of the London of the end of the Second World War.*

Well, yes. Big Brother, for instance. We all knew about Big Brother. The advertisements of the Bennett Correspondence College were a feature of the pre-war press. You had a picture of Bennett *père*, a nice old man, shrewd but benevolent, saying, 'Let me be your father.' Then

Bennett *fils* came along, taking over the business, a very brutal-looking individual, saying: 'LET ME BE YOUR BIG BROTHER.' Then you get this business of the Hate Week. The hero of the book, Winston Smith, can't take the lift to his flat because the electricity's been cut off – we were all used to that. But the 1984 juice has been cut as part of an economy drive in preparation for Hate Week – typical government *non sequitur*. Now we knew all about organized hate. When I was in the army I was sent on a course at a Hate School. It was run by a suspiciously young lieutenant-colonel – boy friend of which influential sadist, eh? We were taught Hatred of the Enemy. 'Come on, you chaps, hate, for God's sake. Look at those pictures of Hun atrocities. Surely you want to slit the throats of the bastards. Spit on the swine, put the boot in.' A lot of damned nonsense.

And I suppose the contradiction of that section of the book is meant to be comic too?

Contradiction?

The electricity has been cut off, but the telescreen is braying statistics to an empty apartment. It's hard to accept the notion of two distinct power supplies.

I hadn't thought of that. I don't think anybody thinks of it. But there you are – a necessary suspension of disbelief, appropriate to a kind of comic fairy tale. And the television screen that looks at you – Orwell had lifted that from Chaplin's *Modern Times*. But it's prophetic, too. We're in the supermarket age already, with a notice saying, 'Smile – you're on TV!'

Did England have television in those days?

Are you mad? We'd had television back in the 1930s. The Baird system, what James Joyce called the 'bairdbombardmentboard' or something. Logie Baird, his name dimly echoing in Yogi Bear. I saw the very first BBC television play – Pirandello, *The Man with a Flower in His Mouth*. You got vision from your Baird screen and sound from your radio. Aldous Huxley transferred that system to his *Brave New World* – 1932, as I remember. Mind you, it's never been necessary actually to have television in order to appreciate its potentialities. The Queen in *Snow White* has a TV screen that puts out just one commercial. In England, Robert Greene has a TV screen or magic mirror for spying in *Friar Bacon and Friar Bungay*. That was about 1592. The

word existed before the thing. In 1948 the thing was back,
I think. It was evident then it was going to be a part of
everybody's life. Among the ingenuous there was a feeling that the faces that spoke at you were really looking.
The TV was intrusive. The first post-war programmes
were more didactic than diverting. The screen was for big
faces, not for the tiny figures of old movies. The adjustment of vision we take for granted now wasn't easy at first
– I mean the ability to take in a Napoleonic battle on a
pocket set. The TV set in the corner of the living-room was
an eye, and it might really be looking at you. It was a
member of the household, but it was also the agent of a
great corporation. I remember a lot of people were shy of
undressing in front of it.
You think this is comic? Listen –

> There was of course no way of knowing whether you were being watched at
> any given moment. How often, or on what system, the Thought Police
> plugged in on any individual wire was guesswork. It was even conceivable
> that they watched everybody all the time. But at any rate they could plug in
> on your wire whenever they wanted to. You had to live – did live, from habit
> that became instinct – in the assumption that every sound you made was
> overheard, and, except in darkness, every movement scrutinized.

No, not comic, but not as frightening as all that. It's the
possibility of being caught out by the electronic eye that
constitutes the real intrusion. Winston Smith isn't pursued to either the kitchen or the toilet – not, anyway, in
Victory Mansions – by Big Brother. (Incidentally, it seems
to me all wrong that he should be allowed to live alone in a
flat. Wouldn't it be a matter of dormitories with a police
thug in the end bed?) There can be plenty of subversive
thought in bed, in the dark. The telescreen is perhaps no
real menace – any more than bugging is to those who
know it is going on. It's a metaphor of the death of privacy. The important thing is that it can't be switched off.
It's like muzak, a perpetual reminder of the presence of
the big corporation, the State, the anti-self.
*But Winston is actually watched. He's rebuked from the screen
by the morning physical-jerks instructress.*
Yes, but the occasion's comic. We're not far from the
Billy Butlin Holiday Camps, so popular in the post-war
days. You were awakened in the morning with jocular
cries from tannoys. You were cajoled into before-breakfast
exercises to loud music.

Did Orwell know about these camps?

No, he died before they got going. And they didn't know about him. But the interesting thing is that they were immensely popular for a time, and that was when the term *camp* and the thought of even harmless regimentation ought to have sickened the average Briton. Of course, they were comparatively cheap. But that wasn't enough to recommend them. Men came out of the army to spend a summer fortnight with wife and family in an ambience which had a great deal of the army about it – reveille, cookhouses, dining-halls, organized diversions, physical jerks (an aspect of army life which most soldiers hated worse than going into battle). There were uniformed camp officers called redcoats – a name uncomfortably close to redcaps, which was what the Military Police were called. And there was always this loud big-brotherly voice from the loudspeakers, exhorting everybody to be happy. Late drinkers-up in the canteen at closing-time were danced off in a cunning conga-line by the female redcoats. The Butlin Holiday Camps proved that the British proletariat was not really averse to discipline. The working man opposed to army life not civilian freedom so much as the infusion of geniality into regimentation. The post-war proletariat accepted the Holiday Camps as readily as they accepted American Army units in English villages, endless shopping lines, the insolence of petty bureaucrats.

And that proves what?

I refuse to draw a moral. The moral that Orwell draws from what he saw of the British working man is terrible and excessive. I insist on looking for comedy.

And for an identification of 1984 with 1948?

Yes, which is part of the comedy, comedy a bit grim at times, positively black. And a touch of pathos. One wants to weep over Winston Smith, so recognizable as an Englishman of the forties bred out of the working class – 'a smallish, frail figure ... his skin roughened by coarse soap and blunt razor blades and the cold of the winter that had just ended'. Inured to cold weather and privation, undersized through a tradition of poverty and bad feeding. He looks out on London 'with a sort of vague distaste. ... Were there always those vistas of rotting nineteenth-century houses, their sides shored up with baulks of timber, their windows patched with cardboard

and their roofs with corrugated iron, their crazy garden
walls sagging in all directions?' The answer is – not
always. This is the London of war-time or just after. It's
certainly not a London of prophetic vision.

*It is, surely. How about the Ministry of Love, of Truth and so
on?*

Well, the Ministry of Truth may certainly be accepted as
the Broadcasting House where Orwell worked during the
war. Headquarters of the BBC. The other ministries
merely have to look like this prototype. In the Ministry of
Love there's that terrible room where the worst thing in
the world happens – Room 101. Room 101, in the base-
ment of Broadcasting House, was where Orwell used to
broadcast propaganda to India. Not far from Broadcasting
House was, and still is, a pub called the George, popular
with BBC employees. Sir Thomas Beecham christened it
the Gluepot, because his musicians got stuck in it. The
name itself has stuck. Now, in *Nineteen Eighty-Four* you
have this place with a bad aura, the Chestnut Tree Café,
where Winston Smith ends up with his clove-flavoured
gin, waiting for the bullet. They're one and the same
place, though the Chestnut Tree Café has a touch of the
Mandrake Club about it, a place where you drank gin of
mysterious provenance and played chess. Strangely, the
bad aura of the George began after Orwell's death. It was
the pub where you had a drink with Dylan Thomas, Louis
MacNeice or Roy Campbell and, on your next visit,
learned they were dead. Notice what the song is that Winston hears coming out of the telescreen as he drinks his gin
and puzzles over a chess problem:

> Underneath the spreading chestnut tree,
> I sold you and you sold me. . . .

We always associated that – not with those unpleasant
words, of course – with King George VI in his scoutmaster
capacity. The song was even turned into a dance, like the
Lambeth Walk, and was terribly and bucolically innocent.
Orwell really poisons the past when he puts in the sneer-
ing yellow note. Not funny. Not comic at all.

*But, otherwise, you'd say that the book was an exaggerated
picture of a bad time, no more?*

Oh, much more, but I have to establish that Orwell
wasn't really forecasting the future. Novels are made out

of sense data, not ideas, and it's the sensuous impact of this novel that counts to me. I mean the gin – giving off 'a sickly oily smell, as of Chinese rice-spirit' (how could Winston know that? That's the author himself, late of the Burma police, getting in the way.) The shortage of cigarettes, and the only cigarettes on the ration are called Victory, the very brand that was issued to us overseas British troops during the war – sporadically. The cheating of the senses with shoddy food, drink and tobacco, the rough clothes, coarse soap, blunt razor blades, the feeling of being unkempt and unclean – it was all there for fictional transference. It was a bad time for the body. One asked for the bread of minimal comfort and was offered instead the stone of progress.

Progress. That brings us to Ingsoc, doesn't it?

Yes. The torn poster on the street, flapped by the wind, with the single word INGSOC on it. English Socialism. I remember English Socialism coming to power in 1945, a landslide victory for the Left. They sang *The Red Flag* at the opening session of Parliament. It drowned *God Save the King* and *Rule Britannia* and *Land of Hope and Glory*. Winston Churchill, war leader and head of the Conservative Party, was first astonished that the country should reject him, the man who had led it through the valley of the shadow to the sunlit uplands of a qualified triumph, and later he spoke of betrayal. The justification of his rejection lay in that very astonishment: he just didn't seem to understand what had been going on.

Why is Winston Smith so called?

We'll come to that. We've some tricky waters to navigate now. Is English Socialism the same as Ingsoc? Did Orwell think it was? And yet he wanted Socialism. We all did. They say that English Socialism prevailed in 1945 because of the services vote. An elaborate apparatus was set up in ships and camps all over the world to enable British servicemen to exercise their citizen's right of suffrage. Very few abstained from voting. A great many – even those who, like myself, had been brought up in a Conservative tradition and were later to return to it – voted Labour without hesitation.

Why?

Oh, Winston Churchill himself had something to do with it. The senior officers liked him, but he wasn't all that

popular with the troops. He'd many of the qualities that
make a people's hero – eccentric colourfulness, a gift for
obscenity and coarse wit, a mode of speech that sounded
more demotic than that of certain of the Labour leaders –
though it was really the aristocratic twang of an earlier
age. He had a large capacity for brandy and cigars. But it
was unwise of him to smoke these when visiting the
troops. Some of us at times would have given our souls for
a puff at a Victory cigarette.

What, apart from the cigars, was the matter with him?

He was too fond of war. Many of us, by the time of the
1945 election, had been in uniform for nearly six years. We
wanted to get out and resume – or begin, most of us – our
real lives. Churchill orated about the dangers of a too-
hasty disbanding of the citizen army. An iron curtain had
come down in Eastern Europe; the Russian ally had
returned to his old role of the Bolshevik menace. We knew
nothing, we simple soldiers, of the new processes of
international politics – the sudden shifts of policy. We'd
thought Russia was our great fellow-fighter against fascist
tyranny, and now she'd become the enemy. We were
naïve enough to imagine that to great statesmen, as to us,
war was a necessary but painful interlude. We didn't
know that great statesmen consider war to be an aspect of
a continuing policy. We'd had enough of Churchill. He
wept when we rejected him.

*But Orwell obviously admired him. He wouldn't have named
his hero for him otherwise.*

No, no, no. It seemed to many of the first American
readers of *Nineteen Eighty-Four* that Winston Smith's name
was a symbol of a noble free tradition lost for ever. But it
was nothing of the kind. It was comedy again. The name
Winston Smith is comic: it gets a laugh from British readers. It also suggests something vaguely shameful, a political amateurism that never stood a chance against the new
professionals.

*The rejection of Churchill must surely have represented a very
small part of the reason for turning to Socialism in 1945. Wasn't
there compulsory instruction in civics during the war? Didn't
that lead servicemen to a wish for a change of government?*

To some extent. The greater part of the British population had never been much interested in politics, but there
was indeed a measure of compulsory civic education dur-

ing the war, especially in the army, with weekly discussions led by platoon commanders on topical material supplied by the Army Bureau of Current Affairs – ABCA, a whiff of the new age, the pregnant acronym. There was even a stirring song that nobody sang:

ABCA –
Sing it or say it –
Leading the way
To a brave new world.
Till over Europe, freed from her chains,
Liberty's flag is again unfurled,
We'll keep aflame
Democracy's torchlight,
Scorching the wings
Of this night of shame –
Freedom to all,
To act and to utter:
ABCA is calling
In freedom's name.

God help us. There were also lectures by education officers or sergeants on what was called the British Way and Purpose. There was, in fact, a self-avowed attempt to revive the idea of a well-informed citizen army on the lines of Cromwell's Roundheads, who are said to have known what they were fighting for. There were also frank borrowings from the Soviet Army, with its wall-newspapers and political commissars or polkoms.

What, on a point of historical interest, were or was the British Way and Purpose?

I'm not sure. It seems to have been divided, even schizophrenic. Or perhaps the Way and the Purpose were not easily compatible. Much of the material provided was embarrassingly diehard, with its glorification of a colonial system already in process of being dismantled, but articulate members of service audiences were at liberty, during the weekly session, to denounce imperialism and influence comrades who had hardly known that a British Empire existed. Other material was about the building of the Welfare State, with a unified national insurance scheme borrowed from Bismarck's Germany by Lord Beveridge, the Liberal, and known as the Beveridge Plan. I think the British Way was democratic and the British Purpose to establish a sort of cautious egalitarianism wherever

possible. I don't know. I do know that some reactionary
colonels refused to allow either ABCA or BWP sessions in
their battalions, saying that it was all 'socialism'.

Were there any revolutionary colonels?

Not in the British Army. There were plenty of
revolutionaries in the rank and file, though, and the odd
lieutenant from the London School of Economics. Generally speaking, however, the British class system found its
most grotesque expression in the British Army. The professional officers of high rank imposed traditional modes
of speech and social behaviour: an officer had to be a gentleman, whatever a gentleman was. Certainly there was, to
say the least, a general antipathy on the part of the troops
towards their officers, a great gulf of manners, speech,
social values, a chasm between those who had to lead and
those who did not want to be led. Thirty-odd years after
demobilization, there are many former other ranks who
enjoy a dream of avenging old insults, injustices, nuances
of upper-class disdain. There remains something still in
the memory of the 'officer voice' – the reedy vowels of
Field-Marshal Lord Montgomery, for instance – which
arouses a hopeless fury. The structure of the army was a
kind of gross parody of the structure of pre-war civilian
society. If a man entered the army as a mild radical, he
approached the 1945 election as a raging one. A Welsh
sergeant summed it up for me: 'When I joined up I was
red. Now I'm bloody purple.' If the British Communist
Party had fielded more candidates, the make-up of that
first post-War Parliament might have been very interesting indeed.

*And this was all it was? The British troops put the Labour
Party in because they didn't like Churchill and didn't like the
way the services were run?*

No, there was much more than that. Along with the
radical emotions there was a kind of utopianism necessary
to fighting men. They had to believe they were struggling
for something more than the mere defeat of an enemy.
They weren't defending a good cause against a bad but a
bad cause against a worse. Modern war disrupts civilian
society and makes it easier to rebuild than to reconstitute.
Rebuilding from scratch to secure long-delayed social justice – that had been a dream of the 1914–18 war, with its
slogan, 'A country fit for heroes to live in,' but the dream

had not been fulfilled. Discharged soldiers in slums or casualty wards, jobless and hopeless, wished they'd been killed on the Somme. It was not to happen again, the British said, and in fact it did not. In 1945, perhaps for the first time in history, the ordinary British people got what they asked for.

Did Orwell get what he asked for?

Orwell was a good Socialist and was delighted to see a Socialist government in power at last.

But his response was to write a terrifying novel in which English Socialism is far worse than either the Nazi or the Russian variety. Why? What went wrong?

I don't know. The English Socialism that came to power in 1945 had nothing of Ingsoc about it. There was power-seeking there, of course, as well as corruption, inefficiency, a love of control for its own sake, a dour pleasure in prolonging 'austerity'. British radicalism has never been able to rid itself of its Puritan origins, and perhaps it hasn't wished to. A typical figure of the post-War Socialist Government was Sir Stafford Cripps, the Chancellor of the Exchequer. He was a sour devotee of progress without pleasure, of whom Winston Churchill once said: 'There but for the grace of God goes God.' He was treated by the common people as something of a joke. Potato crisps were metathesized in his honour, and men in pubs would ask for a packet of 'Sir Staffs'. But he was no joke, and British Puritanism has been too obdurate a strain to laugh off. The Puritanism of 1984, which goes to the limit – not even Sir Stafford Cripps could abolish sex – owes a lot to 1948. Along with the austerity went an insolent bureaucracy, as I've said, and it was the more insolent the closer it was to the ordinary citizen, as in the local Food Office, but there was no Big Brother. Among the first readers in America of Orwell's book there were many who assumed that here was a bitter satire on Labour Britain; even a few of the stupider British Tories rubbed their hands gleefully at what Orwell seemed to be doing for the Tory vote. None of these seemed to know, what was available for the knowing, that Orwell was a committed Socialist and was to remain so till his death. The paradox of an English Socialism appalled by English Socialism remains to be resolved, and the resolution is an intricate business.

I think I can resolve it.

How?

Listen to this extract from The Road to Wigan Pier. *Orwell was looking from the window of a train into the backyard of a Northern slum:*

> A young woman was kneeling on the stones, poking a stick up the leaden waste-pipe. I had time to see everything about her – her sacking apron, her clumsy clogs, her arms reddened by the cold. She looked up as the train passed, and I was almost near enough to catch her eye. She had a round pale face ... and it wore, for the second in which I saw it, the most desolate, hopeless expression I have ever seen.... What I saw in her face was not the ignorant suffering of an animal. She knew well enough what was happening to her – understood as well as I did how dreadful a destiny it was to be kneeling there in the bitter cold ... poking a stick up a foul drain-pipe.

The same image comes in Nineteen Eighty-Four, *you remember. Mrs Parsons, in the first part of the book. Her wastepipe's blocked up and Winston Smith unblocks it for her. It's a kind of Sisyphus image. The hopelessness of the working-woman's lot. Orwell saw that the allegiance of a good Socialist was to the woman struggling with the wastepipe, not to the big men of the Party. And yet how could you help her without putting the Party in power? The Party's in power, but the waste-pipe remains clogged. It's the disparity between the reality of life and the abstraction of Party doctrine – that's what sickened Orwell.*

That's part of it. But put it another way. One of the troubles with political commitment is that no political party can tell the whole truth about man's needs in society. If it could, it wouldn't be a political party. And yet the honest man who wants to work for the improvement of his country has to belong to a party, which means – somewhat hopelessly – accepting what amounts to a merely partial truth. Only the vicious or stupid can accord total loyalty to a party. Orwell was a Socialist because he could see no future in a continuance of traditional *laissez faire*. But it's very difficult to sustain a kind of wobbly liberal idiosyncratic socialism of your own in the face of the *real* Socialists – those who want to push Socialism, with impeccable logic, to the utter limit.

You mean Orwell's Socialism was pragmatic rather than doctrinaire?

Look at it this way. When he worked for the left-wing paper *Tribune*, he had to withstand the rebukes of more orthodox readers who didn't like his writing about literature that seemed to hinder rather than help the 'cause' – the poems of the Royalist Anglican Tory T. S. Eliot, for instance, or the in-grown verbal experiments of James Joyce. He almost had to apologize for bidding his readers go and look at the first daffodils in the park instead of spending yet another Saturday distributing left-wing pamphlets. He knew what Marxism was about. He'd fought alongside Marxists in Spain, but he wasn't, like the redder British Socialists, prepared to blind himself to what Russia was doing in the name of Marxism. His radicalism was of a nineteenth-century kind, with a strong tinge of something older – the dissenting spirit of Defoe and the humane anger of Swift. Swift he declared to be the writer he admired with least reserve, and that Swift was Dean of St Patrick's in Dublin didn't offend his agnosticism. There's a bad but touching poem Orwell wrote – he sees himself in an earlier incarnation as a country rector, meditating in his garden, watching his walnuts grow.

There was more English than Socialism in his English Socialism.

Very neat, and there's some truth in it. He loved his country more than his party. He didn't like the tendency in more orthodox Socialists to inhabit a world of pure doctrine and ignore the realities of an inherited national tradition. Orwell prized his English inheritance – the language, the wild flowers, church architecture, Cooper's Oxford marmalade, the innocent obscenity of seaside picture postcards, Anglican hymns, bitter beer, a good strong cup of tea. His tastes were bourgeois, and they veered towards the working class.

But he couldn't identify himself with the workers. It's horrible that he should seem to blame the workers for his inability to join them. I mean, that total condemnation of the proles in Nineteen Eighty-Four....

He was sick, remember, and hopeless. He tried to love the workers but couldn't. After all, he was born on the fringe of the ruling class, he went to Eton, he spoke with a patrician accent. When he called on his fellow middle-class intellectuals to take a step downward and embrace the culture of miners and factory workers, he said: 'You have nothing to lose but your aitches.' But those were just what he could not lose. He had at heart the cause of working-class justice, but he couldn't really accept the workers as real people. They were animals – noble and powerful, like Boxer the horse in *Animal Farm*, but essentially of a different substance from himself. He fought against his inability to love them by desperate acts of dispossession – making himself down and out in Paris and London, spending the season in hell which produced the Wigan Pier book. He pitied the workers, or animals. He also feared them. There was a strong element of nostalgia in him – for the working-class life he couldn't have. Nostalgia has come to mean frustrated home-sickness. This got itself mixed up with another nostalgia.

You mean for the past. A vague and irrecoverable English past. Dickensian. That vitiated his Socialism. Socialism ought to reject the past as evil. Its eyes ought to be wholly on the future.

You're right. Orwell imagines a kind of impossibly cosy past – the past as a sort of farmhouse kitchen with hams hanging from the rafters, a smell of old dog. As a Socialist he should have been wary of the past. Once you start to yearn for kindly policemen, clean air, noisy free speech in pubs, families sticking together, roast beef and Yorkshire pudding, the fug of the old music hall you end up by touching your forelock to the squire. You oppose to that past a present full of political dogma, policemen with guns, adulterated beer, fear of being overheard, fish sausages. You remember the hero of *Coming Up for Air*. He bites into one of these horrors and says it's like biting into the modern world. There's a part of Orwell which fears the future. Even when it's Socialist, progressive, just, egalitarian. He wants to oppose the past to it, as though the past were a real world of solid objects.

It's the future that's supposed to be subversive. Yet Winston Smith has his subversiveness all in the past.

Well, the past *is* subversive in the sense that it opposes pragmatic values to doctrinaire ones. The human and not the abstract. Take even the least considerable and most neutral-seeming areas – like, for instance, weights and measures. *Nineteen Eighty-Four* is genuinely prophetic in presenting a Britain that's yielded to the metric system. At the end of the war there hadn't as yet been any official proposal to replace the traditional units with the Cartesian abstractions of France, but everybody felt sure the change was on its way. Inches and feet and yards were too much based on thumbs and limbs to be acceptable in a truly rational world. A prole beer-drinker whom Winston Smith encounters complains of having to drink in litres or half-litres: he wants the traditional pint. But despite the protests of traditionalists, Britain had to be given a decimal coinage. Orwell knew this was going to happen: he puts dollars and cents into Winston's pocket. As the British know, the reality is the heavy dollar still called the pound, with a hundred new pence or *p* in it – shameful liquidation – but the dehumanization remains. Americans have a monetary system that carries an aura of revolutionary necessity, and they'll never understand how the loss of the old shillings and half-crowns and guineas wounded British hearts. For the whole point of the traditional system was that it sprang out of empirical common sense, not abstract rationality. You could divide by any number – 3, 4, 5, 6, 7, 8, 9, 10. If you try to divide by 3 now you get a recurring decimal.

7 and 9?

Yes. You added a shilling to a pound and that gave you a guinea. A seventh of a guinea was three shillings. A ninth of a guinea was two shillings and fourpence, or a Malayan dollar. So long as there were seven days in a week, four weeks in a month, twelve months in a year, and an hour divisible by 3 and its multiples, the old system made sense. But it had to go: it was too reasonable, too human. It also committed the grave error of keeping ancient folk traditions alive. 'Oranges and lemons, say the bells of St Clement's. You owe me five farthings, say the bells of St Martin's.' This old song is a mysterious link between Big Brother's London and the ancient buried one of churches and chimes and liberty of conscience. But in 1984 nobody knows what a farthing is. Everybody began to cease to know in 1960. 'Sing a song of sixpence' – it means nothing. Nor does Falstaff's reckoning at the Boar's Head – a capon, 2s 2d; sauce, 4d; sack, two gallons, 5s 8d; anchovies and sack after supper, 2s 6d; bread ½d.

Why does Orwell make Winston Smith wake up with the name Shakespeare on his lips?

Shakespeare, though still not proscribed by the Party, is subversive. God knows what the Newspeak version of him is like, but the Oldspeak Shakespeare is full of private lives and individual decisions. Shakespeare means the past. But note that Winston Smith evokes the past in a far more dangerous way. He buys, for 2 dollars 50, a beautiful book full of blank paper of a creamy smoothness unknown to his modern world – or, for that matter, to present-day Soviet Russia. He also buys an archaic writing instrument – a pen with a real nib. He is going to keep a diary. He feels able to do this with a modicum of safety because his writing-table is in a small alcove out of range of the tele-screen. He first writes at random, and then lets his thoughts wander. He looks down at the page and finds that he's written over and over again, in total automatism, the words DOWN WITH BIG BROTHER. Mrs Parsons, the woman with the blocked-up drain, knocks on the door but, for all Winston knows, it may already be the Thought Police. Going to the door he sees that he's left the book open. 'It was an inconceivably stupid thing to have done. But, he realized, even in his panic he had not wanted to smudge the creamy paper by shutting the book while the ink was wet.' The subversive act and the materials with which it's been performed – these have become one thing. The past is an enemy of the Party. Hence the past is real. After dealing with Mrs Parsons's problem, he comes back and writes:

> To the future or to the past, to a time when thought is free, when men are different from one another and do not live alone – to a time when truth exists and what is done cannot be undone:
> From the age of uniformity, from the age of solitude, from the age of Big Brother, from the age of doublethink – greetings!

We can talk to the past as we can talk to the future – the time that is dead and the time that has not yet been born. Both acts are absurd, but the absurdity is necessary to freedom.

Conversely, freedom itself is thus proved to be absurd.

Yes yes. Freedom was certainly an archaic absurdity to some of Orwell's contemporaries. Britain and her allies had been fighting fascism, which was dedicated to the liquidation of personal liberty, but one of those allies was herself as repressive of freedom as the enemy. When Soviet Russia became a friend of the democracies –

A brief friend.

Yes. That was when those of tender conscience believed the war had lost its meaning. That was when it was in order for Englishmen to love Stalin and praise the Soviet system. There were certain British intellectuals, especially those associated with the left-wing magazine the *New Statesman*, who even preached totalitarianism on the Stalinist model. Kingsley Martin, its editor, for instance. Orwell summed up Martin's view of the Soviet leader something like this: Stalin has done ghastly things, but on balance they've served the cause of progress, and a few million liquidations must not be allowed to obscure that fact. Means justify the end. That's very much the modern view. It was Orwell's belief that most British intellectuals were given to totalitarianism.

He went too far.

Well, consider – it's in the nature of an intellectual to be progressive, meaning that he'll tend to support a political system that will bring rapid changes about in the commonalty, meaning a disdain for the lumbering old democratic process with its tolerance of opposition. A state machine that can pulp up the past and create a rational future. A very intellectual idea. There had been intellectuals who seemed 'fascist' to Orwell, in love with authoritarianism or at least tolerant of it – writers like Eliot, Yeats, Evelyn Waugh, Roy Campbell, even Shaw and Wells – but the intellectuals who were not fascist were usually communist, which – in terms of state power, repression, the one-party system and so on – amounted to the same thing. Terms like fascism and communism represent no true polarity, despite the war. They could both, thought Orwell, be contained in some such name as Oligarchical Collectivism.

And yet any progressive idea is an intellectual creation. Without intellectuals, with their cries for greater social justice, removal of the profit motive, equal incomes, the death of inherited privilege and so on – would there be any progress at all?

But is their talk of progress truly disinterested? Orwell knew enough, as Arthur Koestler did, of the springs of political authority in Europe. No man, it seemed to them, strove for political leadership solely out of altruism. Koestler had been sent to jail by the system he supported. Orwell fought for freedom in Spain, and he had to run for his life when Russian Communism condemned Catalonian Anarchism. Intellectuals with political ambitions had to be suspect. For, in a free society, intellectuals are among the under-privileged. What they offer – as school-teachers, university lecturers, writers – is not greatly wanted. If they threaten to withdraw their labour, nobody is going to be much disturbed. To refuse to publish a volume of free verse or take a class in structural linguistics – that's not like cutting off the power supplies or stopping the buses. They lack the power of the capitalist boss on the one hand and the power of the syndicalist boss on the other. They get frustrated. They find pure intellectual pleasures inadequate. They become revolutionaries. Revolutions are usually the work of disgruntled intellectuals with the gift of the gab. They go to the barricades in the name of the peasant or the working man. For 'Intellectuals of the world unite' is not a very inspiring slogan.

But why was Orwell frightened of the intellectuals? The intellectuals were not running the Labour Government in the late 1940s.

No. The Labour leaders weren't *New Statesman* fanatics. They'd no desire to turn Britain into a miniature Stalinist Russia. But there was a whisper, perhaps more than a whisper, of the danger that comes from more and more State control, a bigger bureaucracy, the devaluation of individuality that inevitably follows a doctrine of equality. Strictly, a Socialist government can only fulfil its ideal of total public ownership if granted a perpetual mandate. The very notion of Socialism is undemocratic, if by democracy we mean opposed parties, a free vote, periodic general elections. Parliament has increasingly the task of pushing through party legislation and ignoring such issues as the rights of the individual, which Members of Parliament are primarily there to protect. Orwell didn't live to see the compromise which English Socialism now represents – a minimum of public ownership, a social-security apparatus that costs too much, a mass of 'equalizing' laws not easily enforceable, and a necessary thwarting of individual, as opposed to collective, endeavour. But, not even in those first heady days of Socialism, could the concept of Ingsoc have begun to germinate – except in some university lecturer's lodgings.

You think it was purely an onomastic trick?

Yes, the taking over quite cynically of an honourable name and then debasing it. Who, after Hitler, can ever mention National Socialism again without a shudder? The link between the English Socialism of 1948 and that of 1984 is purely nominal. We have to imagine this – that a group of *New Statesman* intellectuals has taken over not just England but the entire English-speaking world. As England, or Airstrip One, cannot be more than a satellite of America, the assumption must be that the *New Statesman* oligarchs have first prevailed in the United States and then, armed with power, come home again. Nothing could be more absurd, and Orwell knows it. There's been a great atomic war, but it has left much of Victorian London still standing – absurd again. There are vague memories of political purges in the fifties, but Winston Smith's own reminiscences – and indeed those of practically everyone else – are of the indistinctness of a fading dream. Absurdity. Amnesia seems to have hit everyone, even when they're not exercising 'memory control'. It finds a sort of counterpart in our acceptance that we don't know, nor do we greatly care, how the revolution happened. It's just a necessary device to get the intellectuals into power. Absurd, comic. I'm back where I started.

So you think there's nothing, as it were, nineteeneightyfourish about Nineteen Eighty-Four? *That it was all there waiting in 1948?*

Yes, in a sense. What was merely in the newspapers or the official records – like torture and concentration camps – had to be imported into Britain. The intellectual totalitarianism had to be fictionally realized. But novels are really made out of day-to-day experience, and Winston Smith's frustrations were ours too – dirty streets, decaying buildings, sickening food in factory canteens, the government slogans on the walls –

Slogans? Like FREEDOM IS SLAVERY *and* IGNORANCE IS STRENGTH?

Not quite like those. Those are pure Nazi Germany. But I remember when I came home from overseas army service that the first peace-time government poster I saw showed a haggard sorrowing woman in black, with the legend KEEP DEATH OFF THE ROADS. Naturally, somebody had crossed that out and substituted SHE VOTED SOCIALIST. We were used to posters put out by the Ministry of Information, mostly ham-handed, not subtly ambiguous like the Ingsoc ones. YOUR FORTITUDE, YOUR PATIENCE, YOUR ENDURANCE WILL BRING US VICTORY. You and us, you see. No wonder we all became bloody purple. BE LIKE DAD,

KEEP MUM. That nearly provoked a riot among wage-earning mothers. Slogans had become part of the British way of life. Orwell gave us nothing new.

Wasn't the warning new?

What warning? He was only telling us what Milton told Cromwell's England – hang on to your liberties. Perhaps not even that. He was playing the intellectual game of constructing a working model of a utopia, or cacotopia. How far, he seems to say, can I push things without seeing the careful structure collapse? He'd already made animals play at the Russian Revolution. Another game. He was being the Swift *de nos jours*. Build your own horrible future, enjoy yourself. The thing works, and Orwell has to be pleased. But the pleasure has nothing to do with politics.

Thank you, Mr er – .

Ingsoc considered

It is, without doubt, an oligarchy of refined intellects that is running Oceania. It cultivates a subtle solipsistic philosophy; it knows how to manipulate language and memory and, through these, the nature of perceived reality; it is totally aware of its reasons for wanting power. It has learned how to subdue personal ambition in the interests of collective rule. There is no Hitlerian or Stalinist cult of personality: Big Brother is an invention, a fictional personage and hence immortal, and those who are contained in him partake of his immortality. The oligarchy has learned how to reconcile opposites, not through dialectic, which is diachronic and admits absence of control over time, but through the synchronic technique of doublethink. Ingsoc is the first professional government, hence the last.

Its doctrines are based on a metaphysic, not a mere ethic. To make a political system emerge logically out of a concept of reality is, of course, as old as Plato. The tricky thing about the Ingsoc view of reality is that it is appropriate to a single mind rather than a collective one. Before the metaphysic can assume validity, a collective must learn the technique of thinking in the manner of a single mind.

Solipsism – which derives from Latin *solus* and *ipse* (lone self, self alone) – is a theory that posits reality as existing only in the self, or, more reasonably, states that only the self can be definitely known and verified. This means that nothing in the external world can be assumed to have independent existence. It goes further than mere idealism, which says that mind is real and matter no more than ideas, but does not necessarily reject the existence of many minds and, ultimately, the unifying mind of God. Solipsism teaches that minds other than that of the *solus ipse* cannot be proved to have existence. It does not, however, go so far as to permit temporal or spatial discontinuity within the individual mind, to deny logic, to admit contradiction or inconsistency. If the single mind is real, its memories cannot be illusions. The past is not malleable: it has true existence in the mind and cannot be altered by the present. Mathematical propositions have unchangeable validity, and 2 and 2 always make 4. The collective solipsism of Ingsoc will have none of this. 2 and 2 may sometimes be 4, but they are just as likely to add up to 3 or 5. This sounds like madness. But the Party teaches that madness is an attribute of the individual mind that will not merge itself into the collective one and accept its view of reality. Winston Smith holds fast to simple arithmetic as truth unassailable even by the Party, but part of his rehabilitation consists in learning how to be convinced – not merely to go through the motions of accepting – that 2 and 2 add up to whatever the Party says. Shakespeare, who foresaw most things, foresaw this:

PETRUCHIO:	I say it is the moon.
KATHERINA:	I know it is the moon.
PETRUCHIO:	Nay then you lie; it is the blessed sun.
KATHERINA:	Then God be blest, it is the blessed sun,
	But sun it is not, when you say it is not;
	And the moon changes even as your mind.
	What you will have it nam'd, even that it is,
	And so it shall be so for Katherine.

The self-willed Winston Smith has to be tamed, and O'Brien is his Petruchio.

The Party's solipsism is far saner – or certainly far more consistent – than anything the term was traditionally held to encompass. The *solus ipse* could be said to enclose space, but time lay outside it and was one of the conditions of its existence. But logically the single mind, if it is the only reality, must contain everything, and that includes time. It also includes logic. The senses are the mere instruments that serve the self, and they are subject to error. That sensory illusions exist none will deny: how can we distinguish between illusion and reality? It is unwise to rely at all on the evidence of the senses. The self only, that non-material verifiable entity, can state what is and is not real. To confer on the self the one attribute it requires to be ultimately real – fixed, unchanging, immortal, like God – it is necessary only to make that self a collective one.

There is something in this notion of an undying, omnipotent, omniscient, all-controlling human entity which lifts the heart rather than depresses it. The history of man is the tale of an arduous struggle to control his environment, and failure always comes from the limitations of the individual, whose brain grows tired, whose body decays. Exalt the collective and diminish the individual, and history will be a procession of human triumphs. Which is precisely what the history of Ingsoc is.

If the collective is to function in the manner of a single mind, all its members or cells must agree as to what they observe or remember. The technique known as doublethink is a device for bringing individual observation and memory into line with whatever the Party decrees, at any given moment, to be the truth. It is the given moment that contains reality. The past does not determine the present; the present modifies the past. This is not so monstrous as it appears. The memory of the collective mind has to be contained in records, and it is in the nature of records to be alterable. Take it further: the past does not exist, and so we are at liberty to create it. When one created past conflicts with another, doublethink has to be brought into operation. It is formally defined in the book attributed to Emmanuel Goldstein, Oceania's necessary and hence unkillable public enemy, and entitled *The Theory and Practice of Oligarchical Collectivism*:

> Doublethink means the power of holding two contradictory beliefs in one's mind simultaneously, and accepting both of them. The Party intellectual knows in which direction his memories must be altered; he therefore knows that he is playing tricks with reality; but by the exercise of doublethink he also satisfies himself that reality is not violated. The process has to be conscious, or it would not be carried out with sufficient precision, but it has also to be unconscious, or it would bring with it a feeling of falsity and hence of guilt. Doublethink lies at the very heart of Ingsoc, since the essential act of the Party is to use conscious deception while retaining the firmness of purpose that goes with complete honesty. To tell deliberate lies while genuinely believing in them, to forget any fact that has become inconvenient, and then, when it becomes necessary again, to draw it back from oblivion for just so long as it is needed, to deny the existence of objective reality and all the while to take account of the reality which one denies – all this is indispensably necessary.

The existence of Goldstein's book – a creation of the Party as much as Goldstein himself – may be taken to be an act of doublethink of a very subtle kind. The Party is literally accusing itself of telling lies through the mouth-piece of an invented enemy. It is disclosing the motive of deception behind the telling of the truth. It is conflating two irreconcilable processes – the conscious and the unconscious. It is the repository of all virtue and yet admits the possibility of guilt. Doublethink is being employed to define doublethink.

Doublethink may not be laughed or shuddered off as a chilling fantasy of the author: Orwell knew he was doing little more than giving a formulation to a thought process that man has always found to be 'indispensably necessary' – and not merely a thought process either: we are more accustomed than we know to reconciling opposites in our emotional, even our sensory, experiences. '*Odi et amo*,' said Catullus: I love and hate the same object and at the same time. Orwell himself once pointed out that meat is both delicious and disgusting. The sexual act is engaged in of the free will; at the same time one is driven to it by a biological urge; it is ecstatic, it is also bestial. Birth is the beginning of death. Man is a double creature, in whom flesh contradicts spirit and instinct opposes aspiration. Orwell recognized his own doubleness very sharply. He was both Eric Blair and George Orwell, a product of the fringe of the ruling class who tried to identify himself with the workers, an intellectual who distrusted intellectuals, a word-user who distrusted words. Doublethink, though rightly presented as an instrument of oppression, seems also a very reasonable technique. Our own attitude to doublethink is inevitably doublethinkful.

Hardly a single human experience is unequivocal. The philosophers of Ingsoc are as good as saying: We recognize that human life is partly a matter of juggling with opposites. We wish that new kind of human entity, the collective, to function as a unity. Unity of thought can only be achieved by forging a deliberate technique for dealing with contradictions. (Note that when you came to that word *forge* you had to perform a very rapid act of double-think. You were, in a context that suggested cheating, ready to give it the meaning of falsifying a cheque or making counterfeit money. But then you had to give it the primary meaning of making, fashioning, with an aura of blacksmith honesty about it.) Let us control phenomena, not be controlled by them. Let there be total harmony between the past and the present. What is the past, that inert ill-understood mass of vague events, that it should exert an influence on the sunlit reality of now? It is a question of who is to be master.

Doublethink is a serious enough formulation of a mode of mental control, but it is also a grim joke. Orwell, like the rest of us, is sickened by the lies of politicians, but he knows that such lies rarely spring from genuine cynicism or contempt of the mob. A politician is wholly devoted to his party, and he has to find ways of making the worse cause seem the better. He does not want to lie, but he has to. He can evade bare-faced falsehood by gobbledygook or euphemism, by ambiguity or redefinition. There is only one sin, and that is to be caught out. The people complain of high prices and unemployment, and they are told: 'These are the growing pains of a new prosperity.' Sir Harold Wilson, when prime minister of Britain, was asked to give evidence of economic progress under Socialism. He said: 'You cannot quantify an élan.' The Pentagon is given to using expressions like 'anticipatory retaliation', meaning unprovoked assault. The communists use the term democracy to mean the opposite of what democrats mean by it. Orwell ironically deplores a lack of system, of logic and consistency, in political utterances. Compared to the amateurish evasions of most ministers of state, doublethink has a certain nobility.

Ingsoc may be thought of as being too sure of its own strength to have to stoop to dishonesty. It does not like verbal obfuscation: it insists on the utmost clarity of expression, both written and spoken. To this end it has manufactured a special kind of English called Newspeak. This is characterized by grammatical regularity, syntactical simplicity, and a vocabulary shorn of unnecessary synonyms and confusing nuances. Strong verbs have disappeared, so that all preterites and past participles end in –ed, as in swim, swimmed; fight, fighted; go, goed. Comparison of adjectives is always on the pattern of good, gooder, goodest. Plurals always end in –s – mans, oxes, childs. This rationalization was perhaps bound to occur of its own accord sooner or later, without the assistance of the State, but Ingsoc, claiming total control of all human activities, has kindly speeded up the process. The limitation of vocabulary is a godsend or statesend: there are far too many words in the traditional language. *Bad* is unnecessary when we can have *ungood*, and intensifiers can be reduced to *plus* and, for greater emphasis, *doubleplus*. *Doubleplusungood* is a very efficient way of rendering 'terribly or extremely bad', and *plusunlight* expresses what great darkness is really about.

But the chief aim of the Ingsoc philologists is not to prune the language to a becoming spareness so much as to make it capable of expressing State orthodoxy so wholeheartedly that no shadow of the heretical can intrude. *Free* still exists, along with *unfree* and *freeness* and *freewise*, but the notion can now only be a relative one, as in 'free from pain'. *Free* meaning 'politically free' cannot make sense, since the concept no longer exists. A statement about political freedom, like the Declaration of Independence, cannot well be translated into Newspeak:

> We hold these truths to be self-evident, that all men are created equal, that they are endowed by their creator with certain inalienable rights, that among these are life, liberty and the pursuit of happiness. That to secure these rights, Governments are instituted among men, deriving their powers from the consent of the governed. That whenever any form of Government becomes destructive of those ends, it is the right of the People to alter or abolish it, and to institute new Government. . . .

Orwell says that the nearest one can come to a Newspeak translation is to 'swallow the whole passage up in the single work *crimethink*. A full translation could only be an ideological translation, whereby Jefferson's words would be changed into a panegyric on absolute government.' Let us, anyway, try:

> We say that truth writed is truth unwrited, that all mans are the same as each other, that their fathers and mothers maked them so that they are alive, free from all diseases and following not food but the feeling of having eated food. They are maked like this by their parents but Big Brother makes them like this. Big Brother cannot be killed but he is to be killed, and in his place there will be himself. . . .

Nonsense, like saying that the sun will come out at night. Or, for that matter, that Big Brother is doubleplusungood when, by sheer definition, he cannot be.

In 1984 we are only in the initial phase of the control of thought through language. The State's three slogans are WAR IS PEACE; FREEDOM IS SLAVERY; IGNORANCE IS STRENGTH. Orwell has informed us that the term *freedom* can have no absolute, or political, meaning, and yet here it is, with just that meaning, blazoned on the State's coinage. Moreover, the State is using paradox in an untypically witty manner: it is the last kick of wit, we must suppose, before the endless night sets in. We are being told, very pithily, that war is the normal condition of the new age, as peace was of the old, and that it is through fighting the enemy that we best learn to love the tranquillity of our bondage. To be left to choose our own way of life is an intolerable burden; the agony of free choice is the clank of the chains of servitude to one's environment. The more we know the more we are a prey to the contradictions of thought; the less we know the better able are we to act. All this is true, and we bless the State for ridding us of the intolerable tyrannies of democracy. Men and women of the Party are now free to engage in intellectual games.

Winston Smith's work *is* an intellectual game, and a highly stimulating one. It consists in expressing doublethink through Newspeak. He has to correct errors in back numbers of *The Times* – meaning, in uningsoc terms, to perpetrate lies – and to compose his corrections, which often amount to full news items, in a language which, restricting semantic choice, promotes ingenuity. (Incidentally, we may ask why separate copies of *The Times* are allowed to exist, since the collection of them for destruction must be a great nuisance. Why shouldn't it appear as a wall newspaper?) The fascination is that of composing a long telegram. Indeed, Newspeak is recognizably based on press cablese. Orwell must have relished the exchange between Evelyn Waugh and the *Daily Mail*, when that great popular organ sent him to cover the conflict in Abyssinia: WHY UNNEWS – UNNEWS GOODNEWS – UNNEWS UNJOB – UPSTICK JOB ASSWISE. Newspeak is, God help us, fun. Doublethink is, God help us again, absorbing mental acrobatics. There may be dangers in living in 1984, but there is no need for dullness.

Consider the situation for eighty-five per cent of the community – the proles. There is a war going on, but there is no conscription, and the only bombs that fall are dropped by the government, just to remind the population that there *is* a war going on. If consumer goods are short, that is an inevitable condition of war. There are pubs, with beer sold in litre glasses, there are cinemas, a state lottery, popular journalism and even pornography (produced mechanically by a department of the Ministry of Truth called Pornosec). There is no unemployment, there is enough money, there are no oppressive regulations – indeed, there are no laws at all. The entire population, prole and Party alike, is untroubled by crime and violence on the democratic model. One may walk the streets at night quite unmolested – except, presumably, by police cars on the pattern of Los Angeles. There are no worries about inflation. One of the major issues of our time, racial intolerance, is lacking. As Goldstein tells us, 'Jews, Negroes, South Americans of pure Indian blood are to be found in the highest ranks of the Party.' There are no stupid politicians, time-wasting political debates, ridiculous hustings. The government is efficient and stable. There are even measures devised to eliminate from life the old agonies of sex and the oppressions of family loyalty. No wonder the system is universally accepted. Winston Smith, in his ingenuous obsession with the liberty of being able to say that $2 + 2 = 4$, and his conviction that the entire army is out of step except himself, is a boil, a pustule, a flaw on the smooth body of the collective. It is a mark of charity on the State's part that he should be cured of his madness, not immediately vaporized as a damned nuisance.

During the Second World War, Orwell bravely wrote that neither Hitler nor his brand of socialism could be written off as sheer evil or morbidity. He saw the attractive elements in the Führer's personality as well as the appeal of a political system that had restored self-respect and national pride to a whole people. Only a man capable of appreciating the virtues of oligarchy could write a book like *Nineteen Eighty-Four*. Indeed, any intellectual disappointed with the wretched outcome of centuries of democracy must have a doublethinkful attitude to Big Brother. Given a chance, confronted by the spectacle of hundreds of millions living, joyfully, resignedly, or without overmuch complaint, in a condition of what the West calls servitude, the intellectual may well jump over the wall and find peace in some variety or other of Ingsoc. And the argument against oligarchical collectivism is perhaps not one based on a vague tradition of 'liberty' but one derived from awareness of contradictions in the system itself.

In the cellars of the Ministry of Love, O'Brien tells Winston of the world the Party is building:

> A world of fear and treachery and torment, a world of trampling and being trampled upon, a world which will grow not less but *more* merciless as it refines itself. Progress in our world will be progress towards more pain. The old civilisations claimed that they were founded on love and justice. Ours is founded upon hatred. In our world there will be no emotions except fear, rage, triumph, and self-abasement.... Children will be taken from their mothers at birth, as one takes eggs from a hen. The sex instinct will be eradicated. Procreation will be an annual formality like the renewal of a ration card. We shall abolish the orgasm. Our neurologists are at work upon it now.... There will be no distinction between beauty and ugliness. There will be no curiosity, no enjoyment of the process of life. All competing pleasures will be destroyed. But always – do not forget this, Winston – always there will be the intoxication of power, constantly increasing and constantly growing subtler. Always, at every moment, there will be the thrill of victory, the sensation of trampling on an enemy who is helpless. If you want a picture of the future, imagine a boot stamping on a human face – for ever....

Winston's heart freezes at the words, his tongue too: he cannot reply. But our reply might be: man is not like this, the simple pleasure of cruelty is not enough for him; the intellectual – for only intellectuals with, behind them, a long deprivation of power, can articulate a concept like that – demands a multiplicity of pleasures; you talk of the intoxication of power growing subtler, but it seems to me you refer to something growing simpler; this brutal simplification surely entails a diminution of the intellectual subtlety that alone can sustain Ingsoc. Pleasures cannot, in the nature of things, remain static; have you not heard of diminishing returns? It is a very static pleasure you are talking about. You speak of the abolition of the orgasm, but you seem to forget that pleasure in cruelty is a sexual pleasure. If you kill the distinction between the beautiful and the ugly, you will have no gauge for assessing the intensity of the pleasure of cruelty. But to all our objections O'Brien would reply: I speak of a new kind of human entity.

Exactly. So he does. It has nothing to do with humanity as we have known it for several millennia. The new human entity is a science fiction concept, a kind of Martian. A remarkable quantum leap is required to get from Ingsoc – which is grounded philosophically on a very old-fashioned view of reality and, politically, on familiar state oppression – to Powerman, or whatever the new concept is to be named. Moreover, this proposed 'world of trampling and being trampled upon' has to be reconciled with the continuing processes of government. The complexities of running a State machine are hardly compatible with the vision – not necessarily a demented vision – of exquisitely indulged cruelty. The pleasure of power has much to do with the pleasure of government, in the variety of modes of imposing an individual or collective will on the governed. 'A boot stamping on a human face – for ever' – that is a metaphor of power, but it is a metaphor inside a metaphor. Winston, hearing the eloquence with which the Ingsoc dream is propounded, thinks he hears the voice of madness – the more terrifying because it encloses his own apparent sanity. But madness never encloses sanity; only poetry, which has the surface appearance of madness, can do that. O'Brien is poeticizing. We, the readers, are chilled and thrilled, but we do not take the poem literally.

We all know that no politician, statesman or dictator seeks power for its own sake. Power is a position, a point, an eminence, a situation of control which, when total, confers pleasures which are the reward of the power – the pleasure of choosing to be feared or loved, to do harm or good, condemn or reprieve, tyrannize or bestow benefits. We recognize power when we see a capacity for choice unqualified by exterior factors. When authority is expressed solely through doing evil, then we doubt the existence of choice and hence the existence of power. The ultimate power, by definition, is God's, and this power would seem non-existent if it were confined to condemning sinners to hell. A Caligula or a Nero is recognized as a temporary aberration, a disease that cannot hold power for long because it can choose nothing but the destructive. The evil dreams of a Marquis de Sade derive from an incapacity to achieve orgasm by any regular means, and we accept that he has no choice but to lay on the whips or the burning omelettes. He makes more sense than

O'Brien's sadism freed from the need for orgasm. O'Brien is talking not of power but of a disease not clearly understood. Disease, of its nature, either kills or is cured. And if this disease is not disease but a new kind of health for a new kind of humanity – well, so be it. But we are the old kind of humanity and not greatly interested. Kill us by all means, but let us not pretend that we are being eliminated by a higher order of reality. We are merely being torn by a tiger or pulverized by a Martian deathray.

Reality is inside the collective skull of the Party: the exterior world can be ignored or shaped according to the Party's will. If the electrical supplies fail that nourish the machines of torture, what then? Is the juice, in some mystical way, still flowing? And what if the oil supplies give out? Can mind affirm that they are still there? There is no science, since the empirical process of thought has been outlawed. Technological skills are all harnessed to the making of armaments or the elimination of personal freedom. Neurologists are abolishing the orgasm, and we must assume that cognate specializations are devising other modes of killing pleasure or enhancing pain. No preventive medicine, no advances in the curing of diseases, no transplantation of organs, no new drugs. Airstrip One would be powerless to stem a strange epidemic. Of course, the decay and death of individual citizens matters little so long as the collective body flourishes. 'The individual is only a cell,' says O'Brien. 'The weariness of the cell is the vigour of the organism. Do you die when you cut your finger-nails?' Still, this vaunted control of the outside world is bound to seem impaired when incurable disease asks the mind to get out, it has outlived its tenancy of the flesh. Of course, logically bodies may disappear altogether, and Big Brother will find himself in the position of the Church Triumphant, souls or Soul static in the empyrean for ever and ever, but with no flesh to thwack or nerves to get screaming.

Nature ignored or ill-treated has a way of expressing her resentment, as the margarine commercials used to remind us. Pollution, says the Party, does not exist. Nature will powerfully disagree. Earthquakes cannot be shrugged off with doublethink. Collective solipsism represents a hubris the gods of the natural order would be quick to punish with failed harvests and endemic syphilis. Orwell was writing at a time when the atom bomb was feared more than the destruction of the environment. Ingsoc, though, has its provenance in an even earlier time, the Wellsian one, when nature was inert and malleable and man could do with her whatever he wished.

Even the processes of linguistic change are an aspect of nature, taking place unconsciously and, it appears, autonomously. There is no guarantee that the State's creation of Newspeak could flourish impervious to gradual semantic distortion, vowel mutation, the influence of the richer Oldspeak of the proles. If *doubleplusungood* or, with a *Macbeth* flavouring, *doubledoubleplusungood*, is applied to an ill-cooked egg, we shall need something stronger to describe a sick headache. *Unbigbrotherwise uningsocful doubledoubledoubleplusungood*, for instance. *Bigbrotherwise*, as an intensifier, can be as neutral as *bloody*. Big Brother, being the only deity, can be invoked when we hit a thumb with a hammer or get caught in the rain. This is bound to diminish him. Pejorative semantic change is a feature of all linguistic history. But – one forgets – one is dealing with a new kind of human being and a new kind of reality. We should not strictly be speculating about something that cannot happen here.

We must take *Nineteen Eighty-Four* not only as a Swiftian toy but as an extended metaphor of apprehension. As a projection of a possible future, Orwell's vision has a purely fragmentary validity. Ingsoc cannot come into being: it is the unrealizable ideal of totalitarianism which mere human systems unhandily imitate. It is the metaphorical power that persists: the book continues to be an apocalyptical codex of our worst fears. But why do we have these fears? We are so damnably pessimistic that we almost want Ingsoc to happen. We are scared of the State – always the State. Why?

Cacotopia

'Wherever you are, you always have to work. There's never any excuse for idleness. Nor are there any taverns, public houses, brothels. There are no opportunities for seduction, no places for secret meetings. Everyone has his eye on you. You not only have to get on with your work, you have to make proper use of your spare time.' That is a rough translation from Sir Thomas More's *Utopia*. It does not sound so bad in the original Latin. In colloquial English it has an Ingsoc flavour. The term utopia, which More invented, has always had a connotation of ease and comfort, Lotus Land, but it merely means any imaginary society, good or bad. The Greek elements which make up the word are *ou*, meaning *no* or *not*, and *topos*, meaning a place. In many minds the *ou* has been confused with *eu* – well, good, pleasant, beneficial. Eupepsia is good digestion, dyspepsia we all know. Dystopia has been opposed to eutopia, but both terms come under the utopian heading. I prefer to call Orwell's imaginary society a cacotopia – on the lines of cacophony or cacodemon. It sounds worse than dystopia. Needless to say, none of these terms are to be found in Newspeak.

Most visions of the future are cacotopian. George Orwell was an aficionado of cacotopian fiction, and we may regard his *Nineteen Eighty-Four* as competing in the Worst of All Imaginary Worlds stakes. It has won by many lengths, with the next worst mare of the night somewhat broken-winded. But without that book Orwell might not have felt inclined to compete.

The book is *We*, by E. I. Zamyatin. Orwell reviewed it in *Tribune* on 4 January, 1946, having at last got his hands on it several years after hearing that it existed. It was always an elusive book, and, if it is easily obtainable now in most languages, that is because Orwell was influenced by it. It is not, apparently, to be found in the original Russian. Zamyatin was a Russian novelist and critic who died in Paris in 1937. Imprisoned by the Czarist government in 1906, he was put into a cell on the same corridor of the same prison by the Bolsheviks in 1922. He disliked most governments and leaned to a kind of primitive anarchism. His title seems to allude to a slogan of Bakunin, the father of anarchism: 'I do not want to be I, I want to be We.' This seems to mean that the antithesis of the powerful central-ized State is not the individual but the free anarchic com-munity.

We was written about 1923. It is not about Russia; indeed, it does not portray, even obliquely, any existing political system, but it was refused publication on the grounds that it was ideologically dangerous. One can see why, despite the wildness of the fantasy and the remote-ness of the setting. We are in the twenty-sixth century, and the scene is a utopia whose citizens have so tho-roughly lost their individuality that they are known only by their numbers. They wear uniforms, and are called not human beings but 'unifs'. As the Orwellian telescreen has not yet been invented, they live in glass houses so that the State police, known as the Guardians, can supervise them more easily. They eat synthetic food and, for recrea-tion, march about to the tune of the State anthem, which blares through loudspeakers. There is no marriage, but sex is allowed at stated intervals. For the 'sex hour' curtains are permitted to be drawn in the glass apartments. There is a sex ration-book of pink tickets: one's partner in the act signs the counterfoil. The Single State, as it is called, is ruled by a personage as remote and vague as Big Brother: he is known as the Benefactor. He is voted to power, but he has no opponents.

The philosophy of the Single State is simple. It is not possible to be both happy and free. Freedom imposes the agony of choice, and God, in his infinite mercy, tried to shut out that agony by shutting Adam and Eve into a glorious garden where they had all they needed. But they ate the forbidden fruit of choice, were driven out of the garden and have had to pay for free will with unhappi-ness. It is the duty of all good States to bring back Eden and scotch the snake of freedom.

The hero-narrator is D–503, an engineer who tries to be a good citizen but, to his horror, finds atavistic impulses breaking in. He falls in love, which is forbidden. Worse, he falls in love with a woman – I–330 – who leads an underground resistance movement given to such vices as tobacco and alcohol and the use of the imagination. D–503, who is no true revolutionary, is given the opportunity to be rid of imagination, which the State declares to be a disease, by X-ray treatment. Cured, he betrays the conspirators to the police and watches unmoved while I–330 is tortured. All the dissidents are at length executed – by means of the Machine of the Benefactor, which reduces them to a puff of smoke and a pool of water: literal liquidation. Orwell comments:

> The execution is, in fact, a human sacrifice, and the scene describing it is given deliberately the colour of the sinister slave civilisations of the ancient world. It is this intuitive grasp of the irrational side of totalitarianism – human sacrifice, cruelty as an end in itself, the worship of a Leader who is credited with divine attributes – that makes Zamyatin's book superior to Huxley's.

That reference, of course, is to Aldous Huxley's *Brave New World*, which, like *Nineteen Eighty-Four* itself, was written under the influence of *We*. Orwell rejected *Brave New World* as a possible blueprint for even a remote future: he blamed Huxley for a lack of 'political awareness'. Huxley depicts, it will be remembered, a utopia which, like Zamyatin's, has sacrificed freedom for happiness. Perhaps, recalling Dr Johnson's strictures on the loose use of a term which is made to express the joys of heaven as well as a little girl's delight in a new party frock, the term *content* would be better. Pre-natal biological techniques and Pavlovian conditioning are capable of rendering the citizens of the future content with the lots which the State has bestowed upon them. There is no equality. Society is rigidly stratified, from the Alpha-plus intellectual to the Epsilon-minus semi-moron, but immobility is biologically built into the system. The family, which Freud said is responsible more than anything for human discontent, has been abolished; children are produced in test-tubes; all sex is promiscuous and sterile. It is a totally stable society, in which hedonism is the prevailing philosophy. But Orwell considers that such a society would not be dynamic enough to last long. 'There is no power hunger, no sadism, no hardness of any kind. Those at the top have no strong motive for staying at the top, and though everyone is happy in a vacuous way, life has become so pointless that it is difficult to believe that such a society could endure.'

The pursuit of happiness is, then, pointless. Is liberty? Presumably not the struggle for it. Orwell cannot conceive of a society whose rulers are not motivated by the desire to impose their wholly malevolent will on the ruled. This is 'political awareness'. The dynamic of society consists in a resistance on the part of the ruled to the will of the ruler – welcomed by the ruler as an inimical drive that merits suppression, with all its concomitant sadistic pleasures. In stating that this is what society is like, Orwell has history on his side. Why do men seek to rule others? Not for the benefit of those others. To be convinced of this is to be 'politically aware'.

And yet there have been utopians – H. G. Wells, for one – who believed that the just society could be built. The Wellsian future is derided in *Nineteen Eighty-Four* – a clean innocent vision of a world full of Hellenic (or Mussolinian) architecture, rational dress and labour-saving devices, in which reason is in control and such base emotions as a lust for power and the exercise of cruelty are rigidly kept under. Had Orwell really been an Anglican rector, he would have known what term to use for describing it. He would have said that the rational society, with scientific socialism triumphant, was 'Pelagian'.

The terms Pelagian and Augustinian, though theological, are useful for describing the poles of man's belief as to his own nature. The British monk Pelagius, or Morgan (both names mean 'man of the sea'), was responsible for a heresy condemned by the Church in AD 416 which, nevertheless, has never ceased to exercise an influence on Western moral thought. The view of man which it opposes appears, to most people, monstrously implausible, even though it is part of traditional Christian doctrine. This view states that man enters the world in a state of 'original sin' which he is powerless to overcome by his own efforts alone: he needs Christ's redemption and God's grace. Original sin relates a certain human predisposition to evil to the crime of disobedience committed by Adam in the Garden of Eden. As Zamyatin reminds us, Adam did not wish to be happy; he wished to be 'free'. He desired free will, meaning the right to choose between courses of action – in effect, between courses on which a moral judgement could be made. He did not realize that, once free, he was more likely to choose the wrong than the right. He would consult the gratification of his own ego rather than what was pleasing to God. He thus condemned himself to divine punishment, which only God's mercy could rescind.

Pelagius denied this terrible endowment. Man was free to choose salvation as much as damnation: he was not predisposed to evil, there was no original sin. Nor was he necessarily predisposed to good: the fact of total freedom of choice rendered him neutral. But he certainly possessed the capability, with no hindrance from unregenerate forces within, to live the good life and, by his own efforts, to achieve salvation at the end. St Augustine, Bishop of Hippo, reaffirming the orthodox doctrine of original sin and the need to pray for divine grace, loudly condemned Pelagius. But Pelagius has, in more than fifteen hundred years, refused to be silent.

In secularizing these views of man, we tend to forget about sin and concentrate on what is good for society and what is not. The Wellsian brand of Pelagianism blamed criminal impulses on environment. What priests called 'original sin' was a reaction to poverty, slum tenements, enforced ignorance and squalor. A scientific socialism would extirpate what was called crime. Man was not just morally neutral: being a social animal, he wanted to be a 'good', or responsible, member of society; it was his environment that had been getting in the way. But, if there are secular Pelagians (though not so many as before about 1933), there seem to be no secular Augustinians. Those who deny the possibility of moral progress, who insist on the destructive, libidinous urges in man as an unregenerable aspect of his condition, take, of necessity, a traditional theological stance. If anything can be done to improve man, it must come from without – from God, or the Life Force, or a miraculous extraterrestrial virus brought in by a UFO.

The polarity is, however, not all that rigid. We are all both Pelagian and Augustinian, either in cyclical phases, or, through a kind of doublethink, at one and the same time. Orwell was Pelagian in that he was a Socialist, Augustinian in that he created Ingsoc. It sometimes seems that the political life of a free community moves in the following cycle: a Pelagian belief in progress produces a kind of liberal régime that wavers when men are seen not to be perfectible and fail to live up to the liberal image; the régime collapses and is succeeded by an authoritarianism in which men are made to be good; men are seen not to be so bad as the Augustinian philosophy teaches; the way is open for liberalism to return. We tend to Augustinianism when we are disgusted with our own selfishness, to Pelagianism when we seem to have behaved well. Free will is of the essence of Pelagianism; determinism (original sin makes us not altogether responsible for our actions) of Augustinianism. None of us are sure how free we really are.

Invoking two opposed, but interpenetrating, kinds of theology, we find ourselves flirting with terms like *good* and *evil*. These, cut off from their base, tend to become semantically vague though strongly emotive. It is embarrassing to hear a politician use them, less embarrassing – though still disturbing – to hear him juggling with *right* and *wrong*. Strictly, the moral duality which these words represent is within the province of the State, while good and evil relate to theological permanencies. What is right, what is wrong? Whatever the State says. It is right to hate Eastasia and then, in the next breath, wrong. It is right to eat potatoes in a time of glut, wrong to eat them in a time of shortage. The Conservatives are wrong and we, the Socialists, are right – a matter of premises. The laws of the State are always changing and, with them, the values of right and wrong. The need to oppose unchanging values to the State's flighty judgements makes us ready to say that this enactment is good, even though it is wrong, and that one, though right, evil.

It has always been easier to point to examples of evil than of good. An Augustinian might say: inevitably, since evil is in our nature, and good not. *Good*, anyway, is a word with a wide spectrum of meaning: we are liable to confuse ethical good with what, for want of a better term, we must call aesthetic good. One of the great human mysteries is supposed to be provided by the Nazi death camps. A commandant who had supervised the killing of a thousand Jews went home to hear his daughter play a Schubert sonata and cried with holy joy. How was this possible? How could a being so dedicated to evil move without difficulty into a world so divinely good? The answer is that the good of music has nothing to do with ethics. Art does not elevate us into beneficence. It is morally neutral, like the taste of an apple. Instead of recognizing a verbal confusion we ponder an anomaly, or, like George Steiner, assert that a devotion to art renders men less sensitive to moral imperatives. 'Men who wept at Werther or Chopin moved, unrealizing, through literal hell.' There is no real mystery.

When we say, 'God is good,' what do we mean? Presumably that God is beneficent and works directly on his creation to secure its happiness. But it is difficult to imagine and harder to believe. It is far easier to conceive of God's goodness as somehow analogous to the goodness of a grilled steak or of a Mozart symphony – eternally gratifying and of an infinite intensity; self-sufficient, moreover, with the symphony hearing itself and the eaten also the eater. The goodness of art, not of holy men, is the better figure of divine goodness.

The goodness of a piece of music and the goodness of a beneficent action have one thing in common – disinterestedness. The so-called good citizen merely obeys the laws, accepting what the State tells him is right or wrong. Goodness has little to do with citizenship. It is not enacted out of obedience to law, to gain praise or avoid punishment. The good act is the altruistic act. It is not blazoned and it seeks no reward. One can see how it is possible to glimpse a fancied connection between the goodness of Beethoven's Ninth Symphony – composed in deafness, disease, squalor and poverty – and that of the saint who gives his cloak to the naked, embraces the leper, dies to save others. But Beethoven's goodness is outside the field of action, to which the saint is so committed. Art is a vision of heaven gratuitously given. Being quasi-divine, it is beyond human concerns. Unlike the heaven of Christian doctrine, it is as freely available to the morally evil as to the morally good: the equivalent of St Augustine's God's grace, impartially bestowed. This, to the narrower moralist, renders it suspect.

What, then, is the good act? To clothe the naked, tend

the sick, feed the hungry, teach the ignorant. These separate acts add up to a concern with promoting, or restoring, in a living organism its native capacity to act freely within the limits of its natural environment. These acts are always good, but they are not always right. Ignorance is strength, says Ingsoc. The Nazis said: let the Jews shiver, starve and die. The good act admits no differentiation of race or species in its object. It is good to mend the broken wing of a bird or to save the life of a *Gauleiter*. The goodness of the saint is characterized by total disinterestedness; the goodness of lesser beings may have motives mixed, unaware, not clearly understood; but the good act tends to grow wild and be unrelated to expediency, policy or law. The good intention, as we know too well, may have evil consequences. Charles Dickens, involved in a train crash, went around pouring brandy indiscriminately down the throats of the injured, thus killing several. He was not, however, a murderer. But the capacity to perform the truly good act is related to a high degree of intelligence and knowledge. Progress may be regarded as a gradual increase in human capacity to understand motivation and free good intentions from the evil of ignorance.

Evil, in its purest form, shares with good this attribute of disinterestedness. If good is concerned with promoting the ability in a living organism to act freely, evil must be dedicated to taking such freedom away. If we are Pelagians, we accept that man has total liberty of moral choice. To remove that choice is to dehumanize. Evil is at its most spectacular when it enjoys turning a living soul into a manipulable object. To confer death is evil enough, but torture has always been regarded as worse. The State has a considerable interest in dehumanizing. It tends to arrogate to itself all matters of moral choice, and it does not care much to see the individual making up his own mind. It is essential that men in power maintain a distinction between the will of the ruler and the will of the ruled. The will of the ruler must, ideally, be totally free; that of the ruled of a greater or lesser freedom, according to the greater or lesser autocratic nature of the State. The State is the instrument whereby the ruler manifests power over the ruled. In so far as this instrument must meet as little opposition as possible in performing its function, it may be said that evil as manifested in the State can never be wholly disinterested. But Orwell's cacotopia represents the establishment of an authority so sure of itself that it can afford to find its chief delight in committing evil for its own sake – that is to say, slowly, deliberately, systematically reducing men and women to gibbering subhuman creatures screaming under torture. This is the ultimate cacotopia, to which Nazi Germany, Soviet Russia, and a host of little autocracies have tended but which they have never been able to achieve.

It is perhaps typical of Orwell's wholly secular culture that he could see the possibility of evil only in the State. Evil was not for the individual: original sin was a doctrine to be derided. Orwell's Socialism permitted, even insisted, that man should be capable of moral as well as economic improvement. His Augustinian pessimism only applied to that projection of man known as the oligarchical State. The State is the devil, but there is no God. The view that evil is somehow outside the individual still persists in a West that has discarded all but the rags of its traditional beliefs. Evil is accepted, to be seen in the My-Lai massacre, in the Charles Manson slaughters, in the daily rapes and murders that animate the streets of major American cities. But it is comforting to believe that this evil is not built into the human entity, as Augustine taught, but comes from without, like a disease. The devil and his attendant demons own the monopoly of evil, and they are concerned with possessing human souls and lighting them up with all the panoply of evil, from blasphemy to cannibalism. They can, perhaps, be exorcised. But evil does not grow in man himself. The superstitious feel happier about their own backslidings if they can attribute them to the Father of Lies. The Orwellians blame it all on Big Brother.

Orwell seemed to believe that the real world, as opposed to that of his feverish and genuinely diseased imagination, was moving in the direction of bigger and worse cacotopias. States would grow greater and more powerful. Equipped with the most devilish technology of oppression, they would more and more reduce the individual to a gibbering humanoid. The future presented an unequal contest between man and the State, and man's defeat would be humiliating and total. We must now see if his prophecy is coming true.

State and superstate:
a conversation

How does today's world of international politics compare with the one that Orwell envisaged?

Very different. There are superpowers, but they don't find it easy to exercise control over the lesser states. The lesser states have not been absorbed into the big ones. The post-war age has been remarkable for the spirit of devolution, uncountable acts of decolonization, the setting up of a host of independent tyrannies, oligarchies and genuine democracies. True, we talk much of spheres of influence, interlocking systems and so on, but there are no great centralized blocs on the Orwell model, all sharing similar ideologies. And where does the power lie? The literal power that drives machines sleeps in Islamic oil. To Orwell, the Middle East was to be merely part of the trapezial zone of cheap labour for the superstates to quarrel over. Islam is one of the genuine superstates, with a powerful religious ideology whose mailed first punched Christendom in the Dark Ages and may yet reimpose itself on a West drained, thanks to the Second Vatican Council, of solid and belligerent belief.

Dear dear. But you have to admit that the main outlines of Orwell's prophecy have come true. America, Russia and China will do, surely, for the three great nightmare powers, armed to the teeth, ready for explosion.

But not exploding. There've been no dangerous naked encounters. Logomachies, yes, but no nuclear attacks on New York or Moscow or Peking.

No condition of perpetual warfare?

Two minor wars a year on average, true. India fights Pakistan, Israel fights Egypt, Jordan fights Syria. Shooting matches in Palestine, Cyprus, Kenya, Aden, Java, Indo-

China, Algeria, Angola, Mozambique, Goa, Tibet, Nigeria, Greece, Dutch New Guinea, the Congo. But no engagement of the superpowers, except by proxy. Korea and Vietnam. So-called Russian advisers on the Golan Heights in 1967. Both Russians and Chinese training the guerrillas of the People's Liberation Front in South Yemen. But Russian forces have only been directly and openly involved in their own sphere of action – to counter the East German rising of 1953, to put down the Hungarians in 1956, the Czechs in 1968.

But there's the germ of Orwell's Eurasia – sovietized Europe.

How much of Europe? Western Europe became sick of authoritarianism after not only Hitler but years of Prussianism, Hapsburgism. Russia could only build Eurasia by force. And Russia's scared of using too much force. So is America. The great paradox of the period since 1945 has been the intrepidity of the little nations in the waging of little wars and the reluctance of the great powers to face each other directly.

Those looked to me very much like direct encounters, or very nearly so – the Korean armistice in 1953, the missile business in Cuba in 1962.

But the assumption that Orwell made, and he wasn't the only one – big atomic war to be followed by a thug's agreement to keep a limited conventional warfare going – seems to belong to a very remote past. We all feared the Bomb once: it was our daily nightmare. Look at the literature that came out of the late forties and the fifties. Take Aldous Huxley's *Ape and Essence* with its picture of post-Bomb Southern California reverted to savagery, with mutated freaks killed at birth, seasonal sex, the Lord of the Flies, Bomb-bringer, appeased with prayers and sacrifice. Take L. P. Hartley's *Facial Justice*, with a guilt-ridden post-atomic world in which everybody is named after a murderer and all human enterprise is blocked, because all we do is evil. Take *Dr Strangelove*, as late as the early sixties. Take novels like *Fail-Safe*. Orwell failed to see that the terror would come about before a nuclear war could get started. So did everybody else.

He failed to see, also, that mere atomic bombs would be quickly followed by thermonuclear devices of far ghastlier potential. I suppose you could sum up the nuclear age like this – the big powers scared to act except vicariously, or in minor acts of puni-

tion in their own spheres of influence; the little nations warring around the immobile feet of the giants. The giants aware of the ease with which the ultimate blast could be triggered, aware too of the consequences – not millions of dead people but a macrotonnage of ruined electronic equipment on both, or all, sides; the pygmies innocent in their belligerence.

Not innocent so much as shrewdly aware of how far they can go. And how far their economies will permit them to go. It's interesting to note, by the way, that the Orwell war rationale hasn't worked in the nuclear age. I mean the using-up of the products of the industrial machine in wasteful war, in order to keep the standard of living low. That notion came from Nazi Germany – guns not butter. The American economy has been marked by colossal expenditure on armaments accompanied by an ever-growing consumption of pacific commodities. It's as though the intercontinental missile and the colour television set reside in the same area of economic expansion. In the modern age you can't keep the two kinds of ingenuity apart – the lethal and the allegedly life-enhancing. Indeed, it's possible to sum up part of the age in terms of a synthesis of the two – you know what I mean, the cosy television evening with the Vietnam war as part of the chromatic entertainment. The American war adventures have been tied up with teaching the world the merits of consumption. Nothing Orwellian there.

But something Orwellian in American imperialism – the building of a kind of Oceania with the centres of power, as with Ingsoc, curiously hidden, dispersed and anonymous. The CIA a kind of Thought Police. The doublethink of democracy, self-determination, freedom of speech and action reconciled with bullying and brutality. A free Francophone Canada? Unthinkable, shoot the dissidents. Too much American capital invested in Our Lady of the Snows. A communist government in Italy? Not to be thought of. I, a harmless British apolitical writer living in Rome, was well aware that the CIA was tapping my telephone. Doing their job, in the name of global freedom, the travelling men of the Thought Police.

Let's be sensible. There's nothing in the traditions of the United States which predisposes them to authoritarianism on the European model. The hysterical anti-communism of the fifties can be seen as a symptom, though an unpleasant and dangerous one, of an ingrained hatred of centralized authority. You can't deny that America did a great deal to promote democratic self-determination in western Europe. Truman, Acheson, Marshall Aid. There was a kind of arrogant assumption on America's part that she knew best, that God had endowed her with a moral superiority that was the reward of an enlightened democratic tradition, but that's very different from collectivist tyranny.

Well, one thing is true, and this is that authoritarianism is no monopoly of the big powers. Africa is full of nasty little tyrannies. Territories that were supposed to have groaned under the colonial yoke gained liberation only to set up dictatorships. Go to Singapore, where Mr Lee presides over a clean unmalarial heaven of free trade. His political opponents are in jail or abroad on courses of what is called self-education. The police drag longhaired youths to compulsory barber-chairs. The media have that bland, uncontroversial quality you associate with Franco's Spain – society weddings, bonny babies, kittens in ribbons. Cinematic candour is called pornography. I lived in Malta for a few years in an atmosphere of censored books and banned films, lingerie advertisements solemnly snipped out of imported British newspapers so that the youth of Malta might not be inflamed. The Maltese government confiscated my house, still full as it was of possibly incriminating books and papers. There are a host of repressive governments everywhere, their tyranny animated by the hypocrisy of doing what is considered 'best for the people'. O'Brien's candid admission that Ingsoc seeks power for its own sake is, compared with the small tyrannical liars, positively healthy.

Let's think of the bigger, older, genuine democracies for a moment. What we ought to be looking for is signs of inroads on personal freedom. There's no doubt that technologies of oppression exist, of a kind that makes Orwell's snooping Thought Police seem very primitive. Now what worries me is the difficulty of making up my mind about these technologies. I don't want to be led into condemning technology in itself. Take the computer. Norbert Wiener and Warren McCulloch developed it as an aspect of legitimate philosophical investigation into the way the brain works – see how far a machine can simulate a human brain, and then what's left over is the essentially human – but it was inevitable that cybernetics should become a *useful* science, and we all know how usefulness tends to be

interpreted – in terms of control over what can be controlled, and that mostly means human beings.

*A computer is a neutral thing. Information is a neutral com-
modity. The more information we have the better. That's the way
I look at memory banks and so on.*

But once the State gets hold of computers it's led on to
the inevitable path of amassing information about its citizens. I don't know whether that's bad in itself, but I'm
thinking of what happened in 1971 in safe, free, democratic little England –

You mean the Census?

Look at the things the State wanted to know. Status of
head of household, relationship to other members of
household, how many cars owned, did the cook have an
oven, was the toilet inside the house, country of origin,
country of parents' origin, previous addresses, education,
marital status, number of children, and so on. Some
refused to fill in the form, but the vast majority meekly
complied. 800 tons of paper, 105 000 enumerators,
£10 000 000 of the taxpayers' money. But only 500 pro-
secutions. There was a maximum fine of £50 for not answering questions. Alan Sillitoe, the novelist, gave his age
as a hundred and one and was fined £25. A man of
seventy-three and a woman of sixty-six weren't able to
pay the fine attendant on their passion for privacy, so both
went to prison. Then it was revealed by the department of
the Registrar General that some of this secret information
was going to be leaked to commercial organizations. One
firm said boastfully that it would have details of 90 per
cent of the entire population on its computers by 1980. The
police easily get access to this kind of stored information.
152 800 people who'd been patients in psychiatric hospi-
tals have had the most intimate details of their lives computerized. Intelligence levels, whether or not they've ever
been in prison, the degree of constraint necessary to get
them there, a full diagnosis of the mental ailment, special
slots for details of drug addiction, epilepsy, alcoholism –

*But is there anything really so sinister about the truth? And,
for that matter, about violation of privacy? When young people
copulate openly in public places, who are we to ask that our
biographies go unpublished?*

I don't know, I don't know. But think – the State is only
an instrument. Everything depends on who has control of

that instrument, which can so easily be transformed into a weapon. It's unwise to assume, even with our heightened wariness of tyranny, a continuation of a tradition of liberalism. A new Hitler could arise in Europe and be overjoyed with the information made available by a civil service thinking in the old terms of restraint and democratic rights. Undoubtedly the computers of the world have Jews neatly listed, as well as dangerous intellectual free-thinkers. And even now, suppose a crime has been committed, and a man in middle age is suspected, one suffering from epilepsy with four false incisors –. The nation's blood groups are computerized. The State knows the addresses of all the men with red hair.

You're saying that nobody is fit to be given knowledge. We have to take a chance on this sort of thing. I insist on the neutrality of knowledge. Justice is always as likely to be done as injustice. Besides, I see signs everywhere that the State is losing power rather than gaining it.

In Russia? In China? In the bloody little republics that issue no news?

I mean in those areas where the luxury of freedom has been for a long time taken for granted, as much as clean water and mains electricity. I'm not forgetting, by the way, that the essential thing in life is to live, somehow. That if the only way to get a daily bowl of rice is to be in a stinking jail – well, open up, let me in. That in some parts of the world the antonym to State tyranny is not personal liberty but impersonal chaos. No, I mean the civilized West. America, Britain, western Europe. We've seen no charismatic bull-necked leaders around for a long time. Politicians are generally despised, statesmen derided, a United States president can take a deserved whipping. Orwell believed that the media, especially the new ones like television, would be in the hands of the State, that here was an apt instrument for propaganda, harangues, lordly directives. It hasn't worked out that way at all. Politics can't compete with soap opera or old movies. The posters and slogans we see concern taste-pleasing commodities, not omnipotent Big Brother. We have a bearded Southern colonel who offers us nothing more oppressive than fried chicken, we have handsome open-air smokers of Kool or Kent. The State can't gratify taste or sense or excite sympathetic tears or the rib risible. It knows it can't have our souls. All it can get is our money, and that is, true, a real oppression that didn't seem to interest Orwell (though, I gather, he tried to turn himself into a limited company to protect his royalties from Nineteen Eighty-Four *and* Animal Farm*)*. *The State exerts its power on us chiefly through fiscal tyranny, in the insolence of brutal demands, not graceful requests, in the immorality of taking money for things not necessarily wanted by the payer, and all without contract – give us your cash or you go to jail; as for what we do with it, that's our concern, brother. The State calls up young people to fight wars that nobody wants except the Pentagon and the arms manufacturers. The State shows its ugly face most blatantly in the police, which increasingly uses methods learnt from the totalitarian torturers, but shows itself also more and more not to be an arm of the State so much as a quasi-autonomous force, able to shoot first and ask questions after. But we're not bludgeoned too much into orthodoxy, chiefly because there isn't any orthodoxy.*

What you mean is that there's a lot of power about, but it's not centralized on the Ingsoc pattern. That there are, indeed, forces always ready to diminish State power, though oppressive enough in their own ways. Multinational companies that can make and break governments but don't give a damn about matters of responsibility to thought, art, sentiment, health, morality, tradition. The manipulators, the true investigators into the power of propaganda, meaning doublethink, subliminal suggestion, rendering us unfree in the realm of what we consume. Trade unions. Minority groups of all kinds, from the women's liberationists to the gay sodomites. And where we expect the State, that takes our money, to protect us from the more harmful of the anarchic forces of the community, there we find the State peculiarly powerless.

You mean the gangs that roam mean streets, robbing, raping, putting the boot in. There aren't any of those in Oceania, because the aggressive instincts incident to youth are channelled, as they were in Nazi Germany, into organized robbing, raping, and putting the boot in on the State's behalf. Or perhaps just putting the boot in. What you want is more and more ruthless police, also skilled at putting the boot in. Well, the situation for most of us in the democracies has been neatly contrived by the growth of technology and the advance of violence. What is life? Work followed by television. We dare not go out in the evenings, but why should we, when the whole of life is brought to our hearths?

That's all it is, a coloured TV image – a family hearth.

When we were permitted coalfires we saw far better pictures in them.

*Dullness followed by dullness. Real sleep and two kinds of
surrogate sleep. Perhaps we'd be happier loving Big Brother.*

Don't, for God's sake, say that. Don't even think it.
Because it's precisely when we admit to the inadequacy of
our private lives that the State is only too happy to step in
to fill the vacuum you call dullness. A night out with the
boys of Biffsquad Number Seven, dear. Polishing his
boots. It must have been exciting to put on a swastika
armband and go *siegheiling* at a Nazi rally. Life ought to be
adequately fed and fairly dull. That's civilization. And if
we don't really like the dullness, then we'd best do something about expanding our own inner vision. We can go to
a George Orwell class. Armed, of course, against the more
truculent of our fellow-citizens.

*We're not being fair to the State, I suppose. When it doesn't
scare us we sneer at it. Do you believe the State can be, well,
beneficent?*

The Welfare State, which Britain has but America
hasn't, though it fills the postboxes with welfare checks,
all too lootable. It's good to have National Insurance, but
what happens to the exercise of charity? We can't be kind
to the poor when the State kills the very concept of poverty. Industries nationalized, and the workers become civil
servants, unfireable, hence not giving a damn. Without
tooth and claw, no urge to work. All nationalized industries fail. Anyway, how can the State be beneficent when
it's using other people's money? Bureaucracies are self-
perpetuating. Bureaucracies are haughty and inefficient.
What do we need the State for? For the conduct of a foreign policy, which means having an army, and for the
maintenance of civil peace, which means the police.
Always guns and a filing system.

*Let's accept, anyway, that the State in the free West is not
moving in an Orwellian direction. We read what we wish, look at
pornography on the streets, can buy pieces of plastic ordure,
make love without official hindrance. We howl for greater and
greater sectional liberties and usually get them. Yet the State
remains an ogre. Especially to the young.*

Ah, the young.

Bakunin's children

It is no new thing to mistrust or fear the State. The nineteenth century went further than our own in wishing to dismantle it as an instrument of oppression. Thinkers like John Stuart Mill saw war as a typical emanation of the State, a terrible evil impossible to individuals or free human communities, and a justification in itself for regarding the State as an unnatural monster. Karl Marx found in it the machinery for capitalist tyranny and believed that it would rust and fall to pieces when the proletariat gained power. Michael Bakunin, Marx's contemporary, dedicated his life to the overthrow of the evil giant, and his spirit is still with us – or rather it has been resurrected, often unknowingly, among the young. Marx regarded him as a fool and a poseur, if not a Czarist secret agent. History, a full century after his death, calls him the father of revolutionary anarchism.

Anarchism has, thanks to him, always carried overtones of violence: you can almost smell cordite in the word. But it resolves coolly and harmlessly enough into its Greek elements – *an*, without; *archos*, a ruler. Bakunin, a Russian aristocrat, large, hairy, emotional, good-hearted, contradictory, clumsy, heroic, has somehow stamped the term with his own personality. He was, unlike Marx, incapable of systematic thought, and this led him to the impulsive doublethinkful, or doublefeelful, adoption of incompatibilities in what he thought of as his philosophy. He loved man, he preached universal brotherhood, and yet he loathed both Jews and Germans. His cult of the hero, beard blowing in the wind on the barricades, had a touch of fascism in it. He rejected authority, and yet for a time could preach revolutionary dictatorship on the Leninist model. He was the rank meat in a more rational anarchical sandwich, tastier than the dry bread of theory that Proudhon offered before him and Kropotkin after. Without him, anarchism would have been merely utopian thinking in books little read: he humanized, or heroicized it. He made the anarchist into a Byron.

Bakunin was born in 1814, before Napoleon met his Waterloo. The despotism that still rode over Europe was matched in Bakunin's mother, whose own reputed tyranny was the cause, or so Bakunin said, of his eventual loathing of all restrictions on liberty. Others, with perhaps more reason, have suggested that his childhood was so idyllic that his subsequent anarchism was an unconscious attempt to get back to the Garden of Eden. He was the eldest son in a family of eleven, idolized by his sisters and brothers alike, but aware of the diversity of tastes and talents possible in a small human community, its capacity for being cohesive despite the contrary tuggings of the temperaments of its members. Why could not the greater human society of the city, the nation, eventually the world, partake of the quality of the family? Bakunin confessed, late in life, to an incestuous passion for his sister Tatyana, a snake in Eden, but normal sexual capacity seems to have been curiously lacking for a man of such hairy volatility. He married, but his wife sought other beds and another father for her children. He perhaps dreamed lust and revolution in the same sector of his brain. His words were always fierier than his acts.

He became a cadet in the Russian army and made, apropos of war, a statement that many of us now would be too hypocritical to accept: namely, that men fight not to win but to revel in the glandular releases of danger: battles are better than the brutal monotony of most people's daily lives. On the other hand, he realized that wars also meant stupid discipline and humiliating regimentation, and it was his revolt against this aspect of army life that primed his revolutionary fervour. He left the army and went to the University of Berlin to study Hegel. The Hegelian definition of the human spirit – 'an I that is a we and a we that is an I' – seems to be reflected in Bakunin's own 'I do not want to be I, I want to be We,' which in turn gives a meaning to Zamyatin's title *We*. Hegel's image of history as a moving towards revelation of the truth, a dialectical process of struggle between ideas, not a mere treadmill of events, fired many of Bakunin's generation both to reject a philosophy that was too much set in the world of spirit and to accept a system that could be applied to the world of brute matter. Socialism needed a metaphysical interpretation of history, and Hegel's dialectic provided the structure for building one. Bakunin made an idiosyncratic dialectic for his own use. History was moving towards the building of a better world, therefore new things were better than old. If you destroyed old things, new things came into being to take their place. Ergo, let us all start to destroy old things. This is what makes the term anarchism carry such terrible, and attractive, overtones.

Bakunin took up revolutionary anarchism as a career. 1848 was the great year of European popular risings (that is to say, risings engineered by intellectuals in the name of the people), and Bakunin followed them around, always just missing their great moments. He was too late to be on the Paris barricades, but he showed such revolutionary fervour in the capital of the new French Republic that he was sent off by its government to start a revolution in Poland. He stopped in Prague on the way and organized bloody battles in the streets – oppressed Slavs versus Hapsburg oppressors, with a foregone conclusion. While in Dresden, still not having managed to reach Warsaw, he was caught up in the Saxon rebellion, captured by the forces of the crown, sentenced to death. Reprieved, he was handed over to the Czarist police, incarcerated horribly in St Petersburg, then sent to Siberia. He got away, tried at last to liberate Poland, failed, led the twenty-four-hour revolutionary commune at Lyons, organized innumerable secret societies, contested the leadership of the First International with Karl Marx, and at length tried to die a hero's death on the barricades of Bologna. The Italian rising collapsed in ignominy, so Bakunin crawled to Switzerland to die in his bed. He died disillusioned. He thought the forces of reaction were too powerful for revolutionary anarchism. But anarchism went marching on.

Limping on, rather, with occasional spastic leaps and gibbers. The immediate followers of Bakunin, obsessed with destroying the old so that the new could automatically replace it, threw bombs, set fire to things, assassinated the functionaries of imperialism, and scared not only the bourgeoisie but the proletariat whose anarchic kingdom was supposed to be coming. Anarchism had a bad press as well as severe thrashings from the forces of reaction. Prince Pierre Kropotkin gave it back something of the philosophical prestige it had lost, emphasizing the intellectual, utopian elements, and at the same time rendering it plausible as a doctrine for the working class. And so a philosophy that perhaps only aristocrats could have contrived slowly made a serious impact, especially in Spain, where it was ingeniously reconciled with trade unionism. Collectivism and cooperativism seemed to be working when the Spanish Civil War broke out. It was with Catalonian neo-Bakuninians that George Orwell fought. There were industrious anarchists in Russia at the time of the Revolution, conveniently forgotten in the official Soviet histories. They worked hard for the Revolution but refused to accept a Bolshevik dictatorship. They were shot in Russia as, to Orwell's unforgettable horror, they were shot in Spain. Anarchism is an unacceptable bedfellow to the Marxists and the capitalists alike. It seems to many still to be too romantic, too much a product of its century, to survive. And yet it produces unexpected saints in unexpected places. Sacco and Vanzetti have certainly been canonized, and not only by fellow-anarchists.

Anarchism has come back to the world, but chiefly with the young. It is characteristic, and probably admirable, in young people to wish to dissociate themselves from both socialism and capitalism, since both have police forces, laws, a concern with materialism, and a respect for property. 'Property,' said the proto-anarchist Proudhon, 'is theft.' Young people tend to idealism, which may be a symptom of the disease called adolescence but also produced the Romantic Revival in literature. They also tend to rebel against their parents, who are dull, worried about money, and have an unhealthy appetite for possessions. Their parents are prepared to send them to fight and die for their country, which means property the young do not own and do not want anyway. The State is, and we yawn saying it, a father-figure. The great divisions in the world are not national or religious or economic; they resolve themselves into one division, which is that of youth and age. The division was mildly dramatized for me in West

Berlin a few years ago. Having inspected the whole length of the Wall, I sought a rest and a drink at a table outside a *Bierstube* called *Der Moby Dick*. It was run by the young and patronized by the young. Nobody came to serve me. After half an hour I walked in to the bar and asked why. 'Because,' said a blond young man with a *Herrenvolk* profile, 'you are of the generation that started the war.'

It seemed a fair reason. The fight between youth and age – or, strictly, between puberty and maturity – engenders a dynamic, excites the flow of adrenalin, adds interest to life. It is a more acceptable struggle than the one between classes or nations, and it is romantically bedded in ancient myth. But there is a problem we do not find in the older divisions. When we fight for land or money we are fighting for solid objects in space. The youth–age conflict is a time-war. Youth is time's fool, youth's a stuff will not endure. It becomes maturity or age, its opposite and enemy, and nobody can properly tell at what point the frontier is crossed. Age does not last either, but it ends in death, which is sharp and incontrovertible. Youth is part of a process, but it is important to the young that it be represented as a quasi-permanency, something static, almost spatial. Young people come and go, but youth remains. Any young person needs to achieve definition of his youth through membership of a community of the young. If he is with the young and they accept him, he knows he is young. The old need no communal assurance that they are old, and they expect to die alone.

The youth group is less concerned with doing than with being. It cannot define itself in terms of a continuity of membership, nor is there properly a continuity of culture. The important thing is to sit about and be young together. There are activities on the verge of doing nothing, such as taking mild narcotics or hallucinogens and listening to rock music – both substitutes for art and learning. A bland sense of alienation from the laws and culture of the old can satisfy, with no need of stressing alienation through aggression. Unfortunately, it is the agents of the gerontocracy, or old men's rule, that are aggressive and demand conformity. Youth, content just to be, has to shift from the essential to the existential. The group defines itself in the manner of a mature society – with politics and what is known as a counter-culture. It resembles a commune of the nineteenth century, opposing itself to the established order, though, most unbakuninian, with no hope of over-turning it.

That is, of course, an over-simplification. If the youth movements of the sixties can be described in terms of primitive anarchism, this means that anarchism is capable of too many definitions. There have been some young people who have made an intelligent political rationale out of their sense of alienation, such as the 'pragmatic anar-chists' of Germany and Scandinavia, mostly young intel-lectuals. There was an anarchist youth movement in Yunan province in the People's Republic of China, sup-pressed by the central government in 1968. Bakunin has been specifically evoked by young people in America as well as Europe, carriers of blown-up photographs of the prophet at rallies for the condemnation of everything pro-duced by the old – police forces, television, canned foods, *autoroutes*, war, indiscriminate killing, prisons. Bakunin will serve as the patron saint of any movement that invites voluntary membership and allows equally voluntary withdrawal and is dedicated to harassing the State or else studiously pretending the State does not exist. But the whole purpose of the nineteenth-century anarchic move-ment was to provide a genuine alternative to the State as an instrument of rule or, mostly, oppression. Youthful communes and even mature *kibbutzim* have, whether they will or not, to acknowledge that the State exists: they themselves exist by the grace and favour of the State. There is nowhere today where the State is not.

In any discussion of the political future of the countries of the Free World, we have to consider seriously the danger that the youth movements represent to the cause of traditional liberty. Such a statement will seem nonsen-sical to youth itself, which believes it is the sole custodian of freedom in an age when the old seem desirous of limit-ing it more and more. It is true that age seeks to limit the freedom of youth, but only because this freedom is prop-erly licence. If men are born free, it is only in the Ingsoc sense that animals too are born free: freedom to choose between two courses of action presupposes knowledge of what the choice entails. We gain knowledge through direct experience, like the burnt child fearing the fire, or else through the experience of others, which is contained

in books. The voice of the neo-anarchists is that of the
film-maker Mr Dennis Hopper: 'There ain't nothing in
books, man,' or that of the British pop-singer who said:
'Youth don't need education. Youth susses things out for
itself like.' Dr Samuel Johnson, having listened to an
exponent of primitivism, said: 'This is sad stuff, sir. This is
brutish.' It is cow-like rather than lion-like. It takes a long
time to gain, by browsing over a field, the protein available
in a quick meal of meat. We old offer the meat of education; the counter-culture goes back to grass.

Education consists in taking swift and economical meals
out of the larder called the past. Bakunin, with his eccentric interpretation of Hegel, rejected the past, which was
bad by definition, not being new. The young very logically
reject the past because it seems of no use to people living
in an eternal present. And when the old start to oppress
the young, it is of course in the sacred name of the past
that the bludgeons are raised. The young do not necessarily reject educational establishments, however, since
being taught involves being in communities of their own
kind, with teaching as an irrelevance or as a purveying of
things to be rejected, such focuses of protest being welcome to the idealism of youth.

It is instructive to note how far youthful anarchism has
been able to prevail against central government since the
year of the first appearance of *Nineteen Eighty-Four*. No
student of 1949 could have dreamt that, twenty years later,
university authorities would have been so willing to abdi-
cate traditional discipline. Students have gained remarkable liberties, or licences, by the simple procedure of
demanding them. The question of the old was *why*? Of the
young it has been *why not*? It is difficult, in an establishment dedicated to reason, to give good reasons why student dormitories should not be mixed, promiscuous copulation should not abound, drugs should not be freely
taken. In a society given over to consumption, it becomes,
for muddle-headed academics, difficult to separate learning from other saleable commodities. If students wish to
study petromusicology (the aesthetics and history of rock
music), Basic Swahili, or the poetry of Bob Dylan, they, as
the consumers, must have their way. And it is very
difficult to make out a cogent case for the study of Latin or
medieval economics, or to convince that education is most

valuable when we do not too nicely question its content.

Students must naturally delegate the voicing of their desires and abhorrences to elected leaders. Even anarchists require leaders, as Bakunin recognized, thinking of himself. He assumed, like his successors, that new modes of leadership would be untaintable by the vices of the heads of the old tyrannies and oligarchies; a leader of free men and women would be the articulator of their needs, not their oppressor, since the very notion of oppression belonged to a past destroyed. A phenomenon of our age, and a very bizarre one, has been the rise of the student leaders – young people like Daniel Cohn-Bendit, hero of the barricades during the 1968 Paris student revolt, and Jerry Rubin, founder of the Youth International Party. Names not now well remembered used to be briefly in the news when the Dutch Provos or the Spontaneous Maoists of the French high schools extolled the virtues of shop-lifting, incest and killing as an *acte gratuit.* We should ask what all this has to do with education. The true leaders of youth should be their pedagogues, qualified to inform them what they have to learn in order to survive as members of a civilized community. The logic of youth's eligibility for choosing its own leaders has, inevitably, been pushed to the near limit with children of twelve finding coeval spokesmen for proclaiming their rights. We have not finished with this extension of rights down the age-scale: it is all a matter of finding leaders.

The student leaders reported in the press are ranting extremists of an eclectic kind, mixing Marx and Bakunin, Zen and the Hobbits in bouts of verbalization with no real programme except more and more licence for the young. The danger is always that they can all too easily be manipulated by maturer, genuinely radical, minds that know what they want. The cause of the students becomes whatever universal cause has lately become urgent. To a great extent, the student rebels of Paris in May 1968 were directed by adult agitators. Youth groups are very useful engines: young people have energy and sincerity and ignorance. They have all the qualities that would make them valuable to the professional agitators who want to bring in Ingsoc. The young could easily be made to love Big Brother as the enemy of the past and the old. He is, after all, careful not to call himself Our Father.

The Orwellian world is one that could have a strong initial appeal to the young. It has a striking anarchic feature – a complete absence of laws. It treats the past as a void to be filled with whatever myths the present cares to contrive. It sets up, as a group to be despised, a vast body outside the pale, devoted to past traditions, reactionary and conservative, essentially *old*. Oldspeak is rejected as having no power to express that eternal present which is youth's province as well as the Party's; Newspeak has the laconic thrust of the tongue of youth. The programme, if not the eventual reality, would find its most energetic supporters initially among the young, all happily ready to destroy the past because it *is* the past, and to accept the Ingsoc revolution as it has already accepted the mixed mythology of Mao, Che Guevara, Castro and Bakunin himself. It is the prospect of revolution that counts, with its connotations of the liquidation of the outdated and the glory of the fresh start. What comes after the revolution is another matter.

If, on the other hand, the new strikes even the innocent and ignorant young as somehow suspect, it can only be scrutinized in the light of standards derived from the past. I mean, of course, those sifted nuggets that add up to what we vaguely call a tradition, meaning a view of humanity that extols values other than those of pure bestial subsistence. The view is, alas, theocentric and rests on an assumption that cannot be proved – namely, that God made man to cherish as the most valuable of his creatures, being the most like himself. It is not the aggregate of humanity that approaches the divine condition but the individual human being. God is one and single and separate, and so is a man or a woman. God is free, and so is man, but man's freedom only begins to operate when he understands the nature of the gift.

Human freedom is the hoariest of all topics for debate: it still animates student gatherings, though it is often discussed without definition, theological knowledge or metaphysical insight. Augustine and Pelagius confront each other on the issue of whether man is or is not free; Calvinists and Catholics shout each other down; even in Milton's hell the diabolic princes debate free will and predestination. The pundits of predestination affirm that, since God is omniscient, he knows everything that a man can ever do, that a man's every future act has already been determined for him, and therefore he cannot be free. The opposition gets over this problem by stating that God validates the gift of free will by deliberately refusing to foresee the future. When a man performs an act that God has refused to foresee, God switches on the memory of his foreknowledge. God, in other words, is omniscient by definition, but he will not take advantage of his omniscience.

The arguments for and against free will can be transposed to the secular plane. So much of man is genetically determined, environment limits him as well as his physical and psychological structure; a seemingly free act may well be the end-product of a process determined by a multitude of unconscious and mechanical factors. Man cannot control his response to a reflex. History is a cyclical movement, and man rides the cycle: he revisits old scenes and repeats old actions. Man is a social creature, and society is a negation of individual freedom. And so on. The view of man as an unfree being is hard to combat, and it is supported by Freud, who found that adult acts were motivated by childhood events cached in the unconscious, and Marx, who saw history as a huge steam engine committed to one track and one destination.

The proponents of human freedom accept a great number of limitations on it, but insist that there are areas where it has to operate, or man ceases to be man. First, man's special nature resides in his capacity to make certain judgements on the basis of certain criteria. He can attach these criteria to experience; he learns the criteria from a combination of experience and insight. He is totally free to apply them. Thus, he can freely choose to declare a thing beautiful or ugly, good or evil, true or false. Writing in his diary, Winston Smith says that freedom consists in being able to say that two and two make four, but this is only one of three available freedoms. It is important to keep the three categories separate from each other, so that a thing is not declared ugly because it is immoral or (pace John Keats) true because it is beautiful. There is a whiff of religion in all this: we are reminded that truth, beauty and goodness are attributes of God. But, on a purely empirical approach, nobody would deny that these are valid areas of human judgement.

If man is free to evaluate, he is also free to act on his evaluations. But he cannot evaluate without knowledge, and hence cannot act without it. Education consists in acquiring both the knowledge and the terms of evaluation. Hence we are not free not to acquire an education. It is the first condition of freedom. But education which teaches how to judge and what to judge cannot be regarded as a tyrannical imposition: it is merely tradition, or the past, speaking to the present. If a new political doctrine claims that it is the duty of the rulers to free the ruled from the burden of deciding what is good, true or beautiful, then we know that it has to be rejected, since such decisions can only be made by the individual. When a political party condemns a work of art because it is false (meaning untrue to the party's view of reality) or immoral (meaning untrue to the party's view of behaviour), then we are being given a most spectacular example of trespass on the individual's right to make his own judgements. Such judgements cannot be handed over to a collective: they make sense only in terms of the individual soul.

A human being is free not only to act on his own judgements, but also free not to act on them. Most of all, and this may be the essence of his humanity, he is free to act contrary to his judgements. I am a heavy smoker, but, not finding in myself any of the symptoms of addiction, I consider myself free to smoke or not to smoke. I have been thoroughly schooled in the dangers of smoking and conclude that smoking is bad for me. Nevertheless I defy my own judgement and continue to smoke. The unwillingness to break a 'bad habit' always looks like slavery rather than freedom, but it represents that human doggedness of choice which the Church, if not the State, has always resignedly, even sympathetically, learned to live with. There would be very little literature, whether tragic or comic, without it. The old theocracies of Geneva and Massachusetts offered to free man from his slavery to sin, meaning bad habits, by punishing him. The secular theocracies, or Socialist States, make the same offer, or else substitute 'positive reinforcements' for punishment. They propose taking the health of the citizen, as well as his private morality, into their charge. They cannot properly do this: there are certain judgements which only the individual is qualified to make.

It is out of lack of knowledge of the nature of human freedom, and the conditions which validate its exercise, that many young people are drawn to embrace doctrines of political oppression. If they reject tradition, and the transmission of it through education, they are rejecting their only protection against tyranny. They cannot, in other words, be sure what oppression means. Anarchism, in rejecting the past and assuming that the new is, by a kind of Hegelian necessity, better than the old, opens the way to tyranny. Moreover, the anarchist attributes evil to the State, which is the mere instrument of rule, and fails to acknowledge that the so-called free society must also find a technique for holding itself together. Bakunin saw, more clearly than most of his successors, that danger lay not only in the State but also in any powerful group that knew what it wanted – a fellowship of bankers or scientists, for instance. There is nothing magical about the State, making it uniquely engender a desire to hold on to power. A tyranny can be born out of any social group.

I have seen, in the United States, examples of young people's 'communes' that were dangerous for two reasons. They were based on ignorance of the first principles of agronomy. How to grow grain or look after pigs is something to be learnt out of the past, and the past is rejected. They were ignorant of the nature of the principles which hold a society, however small, together. They assumed the existence of a general will in the group and then found it to be no more than a bag of quarrelling individuals. The strongest of the individuals became a leader and demanded obedience. Often obedience was exacted irrationally and, as it were, mystically. The Charles Manson group was an extreme example of a leader's taking on the properties of a messiah, a kind of bloody Jesus. The acts of violence performed by his followers were fewer in number than those perpetrated by the Nazi State, but one does not measure evil quantitatively. There is no guarantee that the social body that rejects the rule of the State will behave better than those who control the State. Because of the ignorance of tradition on which anarchic bodies are founded, there is every likelihood that it will behave worse.

The anomaly of any commune or *kibbutz* or collective Walden (on the lines of B. F. Skinner's blueprint) is that it both denies and accepts the greater social body: it has torn itself away from the bigger fabric and yet is a pocket of it. Skinner's *Walden Two* grows its own food and generates its own power, but it cannot build either tools or machines. It cannot maintain a symphony orchestra, but it demands the right to hear Beethoven and Wagner on tape or disc. It has a library, but it cannot publish books. The more bizarre youth communes of America have made their dwellings out of Coca–Cola cases and old car bodies – the leavings of the consumer society they detest. Antonioni's film *Zabriskie Point* ended with an apocalyptic vision of the consumer society being blasted, on good Bakunin lines, to smithereens, but the vision was in the mind of a girl with a car and a radio in it. Anarchism is not possible. Bakunin is a dead prophet.

In democratic societies like the United States and Great Britain, whose great crimes in the eyes of the young are consumerism and belligerence, breakaway societies and protest groups often succeed in denting the iron of establishment. In time they modify the laws and even increase bureaucracy. The forces of Women's Liberation and Homosexual Liberation are making it a crime to discriminate in employment rights, which is wholesome and just, but they are prepared also to modify language by fiat, so that if I, a writer, use words that betray even grammatical discrimination, I am in danger of legal punishment. The same is true, of course, of such bodies as Britain's Race Relations Board, which rightly condemns bigotry, discrimination, and 'racist' language but renders the individual not always sure of the limits of his own acts and judgements. The trade unions are a conspicuous example, especially in Europe, of the power that collectives can have within the bigger collective of the nation. Sometimes the power is justly based, sometimes not. A government cannot invoke moral principles when dealing with the perhaps unreasonable demands of a powerful pressure group. And, outside the field of legitimate or tolerated group action, there are the politically motivated kidnappers and skyjackers blackmailing governments in a manner inconceivable on Airstrip One. Soon, we are told, our great cities will be held to ransom. This is the limit of Bakuninism. The cartoon anarchist of the old days, bearded like the saintly founder, carrying like a Christmas pudding a black smoking bomb, has been metamorphosed into a deadly monster. The revolutionaries who want to create Ingsoc differ from traditional anarchists only in lack of innocence and the possession of high intelligence. Ingsoc cannot come about in any of our existing systems of government in the West: it is waiting outside, blessed from heaven by Bakunin.

The individual alone can be a true anarch. Orwell saw this when writing *Nineteen Eighty-Four*, which is an allegory of the eternal conflict between any individual and any collective. Winston Smith, though thirty-eight years old, is very young in his ignorance, though the ignorance is not all his own fault. The only freedom he can think of is the right to say what is true and what is false. As O'Brien rightly says, he has no metaphysics to oppose to the doctrine of the State. Even if he had a coherent system of belief, he could not prevail against the massive engine of the Party. But at least he would have had the stoic satisfaction – like that of the heroes of Seneca – of knowing precisely what he was fighting for in the battle he was bound to lose. The situation is a melodramatic inflation of that which any freedom-loving individual finds himself in today, even in a permissive democracy. The individual, of whom Thoreau is the true patron saint, is always against the State, and his liberties are, inevitably, going to be reduced in proportion as the pressure groups gain more licence. Time that could be given to improving his mind is taken up with form-filling and fighting hopelessly with bureaucrats. His money is taken from him. He cannot travel the world freely, since he is limited as to foreign currency by the exchange control regulations. Comforts like tobacco and alcohol may be taxed out of his reach. But he can still exercise free judgement on epistemological, aesthetic and moral issues and act, or fail to act, on such judgements. He can go to jail because he considers war evil. He can kill, if he thinks, after long consideration, that killing is the only possible response to an attack on his person or loved ones or property. He can steal, commit libel, act or write or draw obscenities. He must, naturally, be ready to suffer for the exercise of free will, even to the lethal limit. 'Take what you want,' says the Spanish *dicho*, 'and pay for it.' The important thing is that he should not act without full knowledge of the meaning of his act. That is the condition of his freedom.

Clockwork oranges

I am aware that there is something intolerably romantic about the above view of human freedom. It posits an inviolable citadel in the human skull, where, however the adversary batters the outer fortifications, the values of individualism subsist. Stone walls do not a prison make. This is very old-fashioned and shows a lack of knowledge of the resources of modern tyranny. The first of the two cinema films made of *Nineteen Eighty-Four* – now, I believe, out of circulation – ended with Winston and Julia shouting 'Down with Big Brother,' while facing the firing squad. This wholly missed the point of the book. The Party is not concerned primarily with liquidating its enemies but with turning them into good citizens. The punishment is not important but the burning-out of heresy is essential. The seventh veil of the recusant mind must be dropped and the final nakedness exposed, ravished, impregnated. And yet, knowing that there is no untouchable citadel, many of us persist in believing, or wanting to believe, that there is a part of every individual soul that eludes the tyrant. Ingsoc knows all about the Christian martyrs, whose bodies were destroyed but voices unstilled. A martyr is, etymologically, a witness. The justice of the new State allows no witnesses.

There are a number of us these days who do not seek deliberately to go to prison but cherish a dream of being sent there to enjoy, paradoxically, true freedom. The stresses of contemporary life grow intolerable, and it is not just the State we blame. There are bills to pay, machines that go wrong and cannot be repaired, roofs that leak, buses that fail to arrive, dull work to be done, an inability to make ends meet, insurance premiums that fall due, sickness, the panorama of the wicked world displayed in the daily press. One longs to be punished, Kafka-style, for a crime that one has not committed but nevertheless is prepared to feel guilty for, and throw over all responsibility. There is a dream of solitary confinement, of writing *Pilgrim's Progress* or *The Ballad of Reading Gaol*. There is even a desire to be bereft of books, paper, pencil, light, and to be forced to sustain sanity by composing in one's head an endless epic poem in heroic couplets. Nor iron bars a cage. What one does in captivity is the true test of how free one is. Ingsoc, however, knows all about the incorrigible wilfulness of the human will and will be cosily with us in the oubliette.

And yet, though Orwell's cacotopia is the epitome of all unfree societies, we hear very little about the scientific takeover of the free mind. What is to happen in 1990 or 2900 or beyond is not clear, but in 1984 there are no signs that the brain is to be altered by surgery or psychotechnic conditioning. Admittedly, we have an episode in the cellars of the Ministry of Love where O'Brien shows Winston that it is possible to have the Party's vision of reality blasted into one's brain.

> 'This time it will not hurt,' he said. 'Keep your eyes fixed on mine.'
>
> At this moment there was a devastating explosion, or what seemed like an explosion, though it was not certain whether there was any noise. There was undoubtedly a blinding flash of light. Winston was not hurt, only prostrated.... A terrific, painless blow had flattened him out. Also something had happened inside his head. As his eyes regained their focus he remembered who he was, and where he was, and recognized the face that was gazing into his own; but somewhere or other there was a large patch of emptiness, as though a piece had been taken out of his brain. ...
>
> O'Brien held up the fingers of his left hand, with the thumb concealed.
>
> 'There are five fingers there. Do you see five fingers?'
>
> 'Yes.'
>
> And he did see them, for a fleeting instant, before the scenery of his mind changed. He saw five fingers, and there was no deformity. Then everything was normal again, and the old fear, the hatred, and the bewilderment came crowding back again. ...
>
> 'You see now,' said O'Brien, 'that it is any rate possible.'

This is nothing more than a trick, though, a demonstration of what the brain is capable of if it tries. And it becomes clear to us that the unfreedom of Ingsoc depends, in a way not at all paradoxical, on the persistence of traditional mental freedom. For, if O'Brien's statement of the Party's programme is to be believed, the exercise of cruelty depends for its efficacy on being able to work on free minds. There may be satisfaction in being cruel to a dog, but it is a lesser satisfaction than being cruel to a human being, especially when that human being is sharply aware of what is happening and why. Ideally, the torturers of the Party would like to take a Shakespeare, a Goethe, an Einstein – with intellect bright and faculties unimpaired – and reduce him to a shrieking mass of flesh and brain tissue.

Evidently the Party uses techniques learnt from Soviet Russia and Nazi Germany to induce states of hopelessness and emptiness, out of which the voluntary confession of crimes uncommitted and the postures of maudlin repentance will come. And Room 101 represents the crude ultimate in mechanistic terrorization, for 'the worst thing in the world' cannot be withstood, no matter what the inner resources of the sufferer. The technique depends on irrationality, the reflex response to a stimulus which varies from subject to subject – rats for Winston, snakes or black beetles or the noise of fingernails on velvet for another, the materials of terror chosen after loving consideration of idiosyncratic phobias. It is spectacular but implausible.

Implausible in its operation, to judge from Winston's response. The starving rats are about to be unleashed on him: they will jump on his face, tear open his mouth and start to devour his tongue. All that will stop O'Brien's opening their cage is Winston's utterance of the right words. He has not betrayed his mistress; now he must ask that she be eaten by the rats, not he. It is enough. The rats are called off. He has now betrayed everything and everybody. He is cured. And yet we know that enforced betrayal is not betrayal at all, that the conscience will quickly enough exculpate itself, blaming instead the machinery of the nerves that is not in the control of the intellect, and that an even stronger fidelity – reinforced by renewed hatred of the manipulators – will ensue. In fact, Ingsoc's knowledge of the techniques of breaking down individual resistance is crude and elementary. Yet this is in accordance with a philosophy based on doublethink. Big Brother both wants and does not want to be in total control. The victim is not a true victim if he is not allowed a modicum of hope.

The victory of the State over Winston Smith is not achieved through a systematic, or Pavlovian, reduction of his personality to the status of a mere mass of conditioned reflexes. As Orwell makes clear, he has to conquer his resistance to Big Brother through the exercise of his own will, with some help from the Ministry of Love. He has to be shown the inadequacy of his own mental resources, which, in comparison with the rigorous metaphysics of the Party, are nothing – a mere bundle of inchoate velleities and catchphrases. He has been shown his essential emptiness, and now he knows that it must be filled with the only thing available to fill it – devotion to the Party and love of Big Brother. Ingsoc depends, then, on a kind of exercise of free will, for acceptance of its authority is nothing unless it is free acceptance.

Winston, during an evening spent at the club, has to listen to an imbecilic lecture on the relationship between Ingsoc and chess. We do not know what the content of the lecture is, but we do know that there is something chess-like about the relationship between the State and its members, as there is something chess-like also in the intellectual techniques which sustain the system. To use doublethink is to play chess – planning a strategy of thought and taking into account its unexpected disruption by an unforeseen move from the Party; to use Newspeak is to play a complex game with a limited number of semantic pieces. The game played by the State against Winston has had prescribed moves if no limitation on length: he has been granted freedom of manoeuvre, but he has had no hope of prevailing against the stronger player. At the end of the story, Winston sits in the Chestnut Tree Café, pondering a chess problem in *The Times* – white to mate in so many moves:

> Winston looked up at the portrait of Big Brother. White always mates, he thought with a sort of cloudy mysticism. Always, without exception, it is so arranged. In no chess problem since the beginning of the world has black ever won. Did it not symbolize the eternal, unvarying triumph of Good over Evil?.... White always mates.

White always mates because the better player has opted for the white pieces. But black is free to win if he can.

In that its citizens are free to play the game of memory control, of working out the devices of orthodoxy, the Orwellian State bears a direct relation to the one in which English Socialism, not Ingsoc, operates. Human souls have not been modified, prenatally or through infantile conditioning, as they have in the *Brave New World* of Aldous Huxley. Orwell rightly saw that the neo-Pavlovian society, with its members incapable of unhappiness through sexual or social frustration, lacked that dynamic of conflict which animates real totalitarianism – a conflict dependent on the individual's awareness of the impairment of free will at the hands of the tyrant. On the other hand, it did not occur to him that the sustention of power could itself be a product of conditioning, that the Alpha-plus executive of the World State could no more break out of his predestined slot than could the Gamma-minus street-sweeper. Orwell was an inveterate proponent of free will, and even made his nightmare out of it. That Huxley's utopia should be based on happiness rather than fear seemed to him to indicate a lack of élan. You cannot have dictatorship without misery.

The techniques for total manipulation of the human soul were in existence in 1932, when *Brave New World* first appeared. Ivan Petrovich Pavlov had four years more to live, he had done his work, and had been able to see something of the possibilities of its social application. Like his fellow-countryman Bakunin, Pavlov was the product of a great phase of intellectual optimism which could not be held back by Czarist repression – indeed, censorship and obscurantism were a positive stimulus to the revolution of thought. Bakunin believed that men were already good; Pavlov believed that men could be made good. A materialist of the true nineteenth-century brand, he saw the human brain as an organ, in Wundt's words, secreting thought as the liver secretes bile, and no more of a mystery to the scientific investigator than any other organ of the body. The brain, seat of thought and emotion, instigator of action, could be probed, cut about, radically altered, but it must always be altered in the direction of a more efficient mechanism, a machine dedicated to the improvement of its owner's functioning as a human organism. This was the ultimate Pelagianism. The perfectibility of man should be not merely a pious aspiration but a scientific programme. He worked on dogs and discovered that their reflexes could be conditioned: ring a bell when bringing food and the dog will salivate: ring a bell without bringing food and the dog will still salivate. The potentialities of this discovery were enormous, and Huxley saw them clearly. In *Brave New World*, infants of the lowest social group must be made to hate consumer goods they can never afford to buy. Children are encouraged to crawl towards highly coloured toys with gurgles of delight; as they start to touch them, electric bells shrill, sirens hoot, electric shocks are given off by the toys themselves. A few sessions of such conditioning, and the children will hate toys. In the same way, in maturity, they can be made to loathe champagne and caviar-surrogate. This is negative conditioning, conditioning employed in the service of rejection, but positive conditioning is used too. Make sweet scents and lovely music arise out of dustbins and the child is ready to be a life-long refuse operative.

The Soviet State wished to remake man and, if one knows Russians, one can sympathize. Pavlov deplored the wild-eyed, sloppy, romantic, undisciplined, inefficient, anarchic texture of the Russian soul, at the same time admiring the cool reasonableness of Anglo-Saxons. Lenin deplored it too, but it still exists. Faced with the sloth of the waiters in Soviet restaurants (sometimes three hours between taking the order and fulfilling it), the manic depression of Soviet taxi-drivers, the sobs and howls of Soviet drunks, one can sometimes believe that without communism this people could not have survived. But one baulks, with a shudder, at the Leninist proposal to rebuild, with Pavlov's assistance, the entire Russian character, thus making the works of Chekhov and Dostoyevsky unintelligible to readers of the far future.

Lenin gave orders that Pavlov and his family should be lodged in capitalist luxury, fed with special rations, and that every possible technical facility should be granted the master, so that he could devise ways of manufacturing Soviet Man. Pavlov went on working with his dogs ('How like a dog is man,' as Shakespeare, if he had read B. F. Skinner, might have said), looking for the seeds of life in the cerebral cortex, afflicting the creatures with diseases of the nervous system in order that he might, with the utmost tenderness (for nobody loved dogs as Pavlov did) cure them. Meanwhile the Soviet police followed up hints about the induction of neuroses, the driving of the Russian soul to breaking-point. And the ancient point was being made about nothing in itself being good or bad, only the way in which fallible human beings use it. Certainly, humanism was being given the lie: man can be changed; the criminal can be turned into a reasonable citizen; the dissident can become orthodox; the obdurate rebel can be broken. But Soviet Man was not made.

We hear less of Pavlovianism these days than of Skinnerism. B. F. Skinner, a practising behavioural psychologist, teaches, and has written in his book *Beyond Freedom and Dignity*, about the conditions under which human society can alone survive, and these involve changing man through a battery of positive reinforcements. It is never enough to demonstrate to man, on the assumption that he is a rational creature, the rational disadvantages of losing his aggressive tendencies and developing a social conscience. Only by associating a particular mode of behaviour with pleasure can it be made to seem desirable. The other, negative, way, whereby people associate an opposed mode of behaviour with pain, is inhumane. But there is something in all of us that is unconcerned with the manner in which circus animals are trained – whether with sugar lumps or the whip; it is the training itself that disturbs us. We make a distinction between schooling and conditioning. If a child plays truant or shuts his ears or throws ink-pellets at his teacher, this at least is evidence of free will. There is something in all of us that warms to the recalcitrant pupil. But to consider hypnopaedia, or sleep-teaching (which also features in *Brave New World*), cradle conditioning, adolescent reflex bending, and the rest of the behavioural armoury, is to be appalled at the loss, even if rewarded with sugar lumps, of individual liberty. Skinner's title appals in itself. Beyond truth, beyond beauty, beyond goodness, beyond God, beyond life. Big Brother does not go so far.

Arthur Koestler, a man who has endured communist incarceration and torture, and hence is disposed to horror at the very thought of brain manipulation, nevertheless now seems to believe that something will have to be done to change humanity if humanity is to survive. The dropping of the atom bombs on Hiroshima and Nagasaki started a new era – one in which we face the possibility of the death of the race. Because of his strange cerebral make-up, the horror created by man can be the means of destroying man: the supreme product of reason is in the hands of unreason. In his book *Janus* Koestler points to the 'paranoid split between rational thinking and irrational, emotion-based beliefs' and suggests that something went terribly wrong in the biological evolution of *Homo sapiens*. He cites the theory of Dr Paul D. MacLean, of the National Institute for Mental Health in Bethesda, Maryland, to the effect that man was endowed by nature with three brains – a reptilian one, one inherited from the lower mammals, and a third, a late mammalian development, 'which has made man peculiarly man'. These three brains will not gear with each other: the term *schizophysiological* has to be applied to man's central nervous system: man is a diseased creature.

'Man can leave the earth and land on the moon,' says Koestler, 'but cannot cross from East to West Berlin. Prometheus reaches for the stars with an insane grin on his face and a totem-symbol in his hand.' It is not just a matter of inability on the part of the neocortex to control the old animal brain that makes man as he is. It is also the fact that he has a remarkably long period of post-natal helplessness, which makes him disposed to submit to whatever is done to him, and this leads to the blind submissiveness to authority which welcomes dictators and warlords. Man does not go to war to satisfy his individual aggressive urges: he goes out of blind devotion to what is represented to him as a cause. Again, language – that time-spanning creation that may be the highest achievement of the higher cerebral centres – abets the irrational, divisive element which expresses itself through war. Language, out of which high art is made, is also, 'in view of its explosive emotive potentials, a constant threat to survival'.

Koestler rejects the 'reductionist' approach to man, which turns him into the pliable matter of Pavlov or Skinner. But he favours the use of drugs:

Medicine has found remedies for certain types of schizophrenic and manic-depressive psychoses; it is no longer utopian to believe that it will discover a combination of benevolent enzymes which provide the neocortex with a veto against the follies of the archaic brain, correct evolution's glaring mistake, reconcile emotion with reason, and catalyse the breakthrough from maniac to man.

Whatever the approach, whatever the therapy, this view of man as a diseased creature is sincerely held, and the need for somebody to do something about him is represented, by Skinner and Koestler alike, as extremely urgent. Man is living on borrowed time; cure, for the night is coming. Strange that the expert beings who are to administer the cure are themselves men. Can we really trust the diagnostics and remedies of these demented creatures? But the assumption is that, though all men are ill, some are less ill than others. Call, for convenience, the less ill ones well, and we have two kinds of being – we and they or, in Prole Oldspeak, us and them. They are ill, we must cure them.

It was the sense of this division between well us and sick them that led me to write, in 1960, a short novel called *A Clockwork Orange*. It is not, in my view, a very good novel – too didactic, too linguistically exhibitionist – but it sincerely presented my abhorrence of the view that some people were criminal and others not. A denial of the universal inheritance of original sin is characteristic of Pelagian societies like that of Britain, and it was in Britain, about 1960, that respectable people began to murmur about the growth of juvenile delinquency and suggest, having read certain sensational articles in certain newspapers, that the young criminals who abounded – or such exuberant groups as the Mods and Rockers, more playfully aggressive than truly criminal – were a somehow inhuman breed and required inhuman treatment. Prison was for mature criminals, and juvenile detention centres did little good. There were irresponsible people who spoke of aversion therapy, the burning out of the criminal impulse at source. If young delinquents could be, with the aid of electric shocks, drugs, or pure Pavlovian conditioning, rendered incapable of performing anti-social acts, then our streets would once more be safe at night. Society, as ever, was put first. The delinquents were, of course, not quite human beings: they were minors, and they had no vote; they were very much them as opposed to us, who represented society.

Sexual aggression had already been drastically burnt out

of certain rapists, who first had to fulfil the condition of free choice, which meant presumably signing a vague paper. Before the days of so-called Gay Liberation, certain homosexuals had voluntarily submitted to a mixture of negative and positive conditioning, so that a cinema screen showed naked boys and girls alternately and at the same time electric shocks were administered or else a soothing sensation of genital massage was contrived, according to the picture shown. I imagined an experimental institution in which a generic delinquent, guilty of every crime of rape to murder, was given aversion therapy and rendered incapable of contemplating, let alone perpetrating, an anti-social act without a sensation of profound nausea.

The book was called *A Clockwork Orange* for various reasons. I had always loved the Cockney phrase 'queer as a clockwork orange', that being the queerest thing imaginable, and I had saved up the expression for years, hoping some day to use it as a title. When I began to write the book, I saw that this title would be appropriate for a story about the application of Pavlovian, or mechanical, laws to an organism which, like a fruit, was capable of colour and sweetness. But I had also served in Malaya, where the word for a human being is *orang*. The name of the anti-hero is Alex, short for Alexander, which means 'defender of men'. *Alex* has other connotations – *a lex*: a law (unto himself); *a lex(is)*: a vocabulary (of his own); *a* (Greek) *lex*: without a law. Novelists tend to give close attention to the names they attach to their characters. *Alex* is a rich and noble name, and I intended its possessor to be sympathetic, pitiable, and insidiously identifiable with us, as opposed to them. But, in a manner, I digress.

Alex is not only deprived of the capacity to choose to commit evil. A lover of music, he has responded to the music, used as a heightener of emotion, which has accompanied the violent films he has been made to see. A chemical substance injected into his blood induces nausea while he is watching the films, but the nausea is also associated with the music. It was not the intention of his State manipulators to induce this bonus or malus: it is purely an accident that, from now on, he will automatically react to Mozart or Beethoven as he will to rape or murder. The

State has succeeded in its primary aim: to deny Alex free moral choice, which, to the State, means choice of evil. But it has added an unforeseen punishment: the gates of heaven are closed to the boy, since music is a figure of celestial bliss. The State has committed a double sin: it has destroyed a human being, since humanity is defined by freedom of moral choice; it has also destroyed an angel.

The novel has not been well understood. Readers, and viewers of the film made from the book, have assumed that I, a most unviolent man, am in love with violence. I am not, but I am committed to freedom of choice, which means that if I cannot choose to do evil nor can I choose to do good. It is better to have our streets infested with murderous young hoodlums than to deny individual freedom of choice. This a hard thing to say, but the saying of it was imposed on me by the moral tradition which, as a member of western civilization, I inherit. Whatever the conditions needful for the sustention of society, the basic human endowment must not be denied. The evil, or merely wrong, products of free will may be punished or held off with deterrents, but the faculty itself may not be removed. The unintended destruction of Alex's capacity for enjoying music symbolizes the State's imperfect understanding (or volitional ignorance) of the whole nature of man, and of the consequences of its own decisions. We may not be able to trust man – meaning ourselves – very far, but we must trust the State far less.

It is disturbing to note that it is in the democracies, founded on the premise of the inviolability of free will, that the principle of the manipulation of the mind may come to be generally accepted. It is consistent with the principles of Ingsoc that the individual mind should be free, meaning free to be tormented. There seem to be no drugs in use on Airstrip One, except temporarily mind-dulling cheap and nasty gin. A strong centralized State, with powerful techniques of terrorization, can keep the streets free from muggers and killers. (Queen Elizabeth I's England hanged rioting apprentices on the site of the riot.) Our own democratic societies are growing weak. There is a great readiness to be affected, in the direction of the loss of authority, by pressure groups of all kinds, including street gangs as much as aggressive students. The lack of a philosophy at the centre (which neither Ingsoc nor Communism lacks) is matched by indecisiveness in dealing with crime. This is human; we leave draconian deterrents and punishments to the totalitarian States. But the eventual democratic response to crime may well be what could be represented as the most human, or humane, or compassionate approach of all: to regard man's mad division, which renders him both gloriously creative and bestially destructive, as a genuine disease, to treat his schizophrenia with drugs or shocks or Skinnerian conditioning. Juvenile delinquents destroy the State's peace; mature delinquents threaten to destroy the human race. The principle is the same for both: burn out the disease.

We must, say both Koestler and Skinner, accept the necessity of change. A new race, *Homo sapientior*, must be created. But, I say again, how far can we trust the therapists, who are as imperfect as ourselves? Whose blueprint of the new man must we follow? We want to be as we are, whatever the consequences. I recognize that the desire to cherish man's unregenerate nature, to deny the possibility of progress and reject the engines of enforced improvement, is very reactionary, but, in the absence of a new philosophy of man, I must cling to whatever I already have. What I have in general is a view of man which I may call Hebreo-Helleno-Christian-humanist. It is the view which the Savage in *Brave New World*, who has been reared in the wilds on a volume of William Shakespeare, brings to the stable utopia of AF 632: 'I don't want comfort. I want God, I want poetry, I want real danger, I want freedom, I want goodness. I want sin.' The World Controller, Mustapha Mond, sums it up for him: 'In fact, you're claiming the right to be unhappy.' Or the right, perhaps, not to find life dull. Perhaps the kind of humanity that can produce *Hamlet*, *Don Giovanni*, the Choral Symphony, the Theory of Relativity, Gaudí, Schoenberg and Picasso must, as a necessary corollary, also be able to scare hell out of itself with nuclear weapons.

What I have in particular is a kind of residual Christianity that oscillates between Augustine and Pelagius. Whoever or whatever Jesus Christ was, people marvelled at him because he 'taught with authority'. There have been very few authoritative teachers in the world, though there have been plenty of authoritarian demagogues. It is possible, just possible, that by attempting the techniques of self-control that Christ taught something can be done about our schizophrenia – the recognition of which goes back to the Book of Genesis. I believe that the ethics of the Gospels can be given a secular application. I am sure too that this has never seriously been tried.

The basis of the teaching is as realistic as Professor Skinner's, though the terms are rather emotive. Sin is the name given to what the behaviourists would like to cut, burn, or drug out. There is a parallel between the cohesion of the universe and the unity of man. This makes a kind of sense out of the doctrine of the Incarnation. In order that the unity of man may be more than a mere aspiration, love, charity, tolerance have to be deliberately practised. The technique of loving others has to be learned, like any other technique. The practice of love is, we may say, ludic: it has to be approached like a game. It is necessary first to learn to love oneself, which is difficult: love of others will follow more easily then, however. If I learn to love my right hand, as a marvel of texture, structure and psychoneural co-ordination, I have a better chance of loving the right hand of the Gestapo interrogator. It is difficult to love one's enemies, but the difficulty is part of the interest of the game.

The serious practitioners of the game, or *ludus amoris*, will find it useful to form themselves into small groups, or 'churches', and meet at set intervals for mutual encouragement and inspiration. They may find it valuable to invoke the spirit of the founder of the game. Indeed, they may gain strength from conjuring his, in a sense, real presence in the form of a chunk of bread and a bottle of wine. If they believe in the divine provenance of the founder, they will be able to strengthen their sense of the need to promote human love to the end of human unity, since this is a figure of the unity of the divinely created cosmos. Men and women must practise the technique of love in the real world and not seal themselves off into communes or convents. The existence of the State is acknowledged, but it is accepted that it has little to do with the real purpose of living. Caesar has his own affairs, which he considers serious but are really frivolous. The practice of love has nothing to do with politics. Laughter is permitted, indeed encouraged. Man was put together by God, though it took him a long time. What God has joined together, even though it be an unholy trinity of a human brain, let no man put asunder. Pray for Dr Skinner. May Pavlov rest in peace. Amen.

The death of love

When Winston Smith takes part in one of the daily man-
datory sessions of Organized Hate, he is aware of how
efficiently the emotion of homicidal loathing is aroused in
himself by a two-minute montage of noises and images.
He is aware too of how the hatred he is made to feel can be
used as an indifferent weapon, pointed at anyone or anything. This was perhaps one of the big discoveries of the
period in which Orwell planned and wrote *Nineteen
Eighty-Four* – that hate could, once aroused, be pointed
like a blowgun at any object that the State decreed was
hatable. It is, of course, necessary for doublethink that
emotions should be automatically transferable from one
object to another, without the necessity to take thought
and consider why the hatable has now become the lov-
able, and vice versa. Eastasia changes, in mid-sentence,
from friend to enemy, and emotional adjustments have to
be immediate. Orwell was doubtless thinking of how the
attitude of his own country to Soviet Russia, once as fiendish as Nazi Germany, now a fellow-victim of Nazi aggression, had to change overnight. The great age of hypocrisy
had begun.

Evelyn Waugh, in the last third of his *Sword of Honour*,
reminds us of how Soviet Russia became not merely an
exemplar of democratic freedom but a vessel of holiness.
The British State ordered that a jewelled sword be forged
in honour of the defenders of Stalingrad, and this
Excalibur was solemnly exhibited in Westminster Abbey.
The Free World, that had loathed Stalin, now called him
Uncle Joe and loved him. When the war was over, of
course, hatred was in order again. The free swivelling-
around of emotions, as in a gun turret, had become one of
the regular techniques of the modern age.

Traditionally, we have always hated a thing because it is intrinsically hatable. Christianity, though it enjoins love of people, commands hatred of certain qualities that may inhere in them – cruelty, intolerance, greed and so on. There was a time when we knew what the hatable qualities were; now we are no longer sure. Traditional vices are presented in the popular press as virtues. A man, film star or tycoon, who has been proud, covetous, lustful, envious and gluttonous and achieved a name in the world through the exercise of such vices, is a hero, not a monster. Tolerance is weakness, cowardice is prudence. The notion of intrinsic loathability no longer exists.

It seems to follow that lovability does not exist either. Love comes into *Nineteen Eighty-Four*, but it is neither the disinterested, generalized love of the Gospels nor the romantic love of nineteenth-century novelists. It is certainly not a love appropriate to marriage vows. Winston receives a note from a girl whose name he does not even know. It says simply, 'I love you.' He at once palpitates with fear and excitement. The love that the girl, whose name turns out to be Julia, claims to feel for him is, we learn, based on a recognition that his political orthodoxy is imperfect, and that his disaffection is ready to be expressed in the only form she knows – a willingness to fornicate. Fornication is forbidden by the State, since it offers a pleasure the State cannot control. To make love physically is an act of rebellion. This imposes on the sexual act a bundle of virtues which it is not, in itself, well able to sustain. But the statement 'I love you' is here as much a mockery of the values traditionally attached to the phrase as is the State's own institution of a Ministry of Love.

The main fictional weakness of *Nineteen Eighty-Four* lies here. There is an insufficiency of conflict between the individual's view of love and the State's. Winston and Julia do not oppose to Big Brother the strength of a true marital union and, by extension, the values of the family. They have fornicated clandestinely and been caught naked in the act. There is a sad moment when Julia, whose sole notion of freedom is the right to be sexually promiscuous, gives Winston a potted history of her love affairs. Winston rejoices in her corruption, and Orwell seems to abet the false antithesis – oppose to the moral evils of the State the moral evils of the individual. And yet, as we know, the history of Orwell's own love life is one of trust and devotion: he was not extrapolating a frustration in his fiction. He was perhaps merely being prophetic. In 1984, whether Big Brother is there or not, the traditional view of love will have disappeared, and through no fault of the repressive State.

One of the achievements of American civilization is the devaluation of the institution of marriage. This has had much to do with the Puritan condemnation of adultery as a deadly sin; the scarlet letter is burnt into the American soul. Divorce is preferable to adultery, divorce sometimes being a euphemism for serial polygamy. But divorce is rarely presented, in American fiction or American life, as the wholly regrettable, unavoidable, last-resort surgical operation of a less permissive tradition. Love is a sort of car that has to be replaced by a newer model. It is an electric light bulb whose hours of illumination are numbered. It is equated, as in the mind of Orwell's Julia, with sexual desire. Sexual desire does not die, but it requires a change of object. Like hatred, it is a gun.

Love, however, could be defined as a discipline. It is big enough to encompass transient phases of indifference, dislike, even hatred. Its best physical expression is sexual, but the expression should not be confounded with the essence, the word confused with the thing. Both Winston and Julia love in the sense that they form a self-contained community whose main activity is the sexual act, the act and its concomitants begetting fondness, companionship, and other benign essences. They know, however, that there is no permanency in the relationship; their only discipline is directed to not being found out. It is a brief phase of superficial tenderness to be ended by punishment. 'We are the dead,' says Winston, and Julia dutifully echoes him. 'You are the dead,' says the voice from the wall. The relationship had death in it from the start. So do many relationships in our permissive age, and the death is not imposed from without; it is self-induced.

Separate the sexual act from love, and the language of love is devalued. An aspect of our freedom is our right to debase the language totally, so that its syntagms become mere noise. Big Brother, though regretting the promiscuity enjoined by our society and abetted by our films and magazines, will be delighted to see the weakening of marital values. Communism has tried to kill the family – with great difficulty in China – since the family is the original of which the State tries to make a grotesque blown-up copy; it is far better for the family to kill itself.

The reduction of love to the sexual act, and then to the promiscuous sequence of sexual acts, has the effect of reducing sexual partners to mere objects. It becomes easy then to regard all human beings, in whatever social connection, as objects, on to whom we can spray whatever emotion is expedient. An object has no individual essence; it is a common noun. Generalization follows – women, not this woman and that; workers, the working class. The shocking demotion of millions of individual souls to a generalized class called the proles is perhaps, after the devaluation of love, the most terrible thing in *Nineteen Eighty-Four*.

If we regard such a bestial corralling as implausible, nevertheless we accept it as the basic condition for the setting up of an oligarchy like that of Ingsoc. If one hundred per cent of the population has to be controlled with Thought Police and telescreens, then the oligarchical State cannot survive: its resources will be insufficient to hold everybody down. It has to assume that the proles are too stupid, cowed, unimaginative ever to represent a danger to stability: if, improbably, a prole demagogue starts preaching revolt, he can easily be picked off. But the whole mystique and technique of Ingsoc accepts without question the inertness of eighty-five per cent of the population. We accept it too; otherwise we would not be frightened of the possibility of the nightmare of Ingsoc's coming true. And by *we* I do not just mean readers of this kind of book; I mean members of the working class who, drinking a pint in a pub after a television adaptation of *Nineteen Eighty-Four*, make jokes about Big Brother watching them. The story is founded on a division that is no mere fictional device, something we are as prepared to accept to get the plot moving as the absence of marine insurance in Shylock's Venice. It was Orwell's revenge on the workers of 1948. They had let him down. More than that, it was an inherited acceptance of an immutable social division that he could no more drop than he could drop his aitches.

The idea of writing *Animal Farm* came to Orwell when he saw a small boy in charge of a Suffolk Punch. What if these great beasts became aware of their power and turned against their puny human masters? The farm animals of the little fable turn against Mr Jones and his family and found the first animal republic. But it was only possible for Orwell to write the book at all by thinking of a revolutionary proletariat as something different from the sort of human being he and his class represented. The common people were different from the middle class, a different sort of animal. They are still a different sort of animal in *Nineteen Eighty-Four*. There is no real human life in them.

Admittedly, Winston Smith cherishes the romantic hope that when change comes it will come from the proles. But it is a vague hope, sentimental and unworthy. If the proles are not to be animals, they are to be a sort of noble savage: they are not permitted to be ordinary human beings, like Winston and his creator. Winston watches a fat prole woman hanging out clothes, singing a popular song turned out by a musicator:

> The birds sang, the proles sang, the Party did not sing. All round the world, in London and New York, in Africa and Brazil, and in the mysterious, forbidden lands beyond the frontiers, in the streets of Paris and Berlin, in the villages of the endless Russian plain, in the bazaars of China and Japan – everywhere stood the same solid unconquerable figure, made monstrous by work and childbearing, toiling from birth to death and still singing. Out of those mighty loins a race of conscious beings might one day come. You were the dead; theirs was the future. But you could share in that future if you kept alive the mind as they kept alive the body, and passed on the secret doctrine that two plus two make four.

'The same solid unconquerable figure ... those mighty loins' – the words are as insulting as the thesis of *Animal Farm*. And the prospect, as O'Brien is to be eloquent in telling him, is absurd.

Either romanticize the worker through deification, which means dehumanization, or despise the worker – they were the only alternatives to an intellectual like Orwell. He had the real Ingsoc stuff in him; he read the *New Statesman* while the workers read *Blighty* and the *Daily Mirror*. The workers did not buy his books. The workers do not buy my books either, but I do not repine. Nor do I make the mistake of supposing that the life of the imagination is somehow superior to the life of the body. The dock-worker and the novelist belong to the same organism, called society, and society, whatever it thinks, cannot get along without either of us.

Orwell was unfortunate in being born on the edge of the ruling class in late Imperial Britain. The gap between himself and the lower orders, who used bad language and smelt horribly, could only be bridged by condescension, by a kind of ritual identification, by the fictional imagination. At the end of his literary career Orwell dropped all pretence of believing in the working class. This, inevitably, meant loss of belief in all men and women, in the possibility of love as a spark capable of leaping over the immensity – five inches or five million miles – between one human identity and another. *Nineteen Eighty-Four* is not a prophecy so much as a testimony of despair. Not despair of the future of humanity; a personal despair of being able to love. If Orwell had loved men and women, O'Brien would not have been able to torture Winston Smith. The great majority of men and women look on like munching cows while Winston screams and the death of freedom is confirmed. This is a monstrous travesty of human probability.

There is no such thing as the proletariat. There are only men and women of varying degrees of social, religious, intellectual consciousness. To view these in Marxist terms is as degrading as to look down on them from a viceregal carriage. We have no duty to cross the gap of blood, education, accent and smell by contracting a penitential marriage outside our milieu, or even by suffering a wet Monday under Wigan Pier. But we have a duty not to turn abstractions like class and race into banners of intolerance, fear and hatred. We have to try to remember that we are all, alas, much the same, i.e. pretty horrible. Orwell has, in *Nineteen Eighty-Four*, opened a gap that cannot exist, and in that gap he has built his improbable tyranny. It rests on air, like a castle in Spain. We are so fascinated by it that we will not use the dissolving power of disbelief and send it silently crashing. 1984 is not going to be like that at all.

Part Two

1985

1 The Yuletide fire

It was the week before Christmas, Monday midday, mild and muggy, and the muezzins of West London were yodelling about there being no God but Allah:

'*La ilaha illa'lah. La ilaha illa'lah.*'

Bev Jones shoved his way through the multiracial shopping crowd past the screaming Diskbutik, the tinselled supermarket, the former pub that was now a travel agency specializing in trips to Mecca but still known as Al-Bulnbush, turned the corner of Tolpuddle Road on to Martyr Street and arrived at Hogarth Highrise. This was where he lived but, he thought glumly, his heart sinking, you would hardly suppose so, not with that gang of aggressive youths barring the way in. Kumina gangs they were called, these terrors of the streets, *kumi na* being the Swahili prefix that meant teen and, by extension, teen-age. Normally they would, at this hour, be terrorizing their school canteens, but there was a teachers' strike on. This was why Bev Jones was not lunching at his own canteen today. His daughter Bessie was home and unattended; his wife Ellen was in hospital. He had to unlock the kitchen and give Bessie a meal. Thirteen years old, physically precocious, she was otherwise young for her age. The National Health doctors blamed it on Yenethlia, a substance prescribed for the easing of childbirth whose side-effects had not been foreseen. 'Nobody's fault,' Dr Zazibu had said. 'Medicine must progress, man.'

Bev grinned ingratiatingly at the seven kumina youths, but his risor muscles responded as though to the massed sucking of lemons. He didn't know any of them; they didn't live here. They were always dangerous, the more dangerous because they were intelligent – more than intelligent, positively learned, some of them. That was the trouble: when the State didn't encourage learning, learning became an anti-social thing. Bev said:

'If you don't mind, gentlemen – I live here.' He was on the second step of the stone stairway; they wouldn't let him get any higher. 'And,' he added, 'I'm in a bit of a hurry.'

'*Festina lente*,' smiled a cocoa-coloured youth in a sweat-shirt that showed a huge-fisted flying-cloaked Shakespeare with the legend WILL POWER. Then they had him pinioned. The Latin-speaking youth went through his pockets, singing Latin: '*Gaudeamus igitur, juvenes dum sumus.*' It was a good tenor voice, unforced, resonant. He did not find much in Bev's pockets – an Interbank credit card, a near-empty packet of Hamaki Mild, a disposable lighter, three pound notes, five deckers (or tenpenny pieces). He pocketed all except the lighter. This he flicked and flared at Bev's eyeballs, as if testing his ocular reflexes. Then he yawned, and his belly rumbled. 'All right, tigers,' he said. 'We eat.' Then he set fire to Bev's hair and let his companions beat it out with their fists. Then they all kicked Bev not too hard, gracefully, balletically. It could have been worse. They went off languidly. When Bev got inside the hallway he saw an explanation of the languor. The Irwin boy lay unconcious near the lift door, near-naked, bruised, not too bloody. It had been a multiple pederastic assault, a sevenfold entry. Poor kid. The Irwins lived on the tenth floor and, naturally, the lift was not working. Bev rang the janitor's bell. Mr Withers came out chewing, marmalade on his chin. He chewed still, looking at the bloodied boy.

'You heard nothing?' said Bev. 'Are the Irwins in?'

'No,' said Mr Withers. 'To both.'

'Saw nothing on your screens?'

'The screens is not working. Still waiting for somebody to come round. It's the committee's job to hurry that up. Aren't you on the committee?'

'No longer,' said Bev. 'You'd better call an ambulance.'

'It's a bloody liberty, the whole business.'

Bev climbed to the third floor. It didn't do, these days, to be too compassionate. You could spend all day and night being compassionate to the victims of street, hallway and apartment assault. Compassion began at home. He came to his own apartment, 3B. Home. It was no good ringing, not with little Bessie. Bessie could not manage the complicated multilocks. Bev gave his name to a dim red eye on a wall panel. The device responded to his voice-print and, from a slot, his keybunch came jangling into his hand. It took him forty seconds to open up.

Bessie sat widelegged on the floor in front of the telly. She wore, Bev saw, no garment under her one-piece school frock. He sighed. She'd been masturbating, no doubt, to some beefcake image on the screen. The screen was now flashing, bleating and exploding with a kid's cartoon film – lethal violence but nobody getting really hurt, let alone dying. The six-year old Porson kid on the twelfth floor, having seen Chickweed the Wonder jump from a 120-floor skyscraper roof without damage, had, in smiling confidence, leapt down the stairwell. That had been a year ago; the Porsons had got over it; they had not even got rid of their telly. Bev said carefully:

'Did you telephone the hospital?'

'What?' Her eyes didn't move from the jerking images.

'The hospital. Where your mother is. Did you telephone?'

'Not working.'

'What is not working?' he asked patiently. 'Our telephone? The hospital exchange?'

'Not working,' she said, and her mouth opened in weak silly joy as a mouse in a hat was crushed with a steam hammer and lived to squeak vengeance. 'I'm hungry,' she added.

Bev went to the telephone in the little hallway. He dialled 359 1111 ('I ill': that was how one remembered the hospital number; the prefix was, of course, a different matter).

A tapevox courteously responded. It said: 'This is Hospital Control. At Brentford General salvage and evacuation are still proceeding. No individual enquiries may be dealt with for at least twenty-four hours. This is Hospital C – '

His heart had hardly settled from its triple agitation. The balletic beating, the Irwin boy, the enforced climb. Now it thumped viciously. He dashed to the telly and began to search the channels. Bessie wailed; she beat his ankles with her fists. He got the news. A man with little chin and much hair was saying, against a background of blown-up flames:

' – is taking a serious view of the matter. It is believed that the fire was started by irresponsible elements who have not yet been identified, though Scotland Yard is already at work on the following up of what are described as significant clues. It is felt that deliberate advantage was taken of the firemen's strike, now in its third week, and of the sympathetic strike that broke out yesterday at army barracks in the London area. In the absence of professional anti-pyro services, said Mr Halifax, Minister of Public Safety, citizens must be on the look out for further acts of wanton incendiarism and, at the same time, should acquaint themselves with the fire precaution information made available by their communication services.' Bev, sobbing, 'Oh my God,' was out of that room and fumbling with the multilocks while the announcer was saying, 'Soccer – tonight's fixtures,' and Bessie, as ever slow on the uptake, was wailing before switching back to her cartoon. An old Popeye was just coming on. She was content. And then she remembered her hunger. But Bev was out of the apartment before her complaints grew loud.

He stumbled sobbing downstairs. The Irwin boy, still unconscious, lay waiting for an ambulance. Mr Withers was probably back at lunch. Bev ran to Chiswick High Street. He saw no taxis. He saw a bus, Brentford-bound, snarled up in the traffic. He boarded it and then remembered he had no money for his fare. To hell; the shock of the sight of the burning sky, his own distress, were not these payment enough? They proved to be as the bus crawled on. The black conductor said: 'You look pretty sick, man. Okay, you pay nother time.'

And then he was there, trying to push through the police, for the police were not at present on strike, and shouting, 'My wife, my wife, it's my wife, blast you.' The sky was puce, damson, gamboge, primrose, daffodil, smoke, flinders of destruction going up like thin black angels, and the heat was a huge shouldering bully. A few windows were square eyes empty of all but flame, sad, at length sadly collapsing. There were a couple of collapsing doctors in singed surgical coats. Beds and stretchers were being loaded on to floats borrowed from the nearby brewery. 'My wife,' cried Bev. 'Mrs Jones, Ellen, Ward 4c.' The doctors shook their heads as if shaking were physically painful. 'You,' cried Bev to an old woman, grey hair burned off, slackly naked under a blanket. 'you know me, you know my wife.'

'Don't let them get away with it,' breathed a known voice.

'Oh, my God, Ellie, Ellie.' Bev knelt to the stretcher that awaited loading. His wife and not his wife. There are parts of the body reluctant to be combusted, but they are mostly bone. He was on his knees beside her and then, desperately sobbing, lying across her, seeking to embrace, picking up a handful of scorched skin and, under it, cooked meat. She could not feel anything now. But that had been her voice. The last thing she said had not been love, I love, look after Bessie, God what a waste, we'll meet. It had been: 'Don't let them – ' 'My dear poor beloved,' he sobbed.

'That one,' said a weary voice high above him. 'for DD. Better out of it. A lot of them would.' Disposal of the dead, evacuation of the living. The brewery floats were chalked DD and EL. Bev was pulled kindly to his feet. 'Can't do anything, mate,' said a kind rough voice. 'It's a crying shame, that's all. It's the world we're living in.'

He went back home. He walked back, seeing in a shop window Bev Jones, his hair singed by a small flame, prophetic, a message, his jaw down, mouth shapeless, eyes fierce. In the hallway of Hogarth Highrise the inert body still lay, awaiting an ambulance that would probably not now come. Bev mounted the stairs.

It was not easy to make it clear to Bessie what precisely had happened, that she was now without a mother, that her mother had been cooked to death by irresponsible elements. That those whose office it was to put out fires had struck some weeks back for more money. That the army had – intimidated or else through genuine ideological conviction of the right to withhold labour – mutinied. But mutiny was an old-fashioned word, its quaint inept syllables (mute, tiny; mew, tinny) to be associated only with old films about the British Navy. It belonged with words like honour and duty. That men and women could withhold their labour on a point of principle was universally accepted as a right, and the right had at last (after certain pointless wrangles about honour and duty) crossed from the shop-floor to the barrack-square. For the moment, he thought, he would say nothing to Bessie. He had quite enough to think about, as well as to suffer, without having to suffer the fatigue of probing for a thinking area in Bessie's brain. Bessie was watching some ancient film about the Americans fighting the Japanese.

She had been eating cereals from a box into which she had poured milk, regardless of leakage, and sprinkled sugar. So much was evident from the floor around her. That was because, in his urgency, he had forgotten to relock the kitchen, in which Bessie could not be trusted. He went quietly to the kitchen now and set about preparing a cooked meal for Bessie. Everybody had a right to a cooked meal at lunch-time. It was long past lunch-time, but the right would stand no nonsense from the feeble arguments of the clock. As for himself, he would not be going back to work today. Tomorrow would be different. Tomorrow would be very different.

He grilled some sausages, reconstituted dried potatoes into a puree, made tea.

'Bessie, dear,' he said, taking her plate in to her. Poor motherless child, watching the Yanks knocking hell out of the Japs. He sat in the worn aubergine-coloured armchair, hands folded, watching her eat. She shovelled it all in near-sightlessly. She belched in finality, scratching her bared pubes. Poor motherless *innocent* child. When THE END came in brassy triumph, he gently switched off the set. She made an animal noise of resentment and put out her hand, but he caught the hand tenderly and said: 'I have to tell you things.'

'But it's Spiro and Spero now.'

'Spiro and Spero, whoever they are, must wait. What I have to tell you is that your mother is dead. She was burnt to death in a fire at the hospital. Do you understand me, Bessie? Your dear mother, my dear wife. We won't see her ever again.' Then he wept, sniffing, *'I'b sorry I cad't help id,'* as he looked for his handkerchief. But the kumina gang had taken that too. His swimming eyes saw Bessie looking at him, mouth open, trying to take it in. She was looking into the future, trying to visualize a life without a mother. She said:

'Who'll cook Christmas dinner for us then?' It was a beginning: she was contemplating a future from which certain familiar amenities had been removed. 'You don't cook as good as mum,' she said. Then she began to snivel. She was taking in more now. 'Poor mum. Poor me.'

'I'll learn, we'll learn together. It's you and me together now, Bess girl.' And he turned eyes of grim pity to her, a child of thirteen who looked twenty and a blowsy twenty

at that, over-ripe for the bearing of moronic workers for
T U K, or The United Kingdom, or Tucland as Bill, the
Symbolic Worker, called it. Bev gauged her capacity to
learn anything other than the numbers on the knobs of the
television dial, a victim of bad medicine, bad air, bad food,
farcical education, a despicable popular culture. A brain
that had reached seven and then stood still. Last year
there had been compulsory fitting of a ring contraceptive
too deep in for her fingers to fiddle with. Well, it was
right, he thought, right. *Don't let them get away with it*. If he
was going to challenge the system, Bessie was not likely to
be much good as a helpmeet.

Having taken in a certain future emptiness, enough to
be going on with, Bessie now partially filled it by switching on the tailend of Spiro and Spero. Bev sighed and
shook his head. Spiro and Spero were a pair of cartoon
dolphins who spoke English on the Chinese model: You
Say He Not Come I Know He Come I Know He Come
Soon.

He knew that shock was going to strike soon, so he
made a cushion. In the kitchen cupboard was a half-bottle
of emergency Australian brandy (Beware of Foreign Imitations). He took it down, sat at the kitchen table, and began
to sip from it. The tap dripped dully, like life. The calendar
facing him showed bronzed naked girls in the snow, their
mouths in a rictus of winter joy exhibiting back-fillings.
DECEMBER 1984. Ellen had ringed 10 December as the day
she was to enter hospital, 20 December as the day she
would probably leave it. It had been a matter of Toye's
disease, tedious tests anyway to see if Dr Zazibu's diagnosis had been correct, and, if the showings were positive,
the excision of the spleen. An altogether safe operation,
Mr Manning the surgeon had said, his eyes belying the
words. Thank your stars, young man, for the National
Health Service. But Bev had looked up Toye's disease in
the Public Library. Not at all altogether safe.

He held back his tears and swigged the brandy. A burnt
sugar taste was the prefix to the big burning word in the
belly, and the word began a vague romantic or sentimental
poem of pure feeling: there's a plan, a meaning, an all-
provident Providence. He let the tears come and began to
enjoy them. Not at all altogether safe. And then he knew
that there was going to be no shock. Nothing unforeseen

had really happened. Toye's disease. ' . . . Removal of the spleen may effect a temporary remission of symptoms but the prognosis is, in 85 per cent of cases, negative.' He had expected Ellen to die, though not so brutally. As for her last words, as for the thing he had to do – well, a matter of principle had now been given sharp teeth. 'My wife's last words, brothers, don't I have to follow my wife's dying request?' But the principle itself had had sharpish enough teeth five years ago, though soon blunted. . . .

His uncle George and aunt Rosa had emigrated to Australia in the 1960s. They'd been happy enough in Adelaide, that rather strait-laced city, going to church, eating oysters; George efficient at his linotype job. Nearly twenty years of it, dinkum Aussies both, never a tear for the England they'd left behind. And then Rosa had become ill in 1978, the very worst illness, a paralysis that meant her being encased in an iron lung as part of the permanent furniture of the sitting-room of the Gloria Soame (so, as his uncle said in a letter, it was called in Stryne or Australian) on Parkside Avenue.

Then, without warning, the electricity workers struck. *Strike* – the right, terrible word. There was no time to rush her and her iron lung to the hospital with its emergency supply. For want of the animating current she died. Was murdered, George had screamed. And then – Ah, it had been in all the newspapers. He had accused Jack Rees, the strike leader, of murder. The union itself took no blame. The strike had been wildcat, unofficial. Yes, screamed his uncle, but who invented the weapon? My curses on the whole union system, to the deepest hell with syndicalism. And, while I'm about it, let me say that no man has a right to withdraw his labour, not in any circumstances, for only by his willingness to work is a man defined as a man. It was in this evident madness that Uncle George shot dead Alfred Wigg, the General Secretary of the Electrical Workers' Syndicate of the Commonwealth of Australia, while Wigg was getting out of his official car outside his private residence. Jack Rees went free. Uncle George was living out his confused and sometimes violent days in a pleasant green place called the Patrick White Retreat.

And there was another thing – a thing that never got into the British or TUK or Tucland papers, a matter of journalistic discretion of bullying or bribery or the quiet invocation of some regulation about public order. On a January day in Minneapolis, Minnesota, USA (which some said, perhaps jocularly, stood for Unhappy Syndicalized America), with the temperature at 35 degrees Fahrenheit below freezing, the entire city's power supplies were threatened with indefinite intermission unless, by presidential fiat, certain extravagant wage claims were immediately granted the members of the Federal Electrical Workers' Union. Fifteen thousand deaths from hypothermia, very hard to hush up, followed defiance of the threat. And then, as had to happen, the workers got what they wanted. Then other workers tried the same hellish technique in other areas of essential amenity – gas, water, fuel oil, food delivery. The National Guard, which still attached a meaning to the term mutiny, had been called out. Struggles with picket lines, shots fired, finally shame and the restoration of order and decency when Big Jim Sheldon's own son was brutally killed. Bev had known all about it. Bev's cousin Bert had long been settled in Duluth, Minnesota. He had written letters. When letters did not get through it was not because of censorship, only because of postal strikes. There had been no postal strikes at that time; the letters had got, or gotten, through.

And so those dying words – *Don't let them get away with it* – were really the echo of an old song. Bev sighed over the near-empty bottle of Australian brandy as he foresaw himself at last translating a long-rumbling disaffection into action. He did not want to be a martyr for a freedom that, anyway, few believed in any more or even understood. But he felt himself, as it were, buying a ticket for a train whose destination he could not know, the sole passenger. All he knew was that the journey was necessary.

2 Tucland the brave

Devlin peered at the computer print-out. 'Bev?' he said. 'That's really your first name? Not an abbreviation for Beverley or something?'

'It could stand for three things,' said Bev. 'Beveridge, Bevin or Bevan. Those were big names when I was born.

In Socialism, I mean. My father was a great Socialist.'

'Beveridge was a Liberal,' Devlin said. 'But, of course, Social Insurance was essentially a radical idea.'

'A radical idea borrowed from Bismarck's Germany,' said Bev. Devlin frowned at him and said:

'You sound like an educated man.' The term itself sounded old-fashioned, but Devlin was a man in his sixties, and his vocabulary had not always kept pace with the development of WE, or Workers English. 'You don't sound like –' He looked down at the print-out. '– Like a Confectionery Operative. And, ah, yes, of course, it's all here. You actually taught European history. At Jack Smith Comprehensive. It doesn't say here why you gave it up.'

'I gave it up because of the Ministry directive,' Bev said. 'It limited the content of history courses rather drastically. The history of the trade union movement was, I knew, not the whole of history nor even the most important part of it. But I kept my feelings to myself. I didn't make any public protest. I just said I wanted to better myself.'

'Ruining children's stomachs,' grinned Devlin, 'instead of improving their minds. That's what the value judgement boys would say.'

'I *have* bettered myself,' said Bev. 'I'm twenty pounds a week better off. And ought to be thirty pounds a week better off in the new year.'

'Except,' said Devlin, 'that you won't be working at Penn's Chocolate Factory in the new year, will you? Not if you persist with this this this atavism.'

'I have to persist. Wouldn't *you*, knowing the filth of the whole bloody villainy that it's become? What started as self-protection has become an immoral power bloc. We dream through it all, and then we wake. It killed my wife, the blasted filthy immorality of it. Do you expect me to put up any longer with the slimy unquestioning sinfulness of it? I *saw* my wife turned into charred bones and scorched skin. And you ask me to support the filthy bloody fireman's immoral bloody strike?''

'Nobody asks you to do anything,' said Devlin gently. He pushed a packet of cigarettes over. Bev shook his head. 'I must give it up myself,' said Devlin, taking one, lighting one. 'Who the hell can afford it any more?' The picture on the cigarette packet was a vivid, if small, representation of a lung eaten up by cancer. Orders of the Ministry of

Health. Verbal warnings had never done much good. 'The firemen go their own way. The army goes its own way. In principle we approve naturally. We approve of the strike weapon. But try and be reasonable. Don't blame your wife's death on a necessary device of syndicalist principle. Blame it on the wanton swine who burnt the hospital down.'

'Oh, I do that,' said Bev. 'But in doing it I attack the principle of evil. Because whoever did it, they were an evil lot of murdering bastards. If they were caught, they'd be made to suffer – no, not suffer, that's old-fashioned, isn't it? Reformed. But even if I could get them and kill them, and you know how I'd kill them – '

'You'll get over that,' said Devlin, puffing away.

'Even if I could watch them burning, screaming as my wife must have screamed, I'd feel impotent inside, unsatisfied, knowing that evil was responding to evil, that I'd added to the sum of evil, and that evil would still go on – illiquidable, indestructible, primal and final.'

'That's not our province,' said Devlin. 'That's theology, church stuff. You put that very well, very eloquent. Of course, that kind of thing is useful, always will be in a way. Used it myself in my early days, except that I'd say things like, "The evils of capitalism must be liquidated, destroyed," Good metaphorical stuff, theological language. Sorry, I was interrupting.'

'Let me put it this way,' said Bev. 'A man is being abused on a public street – robbed, stripped, beaten, even sexually debauched. People stand round, doing nothing about it. Don't you blame the non-interferers as much as the wrong-doers?'

'Not as much as,' said Devlin. 'They're not doing wrong, they're not doing anything. You blame people for doing things, not not doing them.'

'Wrong,' said Bev. 'You probably blame them more. Because the evil-doers are a permanent part of the human condition, proving that evil exists and can't be legislated or reformed or punished out of existence. But the others have a duty to stop evil being enacted. They're defined as human beings by possession of that duty. If they fail to do that duty, they have to be blamed. Blamed and punished.'

'There's no such thing as duty any more,' said Devlin. 'You know that. There are only rights. Commission for

Human Rights – that makes sense. Commission for
Human Duty – bloody nonsense, isn't it? It was always
bloody nonsense, and you know it.'

'Duty to family,' said Bev. 'Duty to one's art or craft.
Duty to one's country. Bloody nonsense. I see.'

'Duty to see that one's rights are respected.' said Devlin.
'I'll grant that. But if you say, "Right to see that one's
rights etcetera," well, it doesn't seem to mean anything
different. No, I throw out your duty.'

'So the firemen have the right to stand by,' said Bev very
hotly, 'when a hospital's burning down, to stand by and
say: "Give us our rights and this won't happen again. Not
till the next time, anyway." I say it's a bigger evil than the
other evil.'

'Well, now,' said Devlin, stubbing out his fag end, 'you
may be interested to know that this fire business at Brentford has already started yielding positive results. The
firemen are sitting down today with the Wages Board.
Tomorrow the strike may be over. Think about that before
you start raging about what you call evil. Nothing that
improves the lot of the worker can be evil. Think about
that. Write it in the flyleaf of your diary for 1985.'

'Write this in your own diary,' said Bev. 'Write: MEN ARE
FREE. You people have forgotten what freedom is.'

'Freedom to starve, freedom to be exploited,' said
Devlin with an old, no longer pertinent, bitterness. 'Freedoms I'm very pleased to see belong only to the course in
history that you refused to teach. You're a bloody-minded
individual, brother,' said Devlin, a growl entering his
tone. 'You're a bloody-minded reactionary, comrade.
You're demanding freedom and, by the dead or living or
non-existent Christ, you're going to get it.' He waved at
Bev the official note that Bev's shop steward had for-
warded to him. 'The old filthy free days are gone, me
boyo,' he said, his Irish coming out, 'except for you and
reactionaries like you. You stopped teaching history and
you've turned your back on history. Do you not wish to
remember that only twenty years ago your union, my
union, did not exist? It was struggling to be born, and, by
Christ, it got itself born and born in pain but also born in
triumph. Men tending the machines that produce chocolate bars and candy crunchies and creamy coconut what-
evertheyare were in a worse bargaining position than the

miners and railway-workers and foundrymen. Why? Because of reactionaries like you, with your value judgements.'

'This is nonsense and you know it.' said Bev with calm.

'You know bloody well what I mean,' shouted Devlin. 'An archaic and essentially bourgeois ladder of values made it dangerous to let the miners strike too long and freeze the arses of the consumers, but what were called inessentials and marginal goods and luxury products could go to hell and the confectionery workers with them. Well, it's all over now, me boyo. When we go on strike the bakers go on strike with us. No response to a reasonable wage increase demand among the chocolate boys and the populace gets no bread. And there's no stupid reactionary bitch who can say let them eat cake, because if you can't have one you can't have the other. And the time's coming, and it won't be long, it may well be before 1990, when every strike will be a general strike. When a toothbrush maker can withdraw his labour in a just demand for a living wage and do so in the confidence that the lights will go off and people will shiver and the trains won't be running and the schools will close. That's what we're moving to, brother. Holistic syndicalism, as Pettigrew calls it with his love of big words. And you have the effrontery and nerve and stupidity and reactionary evil-mindedness to talk about freedom.' He panted hard and fiercely lighted himself another cigarette. Bev spoke mildly. He said:

'I ask only for the rescission of the closed shop. I demand, as a free human being, the right to work without being forced into membership of a union. Isn't that reasonable? People like me, who oppose the closed shop on moral principle – '

'It's not moral principle, and you damned well know it. It's not thought or conviction, it's rage, and I'm not blaming you for the rage, I wouldn't blame any man, but I *am* blaming you for converting the rage into what you think is a belief. What I say is: give it till after Christmas. Get drunk, stuff yourself with turkey, nurse your hangover, then go back to dropping little bits of hazelnut on to your chocolate creams or whatever they are – '

'My rage,' said Bev, 'as you rightly term it, is the mere emotional culmination of a long-growing belief that the closed shop is evil, that it's unjust to force men into being mere cells in a gross fat body that combines the torpid and the predatory, that a man has a right to work if he wants to work without having to jump at the shop steward's whistle, and that, given certain circumstances, a man has a *duty* to work. A duty to put out a fire, if that's his trade. A duty to – ' He was going to say: drop nuts on chocolate creams, but he saw the absurdity of it. And then he did not see the absurdity of it. A child dying and wanting only one thing: a box of Penn's Assorted. And everybody on strike and not a box left in the world, and the defiant worker, braving the threats and the blows, going to his machine – No, it wouldn't work. Principle, principle was the thing.

Devlin got up and walked over to his watercooler. His office was very rational, with flimsy basic furniture in primary colours, and it was very dry and warm. On the wall was a framed poster – the original Bill the Symbolic Worker, not just the first pull but the coloured drawing itself, done by a man called Tilson. Bill was a handsome, tough, intelligent-looking, sharp-eyed generic operative in a cloth cap with curly hair escaping from it, blue-overalled, an indeterminate tool like a wrench in hand. Bev saw, as Devlin stood in the light of the window, drinking water from a paper cup, that Bill might well have been modelled on Devlin when he was, say, thirty years younger. He said: 'Is that you?' Devlin looked sharply and, it seemed, balefully at Bev. He said:

'That? This? Bill? Not quite me. My son.' There was something in his tone that made Bev able to say:

'Dead?'

'Dead to me. With his bloody ballet-dancing and his pansified pretty ways.'

'Homosexual?'

'He might well be for all I know. The bastards he got in with are brown-hatters, bugger them.' Devlin saw he had gone beyond his immediate terms of communication with this bloody-minded one here, who was now grinning rather nastily and saying:

'That must make for a terrible conflict inside you, Brother Devlin – knowing that the prettily pansified are as tightly corseted in their unions as the boilermen and the truckdrivers. Male models, I mean, and dancers, and even the Gaypros.'

'The gay what?'

'The homosexual prostitutes. Minimum rates and so on. I'm old-fashioned enough to get a certain ironic pleasure out of knowing that Bill the Worker there is probably handling a spanner or whatever it is for the first time in his life. What a world you've made.'

'I think this has gone on long enough,' Devlin said. He went back to his desk and picked up the report delivered by Bev's shop steward. 'You tore up your union card in full view of your brothers. You loudly proclaimed your disaffection with the system. Your brothers were tolerant, knowing that you were not your normal self. I don't think, in the circumstances, disciplinary action is called for –'

'What kind of disciplinary action?'

'Read the regulations. Clause 15 section d subsection 12. A fine not less than double and not more than five times your annual subscription. We let that pass. The tearing of the card is nothing. It's like in the old Christian days when people got baptized. Tear up your baptizmal certificate and it doesn't make you unbaptized. You're a union member, and that's it.'

'Until I start to go my own way and not hop to the whistle.'

'You're a union member and you can't unmake it. The records say so and the records are like the tablets of the Mosaic law. But – ' And he looked at Bev sternly, a bald man with a tired and fleshy grey face, droll eyes despite the sternness, a mobile mouth that briefly chewed air or some tiny residue of breakfast cached by a hollow tooth and now released by it. Bill the Symbolic Worker smiled down at Bev with gentle encouragement.

'But,' Bev completed what in effect was meaningful enough. 'when I next neglect to participate in industrial action – '

'There's a strike of the millers on Christmas Eve,' said Devlin. 'I hope you'll have got over this nonsense by then. If not, you can call that the shooting of your bolt.'

'You'll see,' said Bev, getting up.

'It's you that's bloody well going to see, brother,' Devlin said.

Bev left the office of the general secretary of his union, or former union, and took the lift from the twenty-third floor to the foyer, which still had the look of the old Hilton hotel that this building, New Transport House, had formerly been. There was not a single union in the syndicalist network of the whole country that was not represented here, from chimney-sweeps to composers of electronic music for films. A great plaque above the reception desk said THE TRADES UNION CONGRESS OF THE UNITED KINGDOM. Beneath it was a logogram – a simplified map of the country with the simple inscription TUK = TUC. This was why Great Britain had been christened, by a jocular columnist in *The Times*, Tucland. It was a nomenclature seriously and gratefully seized by the great union chiefs, or their copywriters, and it featured in the Anthem of the Workers:

> Muscles as tough as leather,
> Hearts proofed against the weather,
> Marching in friendly tether,
> Cradle to grave,
> Scorn we a heaven hereafter –
> Build it with love and laughter
> Here, firm from floor to rafter –
> Tucland the brave.

Needless to say, few of the workers knew the words. Outside, a warm drizzle just beginning, Bev looked up at the towering stained stucco to the flag flapping at the top – a silver cogwheel on a blood-red background, a hammer and sickle no longer implying a world union of workers but standing for the Advanced Socialists who, in the sacred name of labour, sought to build, or had already in Europe long built, repressive state systems which denied syndicalism. Aneurin Bevan, probably the primary namesake of Bev, since Bev was a son of Wales, as Bevan had been, had once said, though never in public, wise words: 'Syndicalism is not Socialism.' Meaning that when the workers were their own employers there was no one to fight against. In Tucland the ancient division of capital and labour continued to subsist, and would probably do so for ever, whether the capitalist was the private boss (a fast-disappearing figure) or the State.

Bev couldn't help smiling as he strained his neck, still looking upward at the flying wheel, remembering that ownership was incompatible with the philosophy of labour, and that the TUC rented this building from the Arabs. Where would Tucland be without the Arabs? The oil, at a price ever more exorbitant, flowed in from Islam and kept Tucland's industries going. And Islam was not only the hot desert but also the cold ocean, for North Sea oil had been mortgaged to the Arabs for a government loan when the International Monetary Fund had closed its cashboxes to Britain for the last time, and the loan had been called in and the mortgage foreclosed, and the crescent moon banners waved from the chilly derricks. The Arabs were in Britain to stay. They owned Al-Dorchester, Al-Klaridges, Al-Browns, various Al-Hiltons and Al-Idayinns, with soft drinks in the bars and no bacon for breakfast. They owned things that people did not even know they owned, including distilleries and breweries. And, in Great Smith Street, soon would stand the symbol of their strength – the Masjid-ul-Haram or Great Mosque of London. To remind Britain that Islam was not just a faith for the rich, plenty of hard-working Pakistanis and East African Muslims flowed in without hindrance, for the adjustment of the immigration laws (which had had too-stringent quota clauses) in favour of the Islamic peoples was a necessary political consequence of Arab financial patronage. Yet the workers who had forgotten their Christianity were supposed to sing, 'Scorn we a heaven hereafter'. They ought, thought Bev in a flash of insight, to be more fearful than they were of a people that believed in a heaven hereafter.

3 You was on the telly

Like good Muslims, the British millers who produced what Britain called flour – a fine white dust with carcinogens but little nutritive content – struck at sunset, not at dawn. At dawn on Christmas Eve there was no bread, for the bakers locked the doors on their flour-stocks and also went on strike. The confectionery workers went on strike too. Housewives, who were not yet unionized, grew angry when they found no loaves or cakes around and rioted in the High Streets. The Wages Board responded at three in the afternoon by promising favourable consideration of the millers' demands for triple-time pay for night-work, and the strikes were ended half an hour before the Christmas holidays were due to start for regular day workers, so that all could toast the festive season in the boss's time. There was still no bread for Christmas.

Bev, shoulders straight, chest out, legs like water, reported for duty as usual at eight in the morning at Penn's Chocolate Works. There was a picket waiting for him. There were policemen, chewing their straps. The police, though reluctantly, grabbed a man who threw a small stone at Bev, even though he missed.

'Whose side are you bloody rozzers on?' went the shout.

'You know the law as well as what I do,' said the sergeant unhappily. A van from Thames Television drew up. Bev waited. His act would have no validity unless available for the world to witness. This was the new way. It's Really Real when it's Seen on the Screen. Jeff Fairclough got out, hands deep in smart burberry, red hair waving in the breeze. A man with a hand-held camera and a recordist with a Stellavox followed. Fairclough and Bev nodded to each other. He had telephoned Fairclough the previous evening. Fairclough had once been a colleague, a teacher of English until the advent of the new WE syllabus. ('Usage is the only law. *You was* is the form used by eighty-five per cent of the British population. *You was* is therefore correct. The pedantic may reflect that this was the regular form used by pedants like Jonathan Swift in the eighteenth century.') Bev and the team marched through the open gateway. The strikers put on a great act of snarling and cursing for the camera. The sound recordist didn't record. They could get the bloodying and buggering from stock. Bev led the way to the executive wing. Young Mr Penn, very nervous, came forth to meet them. The Stellavox man put his headphones on, switched on, gave a thumbs up to Fairclough, who said: 'Action.'

'Good morning, Mr Penn. I'm reporting for work as usual.'

'You can't, you know it, we're closed. There's a strike on.'

'*I'm* not striking, Mr Penn. I claim my rights as a free man. I'm here to work.'

'You can't. You damn well know you can't. Be reasonable.'

'Are you denying me my basic right as a worker?'

'Don't be so bloody stupid. You know bloody well what the position is.'

'Are you a Quaker, Mr Penn – a member of the Society of Friends?'

'I don't see what the hell that's got to do with anything. Now bugger off.'

'You're dismissing me, Mr Penn? On what grounds? Redundancy? Inefficiency? Insubordination?'

'I'm not dismissing you. I'm giving you the day off.'

'You deny one of the basic tenets of the Quaker chocolate manufacturers – an employee's right to work, his total immunity from any exterior coercion that persuades him not to?'

'You know the position as well as I do. You're in a closed shop. You can do nothing about it and neither can I. Can't you at least go through the motions, man?'

'I'll go through the motions with pleasure. Open up and let me get to my machine.'

'But the power's off. Oh, go away.' Mr Penn was in deep distress.

'You think this is just?' said Bev. 'You think you're being just in the way your ancestral co-religionists were just?'

'It's not the point, I tell you. This is the modern age.'

'You and I, Mr Penn, have entered into contractual relations. As employer and employee. Do you propose breaking that contract?'

'Right,' said Mr Penn grimly. 'Come with me.' And he led the way (the cameraman ahead, walking backwards) to the works. Soon Bev stood by his cold machine among other cold machines, being interviewed by Jeff Fairclough.

'So this, Mr Jones, is your way of denouncing the principle of strike action. Don't you consider you're being rather old fashioned?'

'Is justice old fashioned? Is compassion? Is duty? If the modern way approves the burning to death of innocent people with firemen standing by and claiming their workers' rights, then I'm glad to be old fashioned.'

'You realize, Mr Jones, that you're inviting your dismissal from your job? That, moreover, no other job can possibly be available to you? That the closed shop is a fact of life and applies to every single gainful activity?'

'The individual worker has the right to decide whether or not to withhold his labour. My curse on syndicalism.'

'You've just condemned yourself to permanent unemployment.'

'So be it.'

The camera stopped whirring. The recordist switched off and packed up. 'Was I all right?' asked Bev.

'You was fine,' grinned Fairclough. 'But God help you.'

They left. The picket, held back by unhappy police, jeered and threatened. Bev was given a lift by Thames Television to his bank, where he drew out £150, noting that he now had a credit balance of £11.50. He went to do the Christmas shopping. Poor motherless Bessie must not be deprived of her right to seasonal stuffing. She knew what Christmas was about. Her class teacher, Mrs Abdul-bakar, had told them the whole story. Nabi Isa, last of the great prophets before Mohammed (may his name be blessed), whom it was in order for the Peoples of the Scripture to call Jesus, had been born to tell the world of the goodness and justice of Allah Most High. Therefore you had to stuff and make yourself sick.

Bev was in the kitchen drinking Christmas Eve whisky when he heard Bessie call: 'Dad, dad, there's this man that looks like you.' He went in and saw himself on the news, but he did not hear himself. The appropriate teleworkers' union would have been at work there, threatening strike action if heresy were allowed to be spoken to the world. He saw himself with Mr Penn and at his cold machine for about ten seconds as a brief pendant to the regional news, and he heard the flippant newsreader say something about here's one man that we can wish a merry Christmas to but not a happy New Year, and then, to the tune of Chopin's Funeral March on wa-wa trumpets, they cut to a chalk-scrawled hanged man on a wall. And that's the end of the local news. Bessie said: 'He's like you, dad.' Bev said:

'He has to be, girl. He *is* me.' Bessie looked at her father with an awe she had never before shown: my dad on the telly.

'Why was you on the telly then?'

Bev sighed and wondered whether to tell her all. No, let it wait. Let her have her Christmas stuffing, poor kid. So they sat together that evening chewing dates and cracking walnuts, her eyes glued to the screen, his restless, sometimes closing unhappily, and they saw *White Christmas* with Saint Bing and Rosemary Clooney, and when *Arab Hour* came on they switched over to a new musical version

of Charles Dickens's *A Christmas Carol*, in which Ebenezer
Scrooge was not reformed into a model paternalistic employer but, scared by his ghostly visitants, saw what the
bloody power of the workers was going to be bloody well
like, mate, and celebrated Boxing Day by being cowed by
the new Clerical Workers' Union under its leader, Bob
Cratchit. Then Bev served them both, on the floor in front
of the telly, with the electric fire glowing away, a nice big
cold Christmas Eve meal of ham and mixed pickles followed by sherry trifle he'd made with old dry sponge
cakes and eggless custard, and they drank Australian
sherry (Beware of Foreign Imitations) and big mugs of
sweet tea. There was a late late movie called *The Bells of St
Mary's*, with Saint Bing again as a straw-hatted RC priest
and Ingrid Bergman as a nun, but it was so cut about as
not to make much sense, and then Bessie went to her
squalid bed (Bev had neglected the laundry) and woke her
father up at four in the morning screaming about a man
with claws and three heads. She had wetted the bed in her
fright, and Bev in some unease let her come into his, his
and poor dead Ellen's. The poor girl was naked, having
soaked her already soiled nightdress, and this made Bev
very uneasy. When she had got the nightmare out of her
head (there were other details than the three-headed man,
such as horrid white snakes and hands clutching out of
dirty pools of water) she grew calm and said:

'You was on the telly, dad.'

Then she approached him in a frank amorousness that
he had to fight off. Poor kid, she was going to be a hell of a
problem. He decided to cool her down by telling her what
the situation was. It wouldn't spoil her Christmas: she'd
have forgotten it all by tomorrow morning. He said:

'Listen carefully, Bessie my love.'

'Yes darling, I'm listening. Put your hand there.'

'No, I will not. Listen, bad times are coming. I'm going
to be out of a job. There's going to be no money coming in
at all, not even from the National Insurance. They'll probably throw us out of this flat because I won't be able to pay
the rent. The bad times are coming because it's my stupidity that's making me jobless – that's what they'll tell you – '

'Who'll tell me? Put your hand there.'

'Your teachers and the other kids whose parents will
have told them all about it. But you have to understand

why I'm doing it, Bessie. No man has to be crucified. Jesus didn't have to be. But there are some things that a man can't submit to, and I can't submit to what the unions mean. Do you understand?'

'What's croosy whatever it was? Why won't you put your hand there?'

'Because you're my daughter, and there are certain things not permitted between father and daughter. I want you to understand what I'm telling you, Bessie. Your poor dying mother said: *Don't let them get away with it*. And, although it must seem mad to you, that's why I'm setting myself up against the whole power of the unions. I can't beat them, but I can at least be a martyr to the cause of freedom, and some day, perhaps not till I'm long dead, people will remember my name and perhaps make a kind of banner out of it and fight the injustice that the unions stand for. Do you understand me, Bessie?'

'No. And I think you're mean. Why won't you put your —'

'Well, perhaps you'll understand this, Bessie. You'll have to go into what they call a Girl's Home.'

'A what?'

'A place where the State will look after you, all girls together, until you're old enough to get a job.'

She thought about that for at least a minute, then she said: 'Will there be the telly?'

'Of course there will. No home complete without one, not even a State Girl's Home. You'll get your telly all right.'

'Perhaps they'll have one of these new wide ones.'

'I shouldn't be surprised.'

'They can show the big wide pictures on them, like that one we saw that time with the monsters.'

'You mean *Sky Rape*?'

'Was that what it was called? You and me and mum saw it.' A tone that might have been called victorious came into her voice. 'And now it's me that's here and not mum. Put your hand there. You've *got* to.' Bev turned over wretchedly and pretended to go to sleep. Bessie beat at his back with her fists for a time and then seemed to settle to masturbation. The sooner she got in that Girls' Home the better. The sooner — The first *waktu* of the day started from the Chiswick mosque. No God but Allah.

Next day Bev cooked the stuffed turkey and the cauliflower (it had cost £3.10) and the potatoes and heated up the canned Christmas pudding, while Bessie divided her attention between the telly and her presents – a transistor doll with long provocative legs and an insolent leer, an earplug stereo radio twin set, the Telennial for 1985. After dinner, which Bessie conceded was as good as what mum could do, they listened to the King's Speech on the telly. King Charles III, a rather podgy bat-eared man in his late thirties, a near-contemporary of Bev's, spoke of this happy and sacred time and God bless you all and, at the end, he grinningly wiggled a finger offscreen and Her Majesty the Queen (not to be confused with Elizabeth II, the retired Queen, now Queen Mum) came on, a pretty dark woman with many pearls, also grinning. The King put an arm round the Queen and both waved at the viewers as though they, the viewers, were going off in a train. Then there was *God Save the King*.

In the evening, while they were eating their cold turkey and ham and fried-up spuds and cauli, accompanied by champagne cider, and watching *Holiday Inn*, once more with Saint Bing (whom Bessie took to be a kind of obligatory Christmas presence), the electricity went off. The film rushed at the speed of light to an horizon where it became a pinpoint and then vanished, the electric fire glowed duller and duller and then became irritable noises of contraction. They had no candles, they were really in the dark. Bessie howled and wailed in real anguish.

'*Now* do you understand?' growled her father. '*Now* do you see what I'm fighting against?' She howled that she thought she saw, but the poor motherless child was incapable of generalization. Medicine must progress, man.

4 Out

On 27 December Bev went back to work and at once the all-out whistle blew. Obedient to the contract with the union, the management formally dismissed Bev. Bev went to the Labour Exchange, where he insisted on seeing the Director, not the mere chewing girl underlings with dark after-Christmas rings under their eyes. He informed the Director of his position, and the Director brusquely told him that he could not be registered at the Exchange since he was unwilling to abide by the fundamental condition of employment in any of the scheduled trades, which meant all imaginable trades except that of poet. Formally unemployed and unemployable, Bev went to see about the drawing of unemployment benefit under the provisions of the National Insurance Act. He was told that he was not entitled to anything since he had wantonly rejected employment inasmuch as he refused to accept the conditions of employment as laid down in the Trade Union Enactment (Compulsory Membership) Act of 1979. Bev said:

'I have paid money into the fund. Every week since I began work at the age of twenty – '

'Why did you start so late?' asked the shrewish fat blue-rinsed woman behind the bars, irritably tapping her pencil on the little counter.

'I went to university. I took a degree.'

'Compulsory payment into the National Insurance fund does not automatically entitle you to receive benefits. Certain conditions have to be fulfilled, and you are unwilling to fulfil them.'

'Then what do I do? Do I starve?'

'You fulfil the conditions.'

Bev went to a pub for a half-pint of bitter and a cold sausage with free mustard. He telephoned his Member of Parliament, or rather his secretary, and arranged for an appointment in the late afternoon. Parliament was not sitting: the Christmas recess was on. Mr Prothero would see Mr Jones at his five o'clock 'surgery'.

J. R. Prothero MP was a smart sleek man in early middle age, dressed in tweeds as for a country week-end, smelling of an aftershave lotion that was aggressively urban. He smoked a pipe which he had difficulty in keeping alight; the ashtray before him was a communal grave of dead matches. He listened to Bev's story and said:

'What do you expect me to do about it? Change the law?'

'Laws *are* changed. It's a slow job, I know. The House of Commons, I was taught, is where unjust laws are opposed and just laws propounded.'

'You must have been taught that a very long time ago.'

He had his pipe alight now and sucked two or three times. Then it went out. 'Damn and blast.'

'Why don't you give it up?' said Bev.

'Give what up?' said Mr Prothero with sudden sharp and defensive suspicion.

'Smoking. It's not worth it, with tobacco at £3.50 an ounce, and you obviously don't enjoy it.'

Mr Prothero relaxed. 'I thought you meant – you know.'

'Well,' said Bev, 'You must have asked yourself often enough what use Parliament is. I'll confess I've come to you with no hope. Like a fool, I suppose, living in the past when Members looked after their constituencies. But I have to suck a bitter pleasure out of the hopelessness of it all. I have to go through the motions of believing that democratic freedom still exists. It's like trying to believe in one's wife's fidelity when you see her lying on the hearth-rug with the milkman. Till death us do part. Government for the people. Silly, isn't it? Nostalgia.'

Bev saw that Mr Prothero's inefficiency with pipe-lighting was, in a way, volitional. He kept striking, and, unlike so many of his constituents, he struck to no avail. But the fruitless process gave him an opportunity to put off answering awkward questions or, as now, being even minimally helpful. Still, he said at last, putting down a still cold pipe: 'You can't fight history.'

'Ah, interesting. And who makes history?'

'Movements. Trends. Elans. Processes. Not who, what. What's happened in Britain has not happened through bloody and wasteful revolution. We've gone our democratic way and not, in the process of changing, seen any violent signs of change. And then one morning we wake up and say: The Rule of the Proletariat is Here. What has still not happened in countries where nasty revolutions took place has happened here without trouble. I don't know what Karl Marx would say if he came back, but – '

'Marx would say that the desired thing hasn't happened, that the means of production are not in the hands of the workers, that capitalism has not been destroyed.'

'It's being destroyed,' said Mr Prothero. 'Fast. 'There's hardly a firm in the country that hasn't passed into the hands of the State. The State's the great employer.'

'Exactly. And against the employer is set the employee. The State's the dirty horrible boss and the unions fight it as though it wore a top hat. And they always win, that's the trouble. The government's a mere machine for printing paper money. Look at the state of inflation. And is one single voice in parliament raised against the imminent ruin of the country? It's time some of you risked your jobs and spoke out for liberty and decency and, yes, plain old-fashioned common sense.'

Mr Prothero picked up his old enemy and tried once more to set fire to it. The graveyard of dead matches was rising into a tumulus. He gave up bitterly and said: 'There's the Whips. We just vote in the bills or abstain from voting. Our constituencies aren't regional any more, whatever they're called. Our constituents are a cross-section of the whole syndicalist system. It's no good anyone complaining. That's the historical process nobody can oppose. It's not like in the days of Fox and Burke and Wilkes. There's just two collectives.'

'It might as well be one. The notion of opposition is a farce. Socialists and Conservatives – nothing but names with a nostalgic historical meaning. What difference is there now between your ideologies? Whoever's running the government, the workers can reduce it to impotence. Do what we say or we strike. And,' his voice grew deep and harsh, 'there's a day or two of token resistance in the name of holding back inflation or keeping our exports competitive. Then more money printed with nothing to back it. Token resistance to show the government's really governing. Except that it's not token resistance to those who die of hypothermia or, Jesus Christ help us, hyperthermia.'

'I'm sorry about what happened,' said Mr Prothero pitilessly. 'You must be feeling very bitter. The firemen go back to work tomorrow, if that's any consolation.'

'Unfortunately, I don't have another wife for them not to burn to death. All right, forget it, I have to forget it. I come to you now to ask – to demand, I suppose – that you do something about me. A man jobless and likely to be for ever, unentitled to State benefit, because he's followed the dictates of his individual conscience and refused to yield to the collective will.'

'You know damned well I can't do anything,' said Mr Prothero, clutching his pipe peevishly. 'You're fighting history. I've got more sense than to try to fight it. Strictly speaking I'm forbidden even to open my mouth in a *token* way on your behalf. Because you're outside the law. Union membership is a basic condition of franchise. You're not represented any more.'

'I join the little old ladies and the lunatics and the criminals?'

'There's a Senior Citizens' Union, as you damned well know. Lunatic – criminal – yes, I suppose those terms apply. You're on your own, brother.' It was not clear whether *brother* was used out of Socialist force of habit, or with the contemptuous irony it sometimes carried in old American movies. It certainly conveyed clearly to Bev his condition of brotherlessness. Bev said:

'I expected all this, of course. In a way I'm courting my own ruin. Call me a witness, which, in Greek, is *martyr*. But I had to go through the motions – pretend that an engine is still working when it's only a disregarded item in a museum. I hope my situation gives you bad dreams, Mr Prothero. Screw you. And get rid of that bloody stupid pipe.' Then he went out.

He went back to his flat where Bessie, still on holiday, was eating the remains of the cold turkey with her fingers and gawping at Red, Rod and Rid on the television. He sat down wearily and wondered whether there was anything he could sell to put off the coming day of eviction. There was nothing except Ellen's clothes and a couple of old suitcases. The furniture belonged to the landlord, a faceless collective with computers that would brook no appeal to such human weaknesses as compassion. The eviction notice would come in a week or so, and then the RPs or Rent Police or bullyboys would arrive to enforce the eviction. He did not even own the television set: it was rented from Visionem Ltd. The end of the month, which was also the end of the year, was coming up. Repossession Day. He said:

'Bessie, I think the time has come. Get your things together.'

'What for? It's Dish and Dash in a minute.'

'Very well. After Dish and Dash, whatever they are. You and I must go you know where.'

'Where?' Her eyes had not left the screen.

Bev went to the kitchen and drank the last of the Christmas whisky. Anything to sell here? He opened a

drawer: all landlord's cutlery. Wait, what was this? It was
a flick-knife, rather a good one, sharp and solid, the blade
quick to respond to the flickswitch. It had been put there
to keep it away from Bessie. Where had he obtained it?
Ah, yes – the two six-year-old boys once on this very
street, threatening a five-year-old girl. Why? For no purpose except sheer disinterested terrorization. He had hit
the boys and grabbed the knife. If his MP had, more or less
officially, assigned him to the criminal classes, he might as
well be criminally armed. He put the knife in his trouser-
pocket. Then he went to drag Bessie away from whatever
it was that followed Dish and Dash. She did not wail. it
was only the news. 'Let's be quick,' she said. 'There's *Sex
Boy* on soon.' Home was anywhere, so long as there was a
telly.

5   Culture and anarchy

The new year came in with bitter weather. Bessie was
snug in a Girl's Home in Islington, whence she travelled
daily to school in what her father, having already seen
some of her co-inmates, ironically called a virginibus.
Then she travelled back to tea and the telly. Bev himself
slept where he could – in Salvation Army hostels, in railway termini and, on one occasion, in Westminster Abbey.
His bit of money soon ran out – £7.50 in notes and deckers.
The decker was the old florin that the Victorians had
introduced with a view, later wisely abandoned, to
decimalizing the coinage – ten of them to a sovereign. The
decimalization of the 1960s, to force Britain into line with
the rest of the European Community, had brought one
hundred new pence (called, with proper contempt, *p*),
but these, with the advance of inflation, had soon lost
their meaning. Ten deckers to a pound, and no finer division. Soon, Bev foresaw, the Tucland quid would be like
the Italian lira, only theoretically fissile. For a decker he
could buy a small box of matches, if he wished to, though
he did not see the use. Tobacco, the lonely and idle man's
comfort, was beyond him. A bun or sandwich was at
least £1.00. The Salvation Army gave him, on condition

that he first prayed over it, a bowl of skilly. He grew pretty wretched, dirty and bearded. He had expected to be able to spend much of the day in the reading-rooms of public libraries, but there were not many public libraries around these days, and such as existed still were full of old snoring men.

'The workers don't need libraries,' said a kumina boy. 'They need clubs.'

'I'd club the bastards,' growled another. A small gang of them had stopped Bev with an evident view to bashing and robbing. Bev felt no fear and the boys must have sensed it. He leaned against a torn wall-poster of Bill the Symbolic Worker (some graffitist had added the inevitable cross-bar to the T in TUCLAND), right hand in pocket clutching flick-knife. He smiled and said:

"Sunt lachrimae rerum, et mentem mortalia tangunt.'

They'd surrounded him on that, examining, sniffing, breathing on him.

'You know Greek too, man?'

'Me phunai ton hapanta nika logon. Sophocles,' said Bev. 'From the *Oedipus Colonus.'*

'Meaning?'

'It is best not to be born.'

From some of the boys came a deep exhalation, as from some satisfying inhalation. The kumina leader, black with an Aryan profile, pulled out a pack of Savuke Finns and said: 'You want a cank?'

'Thanks, but I had to give it up.'

'You out of a job? Union mashaki? You antistate?'

'Yes yes yes.'

There were seven of these kumina boys, not all of them black. The leader said: 'Ah.' For across the street, Great Smith Street in Westminster, where the foundations of the new Mosque lay white in frost, an unwise man was walking alone purposively, a man with a place to go to. 'Ali and Tod,' said the leader. The two named walked over and tripped the man expertly, booted him in the left side, then frisked him as he lay. They came back with thirty-five pound notes. 'Right,' said the leader. 'You come, Tod. The rest at Soapy's around eleven, okay?'

'Okay.'

'Okay, Tuss.'

So Tuss and Tod, a yellowish frail-looking boy who

danced up and down with cold, took Bev to the Unemployed Canteen off Westminster Bridge. Here they fed him with ham sandwiches, sausage rolls, macaroons and tomato soup in a cup. The woman behind the counter said they had to show their certificates of unemployment before they could be permitted to take advantage of the low, subsidized, prices, but the boys merely snarled. Tuss said to Bev, while he wolfed:

'You ever heard of Mizusako?'

'Japanese? Inventor of a violin method?'

'That's very good. But you're a couple letters way off. Violence is more like it. Method, yes, a method.'

Tod said earnestly: 'The trouble he said is separating culture from morality. Because culture's developed by societies and that makes it preach social values. I mean, he means, books don't preach villainy. They preach being good.'

'Books shouldn't strictly preach anything,' said munching Bev. 'Knowledge and beauty – they're outside ethics. Who is this Mizusako?'

'He's in jail somewhere in the States,' said Tusa, smoking very aromatically. 'He went the rounds of the campuses preaching disin disint shit disinterest shit shit shit – '

'Disinterestedness?'

'Hell of a mouthful. But yes, that's it. Free learning, free action. He talked of a UU.'

'You You?'

'An underground university. Paid for by robbery, which has to mean violence. Teaching useless things. Latin, Greek, history. We got lousy education, right?'

'Right.'

'Lousy because it's Labour. Lousy because it levels. No clever boys wanted. There's certain things it won't allow, because it says they're no good to the workers. Now it follows that the things they won't allow must be the only things worth knowing. You get that?'

'There's a sort of logic in it.'

'We go to school, we lot, till we're sixteen. That's the law. Okay, we go and we don't listen to the crap they call sociology and Worker's English. We sit at the back and read Latin.'

'Who teaches you Latin?'

'There are these antistate teachers about. You a teacher?'

'History. Very useless.'

'Okay, there are these thrown out of schools for not wanting to teach the crap they're supposed to, right? They wander, like you're wandering. We give then the odd wad like we're doing to you. Then they give us a bit of education in return. Real education, not State school crap.'

'You want something now?'

'One thing,' said Tod. 'How did we get into this mess?'

Bev took a deep breath and then coughed on macaroon crumbs. 'The workers say it isn't a mess. Do your parents say it's a mess?'

'They say nothing,' said Tuss. 'They consume. But it's got to be a mess, because it's so fucking *dull*.'

'I accept that.' Bev couldn't help grinning at the downrightness of Tuss's statement. 'Let me try to explain the mess very quickly and simply. Since the beginning of history there've been the haves and have nots. In politics two main parties developed – one for ensuring that the haves continued to have and, indeed, to have more; the other for turning the have nots into haves. No rich, no poor, just enough for everybody. Levelling, egalitarianism, the just society. Socialism. We have a Socialist State now. We've had one pretty continuously since 1945. Who were the have nots? The workers, the proletariat. They were ground down by the haves, or capitalists. The workers organized themselves into bodies too big for the capitalists to exploit. Unions. Right, the capitalists tried to use non-union labour. The time came when this put them outside the law. The unions had and have the upper hand. The formerly exploited are doing fine. What's wrong with that?'

'There's got to be something wrong,' said Tuss, 'if life is so fucking *dull*.'

'Here's where things went wrong,' said Bev. 'There used to be an Independent Labour Party in England, the old I L P. Then there came a new Labour Party, which destroyed the old. The new Labour Party started off as the political executive of the Trades Union Congress. Part of the union subscription went to the support of the party – very reasonable. Now the aim of Socialism is to socialize. To abolish, as far as possible, private ownership. Instead of railways and mines and steel making huge profits that all go into the pockets of wealthy shareholders, the profits go to the State, which can thus give more money to the workers and put some by for development and improvement. The only trouble is that nationalized industries never make money. Why not? Because there's no urge to make profits.'

'We know all about that,' said Tuss somewhat irritably. 'Bureaucrats and nobody getting fired and sitting pretty.'

'Now I come to the Great Contradiction,' said Bev. 'With a Socialist State you don't strictly need unions any more. Why not? Because the workers are officially in power, and who do they have to defend themselves against? East European Socialism has no unions, and that's logical. But British syndicalism, once started, has to go on existing. It needs its opposite still. Of course, there are still a few private bosses around, but the State is the main employer. You still have the old dichotomy of employer and employee. The workers have to regard their own political executive not as an aspect of themselves but as an entity they have to oppose. They oppose, and the opposition has to give in, because it's not a true opposition. Hence all wage demands are met and inflation flourishes.'

Both boys looked gloomily dissatisfied. 'That explains nothing,' said Tod. 'It doesn't explain the crap we get at school. It doesn't explain us and you sitting here.'

'All right,' said Bev. 'The worker's struggle in the nineteenth century was not solely economic – it was cultural too. Why should the bourgeoisie have the monopoly of taste and beauty? People like Ruskin and William Morris wanted the workers to be *enlightened*. With the Marxist stress on the basic reality of culture and of history too being economic, well – well, pretty wallpaper and free reading-rooms didn't seem so important. Discriminate consumption disappeared as a doctrine. The thing to do was to consume – but what? Whatever gave or gives the easiest gratification. Diluted taste. The manufacturers are always ready with some watered-down parody of a genuine individual creation. To buy should be to gratify. You buy a book you can't understand, and you get angry. You *ought* to understand it, you've paid for it, haven't you? Things have to be made simple, easy sources of gratification, and that means levelling-down. Every worker with money is entitled to the best that money can buy, so the best has to be redefined as what gives gratification with the least effort. Everybody has the same cultural and educational entitlement, so levelling begins. Why should somebody be cleverer than somebody else? That's inequality. There are no nineteenth-century progressives around, telling the workers about the beauties of Homer's verse. As you know, some of the old workers actually learned Greek. And Hebrew. It was called self-improvement. But that means some selves improve and others don't. Monstrous inequality. Hence your lousy school curriculum. Hence the dullness. Napoleon may have been a monster, but at least he wasn't dull. What can great men like Julius Caesar and Jesus Christ do for the worker?'

'We're not in jobs,' said Tuss bitterly, 'and we never will be. We're not sheep, we don't follow the ram's bell. We face a life of crime and violence. Culture and anarchy. I wish to Christ I could get them to fit. Read Virgil and then rip some guy up. I don't like – what's the word?'

'Inconsistency,' said Tod.

'You can't avoid it,' said Bev, though uneasily, 'if you're human. You're committed to crime if you're against the Workers' State. My MP told me that.'

'Crime of two kinds,' worried Tuss. 'Robbing Robin Hood style, like you saw tonight. The *acte gratuit*.'

'Who told you about the *acte gratuit*?'

'A guy called Hartwell,' said Tuss. 'He talked to us some place, I forget where. A great man for the gin. He told us about Camus – a French Algerian guy, a footballer, you may have heard of him. This guy kills a guy and then he knows he's a human being. He's done a thing there's no reason for doing and he sees that that's what makes him free. Only human beings can do the *acte gratuit*. Everything else, and that means the great fucking big universe and all the stars, it all has to follow like laws. But men have to show they're free by doing things like killing and chopping.'

'What we do isn't *gratuit*,' Tod said. 'It can't be. If we're antistate we have to be properly antistate. That means kicking against the law because it's a State thing. Like Latin and Greek are antistate things. So violence and Shakespeare and Plato go together. They *have* to. And literature teaches revenge. When I read *Don Quixote* I went round slashing every guy that wasn't thin and tall and a bit dreamy. I left the little fat ones alone too.'

'What's that big Greek word you said yesterday?' said Tuss to Tod.

'Symbiosis?'

'That's it. Without us how would the Christniques get on?'

Bev's head reeled. All these things happening. 'Explain,' he said.

'These kids,' said Tuss, 'that started the UC or Underground Christ. In that bit of the District Line that's been closed up. They have what they call a love supper, with real shagging, boy and girl, boy and boy, but the feast bit is only mkate and the odd drop of vino. Sometimes we nick it for them. They say the bread and wine is really Jesus. Then they go out looking for trouble.'

'Christian violence?' said Bev, now ready to believe anything.

'No no. They go out wanting to be cracked. Then they practise the Christnique of loving your enemies. That's where we come in. We get sort of friendly, that's the trouble, don't slash hard enough. Let them get their own vino,' he said with sudden viciousness.

'The only things of importance,' Bev said, still with uneasiness, 'are subversive. Art is subversive. Philosophy too. The State killed Socrates.'

'Yeah, I know,' frowned Tuss. ' "Crito, we owe a cock to Aesculapius.' ''

'*O Kriton*,' translated Bev back, '*to Asklipio opheilmen alektruona*.'

'Again, again,' urged Tuss, grabbing Bev's worn greatcoat lapel. 'Christ, those are the real words, that's really the poor guy talking.' Bev, who still owned a stylo, wrote it down in Roman transliteration on Tuss's cigarette pack. Tuss devoured the words, then he said: 'I get a shiver when I read the words in English. Right down the backbone. Now it'll be a shiver all over. I had to bash up those Greeks that ran the stinking restaurant in Camberwell. Because of that. Then I found the guy that ran it was called Socrates. Mockery, I said, and I put the boot in proper.'

Bev shivered inwardly when the image of the ravished and torn Irwin boy came back to him. He'd suffered and died because he wasn't a character in literature? Or perhaps he wanted it, an extreme Christinique? Who knew anything of the dark heart of man? 'Aren't you afraid of getting caught?' he asked. 'Of being put away?'

'No.' Tuss shook his head many times slowly. 'Not scared. It's the final test, to see if you can live like alone inside your skull. That's one reason for stocking it up, to see if it can feed off itself. That's real freedom, being alone in a cell and there's all your brain to travel in, like a country. But nobody gets caught. The nguruwes keep out of our way.'

'I don't know the word. Police?'

'Pig in Swahili. The chanzirim – that's Arabic, that's worse – they don't want blood on their uniforms. *O Kriton*,' he began to read, '*to Ask* – '

' "Pay the debt, therefore. Do not neglect it," ' said Bev. 'That's how it goes on.'

'Give it me in Greek. Give it me real. I want the past in front of me like it was all really there.'

'I can't remember the rest,' said Bev, 'sorry. You're right about the past. We owe no debt to the present or the future. Keep the past alive, pay the debt. Somebody has to do it.'

6   Free Britons

It was the following night that Bev, frozen, came to a disused factory off Hammersmith Broadway. In the factory yard, railed and gated off from the street, ragged men sat round a fire. A reek of charred meat flooded Bev's mouth with saliva. The gate was open.

'No room, no room' said a scholarly-looking man in a stained and ancient British warm, tartan trews and muddy Wellingtons. But his eye was kindly. Bev, without invitation, sat on an old oil drum.

'Antistate?' he said. 'All?'

They looked at him warily. 'Your vocation?' said the scholarly-looking man. Bev told him. The man nodded. 'My name is Reynolds,' he said. 'I am fifty-nine. Had I been willing to keep my mouth shut for a month or so longer I would have retired in the normal way and received my State pension. Comprehensive School, Willingden. Senior teacher of literature, sir.'

'Look, prof, we've heard all this,' whined a bulge-eyed man with a perfectly round head shorn and shaven, as if against ringworm.

'You cannot hear it too often, Wilfred. Besides, I'm addressing Mr Jones here. The set books laid down for the advanced level of the State Leaving Certificate examination were as follows. Poetry: the lyrics of a boy called Jed Foote, member of a singing group called The Come Quicks that sang them; a volume of songs by somebody, American I think, called Rod something. Drama: a play called *The Mousetrap* by the late Dame Agatha Christie – still apparently running in the West End forty years after its premiere. Fiction: a novel called *The Carpetbaggers* – or to be exact *A Shorter The Carpetbaggers* by Harold Robbins, and some nonsense about the errors of social climbing by Sir John Braine. I ask you. Literature. I resigned.' He looked round the circle as for applause.

'Most courageous,' said Bev. 'Might I have a little of that meat there? I'm starving.'

'Let him nick his own,' snarled a black man.

'Charity, charity,' said Reynolds. 'He will do his share of nicking tomorrow, if he joins our band. Here, sir, this is chuck steak and hard to masticate but nourishing. I think a roasted onion rests somewhere among the bluebleak embers.' He picked for it with an iron rod and rolled it out towards Bev. It was oozing juice through its black overcoat. Bev ate gratefully. Wilfred grudgingly, at Reynolds's ocular urging, lent Bev a bottle of rotgut, a coughing fit in every globule. They talked and ate. A thin man with a cap named Timmy read, to general groans, from a worn pocket copy of the New Testament.

'Every bleeding night we have this,' said Wilfred.

'It's to drill it into you,' said Timmy. 'The bargaining principle is forbidden the workers by the Lord hisself. "Didst thou not agree for a penny?" That's clear enough and it's the word of God, so stick it up your jaxy and keep it there.'

'If there's to be reading aloud,' said Reynolds, 'hear the word of Alexander Pope.'

'We don't want no RC stuff,' whined Wilfred.

'You see?' said Reynolds. 'You join the ignorant. Banned in the Ealing Public Library because the Library Committee chairman said some nonsense about the Secular State and if you want Popes go to Rome. But you will listen, my friend.' He read out with evident pleasure:

'Lo! thy dread Empire, CHAOS, is restor'd;
Light dies before thy uncreating word;
Thy hand, great Anarch! lets the curtain fall
And universal Darkness buries All.'

'CHAOS,' said Bev. 'Consortium for the Hastening of the Annihilation of Organized Society. Pope didn't have to fight society. He gloried in exalting it. The elitist society, of course. Meanwhile the loaf-stealers hanged and the beggars scratched their sores.'

'Do you mind?' said the religious man. 'I'm eating.'

Reynolds said: 'And yet what springs out of universal justice? The universal darkness Pope never knew. Pope knew what the great enemy of life was and is.'

'Dullness,' said Bev.

'Ah,' said Reynolds with pleasure. 'No dullness now. Welcome, Szigeti, welcome, Tertis.' Two men with fiddle cases joined the group. One of them produced a kilo of pork sausages from his overcoat pocket. 'Prick them first,' said Reynolds. 'I can't abide burst bangers.'

The newcomers ate and then opened their cases. A violin and a viola. They played a charming duo by Mozart and then a Bach two-part invention. Their standards were high; they were very mature men; they were professionals without union cards. Tertis said;

'You could see how it was going to go back in 1977. Covent Garden, I was first viola. They stopped the damned opera after the second act. Said it was going on too long. They wouldn't accept overtime, all goes in tax anyway they said. I protested.'

'That was nothing,' said the violinist. 'They blew the whistle three bars after the start of the last movement of the Ninth. The singers needn't have come. And the whistle wasn't pitched in the right key, either. Royal Festival Hall, September '79. Jesus help us.'

Don't let them get away with it. Bev's wife's voice crackled out of the fire. 'What do we do?' Bev asked.

'We wait,' said Reynolds. 'We wait for one of history's

little surprises. I propose turning in, gentlemen.' To Bev
he said: 'This factory closed down when it couldn't meet
the '79 wage demands. The government didn't find it
worth while to take it over. It was a mattress factory. We
found plenty of mouldering mattresses in the warehouse.
If you sleep here, you will feel very much like the filling of
a sandwich. Trevor,' he said sharply to the black, 'you said
something about knocking off some blankets.'

'Not easy, man.'

'You must really take our situation more seriously, Trevor.' To Bev: 'Have you any particular speciality, sir?'

'In thieving?'

'We don't like that word. We prefer euphemisms like
nicking, knocking off, finding, scrounging. Were you ever
in the army?'

'I was born,' said Bev, 'at the beginning of the Long
Peace.'

'I see. The army gave me, brief as my service was, a
wholesome attitude to property. Well, we'll see. Come, let
me find you a place to sleep.' He produced a candle-end
and lighted it at the fire.

The empty hull of the factory was cavernous and rusty.
It rang hollow and forlorn. Reynolds lighted a smoking oil
lamp with his end of candle. He showed Bev how to sleep
– on a mattress with two other mattresses laid over him
laterally. Bev felt warm but dirty. 'Does one wash?' he
asked. 'Surely, successful nicking depends on a decent
appearance?'

'For retail winning, yes. For wholesale, filth does no
harm. When a meat truck is unloading, you present a dirty
shoulder and receive a side of beef, then you take it into
the store or shop in question and leave the back way.
Sometimes there are problems. We can give it to you the
easy way tomorrow, if you wish. A beard does no harm. A
cat lick in cold water. But decent dress is essential for the
knocking off of supermarket goods. We have what we call
the C and A. Wilfred's little pleasantry – the Coat and At.
Kept clean and ready in plastic. No shortage of plastic,
plastic everywhere, free and indestructible, like God. Ah,
on cue, as they say. Father Parsons, Dr Jones.'

'Mister, mister,' protested both at the same time. Parsons, who had just walked in, evidently drunk, inclined
courteously, a skeletal man well muffled, nearly seven feet

high. 'A very nearly altogether satisfactory evening,' he said. 'Some of the violent youth of Camden Town stood me whisky in exchange for a swathe of church history. They were sincerely interested. Very pro-Latin. Very much against the Lord's Supper as mere commemoration. Then the landlord of the pub said no religion in here and no politics neither. One of the youths said what else is there worth discussing, up your pipe mate or some such locution. Trouble, fighting, a timid brace of policemen. It spoilt the evening rather.' He yawned with loud relish: 'Yarawwwgh.' He fell on his mattress fully clothed and slept. One by one, two by two, the cheerless cavern filled with sleepers. Snores, chokes, groans, odd muttered or screamed words. No life, thought Bev before he too drop-ped off, no life for anyone.

In the morning black Trevor stole milk and yoghurt from a dairy float for breakfast. Bev washed in an oil drum half-full of rain water, wiped himself on what Reynolds called The Towel. Then he was dressed in the Coat and At – a decent nicked burberry and a pert trilby – and was ready for knocking off a few supplies from a supermarket. 'Observe the poacher's pockets,' said Reynolds. 'Win, for the most part, flat things. Here is one pound.' He ten-dered a note cheery with the boyish smile of King Charles III, merry monarch. 'You obviously have to buy *some-thing*.'

So Bev, heart beating hard, his first crime ever, entered the nearest Foodmart and stowed dehydrated soups and vegetables, sliced bacon, pressed meats, cheese. The place was full of shopping women. One, in metal curlers and head scarf, was saying to another: 'There's nothing in the papers anyway, except that I like the cartoons, but it's Coronation Flats on the telly tonight, and I think they ought to have more consideration, the rotten lot.' It appeared that all the communication media had struck. Why? Bev bought a kilo wrapped loaf for £1.00. None remarked on his bulges. He went out elated.

The fire in the factory yard was going nicely. Reynolds knew all about the strike. 'Tea bags?' he said to Bev. 'Good, we'll brew up in that filthy kettle. I like the tang of rust. Yes, well, this was warned of. As you know, only card-carrying members of the National Union of Journal-ists are permitted to write for the newspapers and periodicals. In *The Times* last week there was a review of some work – American, inevitably – on Egyptology. The review was inept, ignorant, illiterate, but its author was an NUJ man. *The Times* had the effrontery to publish a very long letter – fifteen hundred words or thereabouts – by some wanderer like ourselves, pointing out the ineptness, ignorance and illiteracy. Frankly, I don't see how it got past the printers. Hence the strike. Hence the shutting down of radio and television services. There has to be an abject apology. Oh, and also some kind of gratuity to NUJ funds to sweeten the sour insult.'

Derek, a fair youth in decent clothes, came to the fire smiling. 'I've got a job,' he said. 'Start tonight.'

'That's not bleeding possible,' said Wilfred.

'All too bleeding possible,' said Derek. 'A private press, flat bed, very hush hush. Tosh, you know Tosh, met him just off the Broadway. Gave it me out of the corner of his mouth. A bloke, well-dressed said Tosh, slash speaker, gave him a quid and asked if he knew about printers. Hush hush, like I say. Private residence. On Hooper Avenue. I get met at the corner of the street. Nine tonight.' His hands were already going through the motions of loading a stick with type.

'How much?' asked Reynolds.

'Five quid above union.'

The long day proved not to be as dull as Bev had expected. There were intellectual discussions with Reynolds, Father Parsons, and a new man, an Assyriologist useless to the State, named Thimblerigg. Wilfred nicked or won a small sack of potatoes for roasting in the fire. A clarinettist warmed his instrument by that fire and then played the first movement of the Brahms sonata. Father Parsons, clerical collar on, got altar wine from a religious supplies store on forged credit. Trevor came back from foraging with two plastic-wrapped blankets from a street market. 'More tomorrow, Trevor,' said Reynolds, fingering the synthetic wool.

The following morning the streets were full of copies of a new newspaper, distributed free. Father Parsons brought it in with the milk. It was called *Free Briton*, and there was a copy for each of the company that sat sipping tea from old cans and toasting bacon and bread on the fire. There were only four pages; the type was of an almost forgotten elegance that went piquantly with the inflammatory contents. It was a newspaper without news, except of the proposed formation of the Army of Free Workers. Reynolds read part of the editorial aloud for Trevor's benefit, Trevor being but a slow reader:

' "This once great country has suffered enough from the indolence, insouciance and downright obstructiveness of the workers' unions. . . ." '

'What them big words mean, man?'

'Never mind, Trevor. Let me summarize. There is a gentleman here who calls himself Colonel Lawrence.' Reynolds mused a moment. 'Pseudonym? It could be his real name, of course. Still, it suggests – never mind. This gentleman, Trevor, is forming a private army. As His Majesty's Forces are no longer trustworthy, being unionized and ready to go on strike at the first strangulated note of an ill-blown bugle, there is need, says the good colonel, for a trustworthy paramilitary organization that stands outside the law – law, however, which Colonel L. proposes be changed by a great outcry of the people, backed and encouraged by the Free British Army, as it is to be called. This army is already partly officered, but it awaits recruitment to the ranks. The ranks are as follows: private freeman, free two-striper, leader of thirty, company democrat, battalion democrat-major. The commissioned ranks seem orthodox enough – junior captain, senior captain, major and so on. The promotion rate is rapid and depends on ability rather than mere time-serving. The pay rates seem to me unbelievable.'

'How much, man?'

'Private freeman gets £150 a week, but pay is geared to inflation levels.' Reynolds was thoughtful again, frowning. 'The aim of the Free British Army is to maintain essential services when strikes hit this dear dear land, as the colonel calls it. Free soldiers take a solemn oath – to obey their superiors in everything. They vow to serve their country unquestioningly. There is even an army song – *I vow to thee, my country, all earthly things above*. Familiar, that. A very fine tune, I seem to remember, by some Swede or other.'

'Gustav Holst,' said the violist Tertis. 'Pure English, despite his name. The tune comes from *The Planets*. The Jupiter movement. E flat, three-four, maestoso.'

'And where do you sign on, man?'

'Trevor,' said Reynolds earnestly, 'I hope you are not thinking of joining a fascist organization. Freedom, Free Briton, private freeman – eyewash. This Lawrence man wants a kind of Hitlerian takeover. I beseech you in the bowels of Christ, keep away from it.'

'I could use that kind of money, man.'

'Where is the money coming from?' asked Bev.

'Obvious, I should have thought,' Reynolds said. 'Look on Page 4 – at the bottom.' Bev looked and read:

> Let us be ever mindful of a truth that the Syndicalist State counsels, nay forces us to neglect. Above our duty to country stands our duty to God, and the higher duty contains, in a mystical sense, the lower. God made us to fulfil on earth in human action the divine attributes of which our natures partake – to put beauty, truth and goodness above getting and spending. I do not mean the cricket-playing gent- lemanly God that the Anglicans have created. I mean the God of the prophets, from Abraham to Mohamed. . . .

'Now,' said Reynolds, 'do you see where the money's coming from?'

7   Nicked

Bev was too ambitious. Young in nicking or knocking off, he was over-encouraged by his little successes in super- markets. He should not have attempted to win that £15 bottle of Burnett's Silver Satin from the drinkshelf. The telescreen caught him tucking it away. When he joined the pay-line with a 50p half-kilo brown loaf he was himself joined by a hard-faced handsome girl with attractive streak-blonde hair, not unlike poor Bessie's. She said:

'That bulge in your pocket. May I see it, please?'

'What bulge? Where? Private property, mine. I regard this as an intolerable infraction of.'

'You were observed taking a bottle of gin from that shelf. Do you propose paying for it?'

'I propose putting it back.' Bev took out the bottle and tried to make his way to where he'd nicked it from. There were a lot of people looking at him. One old woman tut- tuttutted. 'Having counted my money I discover that I haven't enough after all. It's terribly expensive.' The girl barred the way. The supermarket manager appeared, grim as a surgeon in a white coat. 'Putting it back,' Bev said, 'if you'll kindly allow me.' But they wouldn't allow him. The manager said:

'All right. Caught red-handed. Get the police, Miss Porlock.'

'Yes, Mr Allsop.' She went, a pretty-legged girl.

'Look,' said Bev, 'you're making a fool of yourself. I've stolen nothing. It would be theft if I got it past the pay-desk, right? But I haven't. You'll have a hell of a job proving anything.' And he tried again to put the bottle back where he'd scrounged it from. The manager pushed him. The manager called:

'Alwyn. Geoffrey.' Two other men in white coats came from their work of shelf-packing. It was as though Bev were going to be forced into submission to a dangerous surgical operation. He panicked and tried to leave, gin bottle in hand. Then he turned back on a reflex of honesty and tried to give it to Alwyn, who looked sympathetic, a sly nicker himself probably. Alwyn, as if to disclaim complicity, thrust it by. 'Grab him, Geoffrey,' said Mr Allsop. Alwyn, who was now shown to be really Geoffrey, laid hands on Bev. Bev was not going to have that. He fought off the hands with the bottle's firm base. Miss Porlock arrived with two policemen, young men with gangster moustaches. They came for Bev and breathed hot sweet tea on him. They grabbed. Bev was not going to have that. He raised his bottle once more. The bottle was seized by one of the constables and given to Miss Porlock. Bev fought. The customers watched. This was as good as the stricken telly, almost. Bev tried to shove through the customers in line at the paydesk, some of whom shoved him back. The police got to him again. Bev scratched. His nails had not been trimmed since Christmas. He achieved a bloody hairline on a left cheek. 'Ah no,' said the constable, 'not that, chum.' They got him with a knee in the groin. They frogmarched him off.

The sergeant at the station two streets away supped tea and nibbled a cream horn while he wrote down Bev's various misdemeanours in a large slow hand: attempted robbery, resisting arrest, assaulting a policeman, being in possession of a weapon (they had found the flick-knife),

having no fixed abode. 'Gertie,' said the sergeant to a
policewoman, 'get this geezer's testiculars from CR.' CR
was Central Registry, where Bev's entire curriculum vitae
lay waiting in a computer for instantaneous disgorgement.
'Jones, B.'

'Number?' said the policewoman.

'What's your number, cock?'

'Union number? Birth registration number?'

'All your numbers, chummy.'

'To hell with numbers,' said Bev. 'I'm a human being,
not a bloody number.'

'Be reasonable,' said the sergeant, 'the whole place is
swarming with Joneses. Very difficult to find, even with a
B. Come on, lad, co-operate.'

'Why should I help a bloody machine?' said Bev. One of
the two constables thumped him.

'Right,' said the sergeant, writing. 'Uncooperative. Let's
have your fingerprints.' They forced him to press inky
whorls on a card, and the card was taken off to be photo-
telexed to CR. 'You forgot anything?' said the sergeant to
one of the constables. 'Sure you got the story right? You
forgot to say he pulled the shiv on you.'

'It's a lie,' said Bev.

'You have to co-operate,' said the sergeant kindly. 'Co-
operation is what life is all about, my son. Take him away
in the usual manner, lads.'

Bev was, in what he took to be the usual manner,
thumped towards the cells. He thumped back. The
sergeant, sighing as though at the irredeemable folly of
man as represented by Bev, made a new entry. The charge
sheet had grown to quite a sizeable document. 'Right,'
said the constable whom Bev had scratched in the supermarket, 'you wait here, cocker, till court in the morning.'
He shoved Bev in a small heaven of warmth and cleanli-
ness, with two made-up bunks and a chamber pot. There
was even a basin of water and a rough towel and a hunk of
green soap. As for the iron bars, it was the rest of the crazy
and evil world that was shut in, not he. He stripped off
and washed all over. He was given a plate of blind hash
and a mug of sweet tea by a surly man in an apron. He lay
on the upper bunk and meditated. The early winter dark
came and dim fluorescent lighting simpered from the ceiling. He slept.

He woke to hearty noise. Two different constables and a new sergeant were thrusting into the cell with some difficulty a soiled and drunken man. They apparently knew him well. 'Come on, Harry,' said the sergeant, 'be a good lad. Your bunk's nice and ready. Get your bloody head down.' The man's head was not in fact bloody, but it was bald and scarred and contained areas of crinkly skin as though it had at some time been burned. The man sang:

> 'They shoved him down and they shoved it up
> Till his cup was well-nigh overflowing,
> And this went on till the crack of dawn
> And all the time their cocks were crowing.'

He interspersed his blurred and tuneless lines with, 'Fuck you, matey,' and, 'If it isn't old Bert, Bert's my pal Bert is,' and, 'Just one more and make it a boilermaker,' and, 'I've supped some stuff tonight, I have that.' He was thrown on to the bottom bunk. Bev sighed, foreseeing a sleepless night. The sergeant, a thin man with the look of a Methodist minister, said:

'We know all about you, you non-union bastard. I've read your little dossier and filthy reading it is. You've got old Ashthorn on in the morning and I hope to Christ he pulverizes you.' He then locked the cell-door, saying to the drunk: 'That's right, Harry, keep that swede well and truly crashed.' Harry snored. Bev tried to go back to sleep. The snores turned into the pleasant sound of a sawmill in a country place: the sun was hot, even for August, and he and Ellen sat on the bank of the stream, their feet laved by the kindcold flinty element. Little Bessie, four years old, chased a red admiral. How beautiful Ellen was: clear skin, wide green eyes and snub nose, laughing wide mouth; her body spare but shapely in its pippin-russet brief summer dress. A covey of partridges drummed. The sawmill had stopped. Bev was shaken very roughly awake. Harry was on his feet, shaking.

'You got a drop for an old pal?' he said. 'I've a thirst that rasps. I can bloody hear it rasping like a real rasp.'

'There's water over there,' said Bev, trying to turn over.

'Water? Water for me? Handled thousands of millions of gallons of the bloody stuff in my time, but never not one drop down the gorge except by accident. All right, if you won't help, you won't, so bugger you, matey.'

Bev, wide awake now, said: 'What's that about water?'

'Never touch it, me, except by way of the job.'

'And what would the job be?' asked Bev, getting down from his bunk. 'Would it be by chance the job of a fireman?'

'Hit it first time, matey. Station B15. Here, I'm fucking parched.' He went to the cell-door and yelled through the bars: 'I'm dying of bloody thirst. Beer'll do. I know you've got a dozen Charringtons there, I saw them, you bastards.' There was no response. All was dark. Bev, now standing, his arms loose, said:

'Murderer. You murdered my wife, you bloody murderer.'

'Eh?' Harry turned in tottering surprise. 'Don't know your wife, matey. Never murdered a woman in my life. Killed one or two with kindness, but that's different. What you on about, then? Christ, I suppose I shall have to.' And he went to the water jug, raised it, glugged it down. 'Terrible stuff,' he panted.

'You struck,' said Bev. 'You let the Brentford Hospital burn down. My wife was a patient there. I saw her. I saw her just before she died.' He came for Harry with thumbs ready to gouge. Harry was drunk, also pot-bellied, but he had no difficulty in knocking Bev's hands off.

'You're barmy,' he said. 'We don't start fires, we put 'em out. You get that, you see it?'

'You didn't put this one out. You murdering bastard.' He struck out but missed Harry's face. It was the sort of face that might look better upside down. 'You went on strike and let people die in agony.'

'Look,' said Harry, 'blame the bastards that set fire to it, right? It was the murdering Micks, the IRA. One of my mates heard them on about it in a boozer in Shepherd's Bush. He lunged and got done for his pains. We don't like fires, matey. The fewer fires there are, better we're pleased. So don't start on about that business, get it?'

'You went on strike,' said Bev, 'that's all I know. She was just burnt bone and scorched skin. My wife. That's what you did with your bloody strike.'

'Listen,' said Harry, now rather sober, 'you got to jump when they say, right? You hear the bells going down and you shin down the pole and don't ask questions. Same when they blow the whistle. You're going on strike, they say. Right, so that's what you do. If you don't, you're out of it, right? I've got five kids. I've got a missis that'll play screaming buggery when I get home tomorrow morning. I've got a job, and it's the thing I can do. I got to do it. I need the money, and what with prices shooting I need more all the time. So you put the fear of Jesus into everybody by going on strike, and then you get what you want. What's wrong with that? Besides, it's not me and my mates that says right we'll strike. It's what they tell us to do and we have to do it.'

'You bloody murderer,' said Bev, feebly, doubtfully.

'I know how you feel. The fire should have been put out, right. We thought the army was doing it. Christ, that's what an army's for. Then those bastards strike, what we didn't expect. We don't want their bleeding sympathy. Scared shitless of the job is what I'd say, so they get out of it by talking of the cause of our civilian brothers. In the army you're supposed to jump to it and get fucking shot if you don't. My dad always said that, he was in the Desert Rats as they were called, and by Christ he was right. Look, I've slept it off, I want out.' He began to rattle the bars loudly, yelling: 'Bert, Phil, Sergeant MacAllister.' Bev sat on the one rickety Windsor chair and sobbed without tears.

8 Sentence of the court

Old Ashthorn presided, as foretold, in Number 3 Court. He was a fierce wattled martinet in his seventies, bald but with clumps of hair like wool-balls above his ears. Next to him sat an assistant magistrate, a plain flat-chested woman with a drab hat on. The clerk of the court was loud and insolent. Bev was addressed as plain Jones. The constable with the bloody hairline on his cheek, which, Bev could have sworn, had been cunningly emphasized with lipstick, read out the charges in the gorblimied form that the desk sergeant had dressed them up in. They sounded pretty bad. Miss Porlock from the supermarket confirmed everything except what was supposed to have happened at the station. The clerk of the court handed up the flick-knife to old Ashthorn who, with frightening expertise, kept shooting in and out the blade, on which dried blood stains had been imposed, presumably by the police. He dared Bev to say something in answer to the charges.

'I admit the attempted theft,' said Bev. 'But I have no job. The Workers' State denies me unemployment benefit. I have to live. I have to steal.'

'You have to steal *gin*,' said old Ashthorn, flashing the bottle (Exhibit A) in the artificial light. 'Not bread, but gin. And a very good gin, too.' He made a cage of his long skeletal fingers and beetled very sternly. His colleague read everything on the label of the bottle. She nodded, as in awe, at the long claim to excellence. 'You tried to evade lawful arrest,' said old Ashthorn. 'You carried a bloody weapon.'

'*Not* bloody. That knife has never been used.'

'Speak when you are spoken to, Jones,' cried the clerk of the court.

'That's precisely what I did,' said Bev. 'He spoke a lie, and I corrected it. Is there something wrong with that?' The assistant magistrate whispered something at great length to old Ashthorn, who kept nodding and nodding.

'You have broken the law,' said old Ashthorn. 'Society must be protected from people of your type.' Bev came as rapidly to the boil as a pan full of alcohol. He said:

'My type? What do you mean, *my type*? I'm a scholar forbidden to transmit my scholarship. I'm a widower whose wife was burnt to death while the firemen of London sat on their arses and picked their teeth.'

'You will apologize to Mrs Featherstone for using that word,' bellowed the clerk of the court.

'I apologize, Mrs Featherstone,' said Bev to the assistant magistrate, 'for using that word. Words are terrible things, aren't they? Far more deadly than fires allowed to burn on while firemen sit on their fundaments. I am not a *type*, your worship or honour or whatever you like to be called. I'm a human being deprived of work because I stand by a principle. I object to being a unionized sheep.'

'You understand what you are saying?' said old Ashthorn.

'Perfectly well. Justice has been corrupted by syndicalism. Not only justice in the wider sense but justice as meted and administered in the courts. Send a union man to jail and you have a strike on your hands.'

'This is insolence,' said the clerk of the court loudly and insolently.

'Shall we say,' said old Ashthorn, 'that it is merely untrue? Shall we also,' he said to Bev directly, 'be reasonable? The law is founded on reason. It would be unreasonable to fine you, since you have no means of paying a fine. This is your first offence – ' He checked with Bev's cybernetic *curriculum vitae*. 'It seems to me evident enough from your behaviour that you have not previously been in a court of law. I am not empowered to send you to prison. Even if I were empowered, a spell of imprisonment would in no wise alter your situation. You are, you say, forced to steal. Justice *in the wider sense* demands that your circumstances of life be so modified that the urge to commit crime is quelled and eliminated. You are to be placed on probation. Mr Hawkes,' said old Ashthorn, 'would you be good enough to explain the probationary process to the er er to the.'

A brightly polished man stood up. Bev had thought him merely to be an idle frequenter of court-rooms; now he was revealed as a court officer of some sort. He was chubby, beautifully dressed, self-satisfied in the manner of a Welsh tenor singing *Comfort ye my people*. His accent was Welsh. He said: 'Yes, your honour.' He smiled at Bev. He said: 'Let us substitute for the term probation the more meaningful word rehabilitation. Have you heard of Crawford Manor?'

'No,' said Bev, 'I have not.'

'*Sir*,' said Mr Hawkes, completing Bev's statement for him but with a kind of apologetic good humour. 'Crawford Manor is a rehabilitation centre set up by the TUC and part-financed by the Treasury. You will be given an opportunity to reconsider your position. You will in no manner be coerced into a resumption of your former union status. Your course of rehabilitation will, it is trusted and, indeed, foreknown, present the nature of *rights* which you seem to regard as tyrannous impositions so cogently that you will, I have no possible doubt, be only too eager to be welcomed back into the comity of the nation's workers. Have you anything to say?'

'I won't go,' said Bev.

The magistrate said: 'I'm afraid you have no alternative.'

'Your friend here,' said Bev, 'said there would be no coercion.'

'No coercion in the rehabilitation process,' smiled Mr Hawkes. 'But I fear that enrolment is compulsory. After all, can you deny that you have broken the law?'

Bev considered that. He saw that there had to be dragging of some kind – a fine from his pocket, his body to a jail. You committed a crime, you accepted the dragging consequences if caught.

'All right,' said old Ashthorn, 'next case.'

The constables looked murderously at Bev as he left the box. Mr Hawkes smiled.

'I go now?' said Bev sullenly.

'You go in three hours time. You take the 13.20 from Charing Cross. Crawford Manor is just outside the village of Burwash, in East Sussex. There will be transport for you and the rest of the party from Etchingham station. Mr B – '

'What a mess,' Bev interrupted. 'there was a time when the powers were separated. Now you bastards control the judicature as well as the – '

'Mr Boosey, as I was trying to say, awaits you outside this court-room. He is your conducting officer.' Mr Hawkes suddenly changed his tone and his manner. He said in a low sibilant voice: 'See sense, *wus*. You can't win, boy. Got you we have then and don't bloody forget it.'

'Fuck you, shitbag,' said Bev.

'Better that is, boy *bach*. Talking like a worker you are now. Go on, *bachgen*, take your non-unionized pong away.'

9   A show of metal

There were twenty-one of them on the train, including Mr Boosey, a man like a failed private detective who sat nursing a big mottled fist like a weapon he was dying to use. But, yawning and stretching on Charing Cross station, he had revealed, perhaps intentionally, a leather holster under his jacket. Most of the party doubted that there was a gun in it. This was England, where only criminals went armed.

Most of the twenty were men of education, few of them very young, some mild and hopeless, hanging on to principle like an expired credit card. But there were some religious fanatics, including a Scot with jutting brows who set himself to provoke Mr Boosey from Tonbridge on:

'Sae, ye dullyeart horse-punckin, ye'd hae it that the Laird's worrrd is kilted in a tippit?' He waved his Bible at the Lord's creation beyond the window, mostly concealed as it was by broken factories and dirty smoke, 'Eh, rawny banes?'

'I dinna ken what you're jabbering aboot, Joke,' said Mr Boosey. 'If it's a pee you want you'll have to wait till we get there.'

'Ach,' the Scot sneered, 'he's nocht but a quean's bycomes an' a drutlin' druntin' para-muddle.' He then turned to high-pitched Kelvinside English and said: 'What I wish to convey, brother, is that you and your lot have decided that the Word of the Lord God is all washed up and if the Lord Jesus was alive today he'd be leading the carpenters out on strike.'

'If you want to shout the odds about what's in the Bible, wait till you get where we're going. I'm just taking you there, right?'

A young half-starved-looking Midlander with great pale eyes began to sing *Onward Christian Soldiers*. Nobody joined in. He said, in a Black Country whine: 'Throwing us to the lions. The twentieth-century martyrs.' Nobody said anything. Mr Boosey took out some throat tablets but did not offer them around. He began to suck. The Scot said:

'Ach, yon thieveless sook-the-blood. Ye scaut-heid reid-een'd knedneuch mawkin'-flee.'

'You watch your tongue, Jock,' sucked Mr Boosey.

The train stopped at Tunbridge Wells. A tall member of the party in a black raincoat stood up and said: 'We change here, surely.'

'Sit down,' said Mr Boosey. 'I checked. We don't change.'

'Are you ordering me to sit down?'

'I'm telling you.'

'I think,' said the tall man, looking very coolly at Mr Boosey, 'I'll get out just the same.'

'Try it,' said Mr Boosey. 'Go on, just try.' And then it was confirmed that the leather holster beneath his jacket was not just for show. Mr Boosey pointed at the tall man a black oiled Sougou .45. The man sat. All marvelled. Mr Boosey said:

'You lot have got to remember that you're criminals.'

Bev said, marvelling: 'I never thought it possible. Gun law. Tell me, Boosey, what kind of a hermaphrodite are you?'

'Watch it,' said Mr Boosey. 'I've got a handle to my name.'

'Aye, that's guid. A scrat.'

'I mean no sexual insult by the term,' said Bev. 'Kipling used it of the Royal Marines, His Majesty's jollies, soldier and sailor too. You're an officer of the law and an officer of the TUC. A confirmation of achieved tyranny in a train going to Etchingham.'

'Batemans,' said a man in dark glasses, 'has been taken over. You'll see when we get to Burwash. The poet of empire's home is now a regional computer centre. May Puck of Pook's Hill split it with an electronic murrain.'

'Look, you lot,' said Mr Boosey, with quiet ferocity. 'I'm doing a job, get it?' He looked across the aisle to take in the rest of his party, even those who sat reading the *Free Briton*, good as gold. 'A job, that's what I'm doing. A job.' He seemed to have nothing further to convey. A uniformed guard came down the aisle calling:

'Everybody out. Train proceeds no further. We're on strike.'

The probationer criminals were interested in Mr Boosey's response to this. He should by rights have said, 'Good, brother.' Apparently, the day of holistic syndicalism not having yet arrived, he was not expected himself to go out on strike with the rest of the Conducting Officers' Union or Guild or whatever it was. But he was surely not expected to frown in irritation.

'Lead us,' said the tall man in the black raincoat, rising again. 'Lead us, brother, whither thou wishest to take us.'

'Look,' said Mr Boosey to the guard, 'will the telephones be working?'

'Working just now when the news came through from the Transport Union, but if you want to phone you'd better put some jildy in it.'

'Kipling,' said the dark man in glasses, 'is not dead.'

'But if it's a bus or something you're after,' said the guard, 'you know the position as well as what I do.'

'Jesus Christ,' said Mr Boosey.

'That is not the tone of a believer,' said the boy from the Midlands.

'You're right there, lad,' said the guard. 'Come on, let's have you all out.'

Mr Boosey looked dangerous as he got his charges out on to the down-line platform of Tunbridge Wells Central. It began to rain. There was distant thunder. A swarthy squat man who had not previously spoken said:

'Tonnerretruenotuonotrovaotunetdonnerdonder – '

'Shut it, you,' snarled Mr Boosey, 'do you hear?' The guard hovered, interested.

'Foreigner, is he?' he said. And then: 'You going up to the Manor, as they call it? Because if you are it looks as if you'll have to walk there. March them along the line, no law against it. Quickest distance between two points.'

A ruddy man with a very dirty raincoat and a copy of the *Free Briton* sticking out of its pocket said jocularly:

'Get fell in, you horrible lot.'

Before Mr Boosey could take charge, the squad had gleefully gotten down on to the rails and started to march south. 'Here, here, bugger you,' called Mr Boosey. The guard was amused.

They moved in double file. Bev's partner was the tall man in the black raincoat, a former county librarian, his name Mr Mifflin. It rained drearily. Mr Boosey cursed. At Stonegate the ruddy man said: 'Five minutes break every hour. Army regulations.'

'Keep going. You're not in the frigging army now.'

Near Etchingham Mr Mifflin said: 'Shall we make a run for it?'

'He has a gun.'

'True. Let's see if it's loaded. *Now.*'

The gun was loaded. Bev felt something whistle past his ear. He and Mr Mifflin came back sheepishly from the green embankment they had attempted to mount. 'Now you know,' sweated Mr Boosey. 'Now you know that the time for your bleeding childish nonsense is over and done with. Now you know who's bloody well in charge.'

10   Two worlds

Mr Pettigrew stood near the blocked-up fireplace of what
had once been called the Joshua Reynolds salon and surveyed his audience of 150. They all knew who he was:
they could not, in spite of themselves, but feel flattered.
The great TUC theorist, the permanent chairman of the
TUC Presidium, lean, tow-haired with an equine forelock,
younger-looking than his forty years, beamed at them and
eyed them dimly while he polished his glasses on his tie
(blood-red with gold flywheels). He put his glasses on and
the eyes, clicking into focus, were seen to be sharp and of
a terribly clear grey. Formidable eyes, thought Bev. Mr Pettigrew said, in a reedy donnish voice:
   'Brothers.' Then he smiled and shrugged with great
grace. 'I find it hard to use the term with the requisite
sincerity. Sisters. No, it won't do, will it?' The seventy-
odd women in the audience seemed to agree. Giggles,
little chortles. 'To call a female fellow-worker *sister* seems
to announce the preclusion of what our American friends
call a meaningful relationship. There is room for many
things in what is rather absurdly nicknamed Tucland, but
I don't think incest is one of them.' Laughter. Careful,
careful, said Bev to himself; don't laugh, don't be seduced
by the charm, he's the enemy. 'So I say: ladies and gentlemen. There are no officious shop stewards standing by
the walls to rebuke me.
   'Ladies and gentlemen, you have been summoned here
because you are exceptional people. You would call
yourselves, perhaps, individualists who put the single
human soul before that strange abstract group entity called the Workers' Collective. You have known struggle,
you have known pain. The principle of the unique importance of the individual soul, the untrammelled free individual will, has led most of you to a state of desperate
loneliness – the loneliness of the outcast, the criminal, the
vagrant, the sane soul shrieking through the prison bars
reared by the insane. I know, none better. You have faced
every day and, more terribly, every night in the distortions

of bad dreams, the intolerable human dilemma. I have
faced it also, perhaps with less courage than you.

'What is the nature of the dilemma? It is this. That
humanity craves two values that are impossible of recon-
ciliation. Man – or, to use the term recommended by the
Women's Liberation Movement, Wo Man – desires to live
on his, sorry, zer own terms and at the same time on the
terms imposed by society. There is an inner world and
there is an outer world. The inner world feeds itself with
dreams and visions, and one of these visions is called
God, the enshriner of values, the goal of the striving single
soul's endeavours. It is good, nay it is human, to cherish
this inner, private, world: without it we are creatures of
straw, unhappy, unfulfilled. *But*, and I must empha-
size this *but*, the inner world must never be allowed to
encroach on the outer world. History is full of the wretch-
edness, the tyranny, oppression, the pain occasioned by
the imposition of an inner vision on the generality. It
began, perhaps, with Moses, who had a vision of God in a
burning bush, and, through it, initiated the long trial of
the Israelites. St Paul sought to impose his idiosyncratic
vision of the resurrected Christ on an entire world. So
with Calvin, Luther, Savonarola – need I go on? And in
the secular field, we have seen, or read of, the agony
caused by the enforcing of some mystical conception of the
State on millions in Europe, on untold millions in Asia.

'Do I make myself at least a little clear? I have nothing
against the inner vision so long as it is controlled by mer
who holds it, kept sealed from the outer world, cherished
behind locked doors. The outer world cannot accept the
inner vision without pain, for the values of the outer world
are of a substance so different from the inner one that they
cannot meet – as phosphorus and water cannot meet –
without dangerous conflagration. Now, you will ask, what
are the values of the outer world? They are simple, and
their simplicity is the inevitable attribute of a generality.
They consist in what all Wo Men possess in common – the
need to live, which means the need to work and to be paid
for that work. When we speak of a Workers' State, a
Workers' Collective, we would, if we could, expunge from
the term the cynical political connotations which have
been added to it by the Marxist oligarchs. By a Workers'
State we mean no more than a system in which the basic

human right is permitted to prevail – the right to work and to be adequately paid for that work. The very concept implies, perhaps, a contradiction. For if the State is the possession of the workers, then the worker's long struggle for justice has been won, since the means of effecting justice is in zer hands. But every day sees signs of the continuation of the struggle, and the struggle will go on for ever. The opposition between Employer and Employed is a basic tenet of our system. The State becomes increasingly the Employer, hence, by simple logic, what is theoretically for the worker is in practice against mer. I repeat, this dichotomy is essential. Essential, because a dynamic is essential to sustain the progressive amelioration of the worker's lot, and only out of opposition can a dynamic be generated.

'It should be clear to you now, I think, that this simple philosophy of the worker's rights does not have to be identified with the philosophy of Socialism. It is true to state that Socialism favours the workers more than the happily defunct metaphysic of grab and capitalist privilege; indeed, the Socialist movement, as I need not remind you, is the movement of Labour, is based upon justice for the worker. But a movement is different from an enthroned system. A Socialist government, especially one that rules virtually, like our own, without opposition, has ceased to struggle. And yet, to sustain its dynamic, it is obliged to struggle. Thus, it struggles to increase the Gross National Product, to stem inflation, which means, in effect, to discipline the worker. Dedicated to Work, it has no especial trust in the Worker. On the other hand, a basic philosophy held in common by the Workers' Collective and the Socialist Executive ensures that the principle of simplification, of the consultation of the need to satisfy, through the machinery of government, certain fundamental requirements of the Worker, is more or less adequately fulfilled. I mean, of course, the provision of a national health service, an educational system that meets the general need but eschews the special ones of the inner world of individualists like, ladies and gentlemen, your good selves. And, of course, a social security network from which you, ladies and gentlemen, have – through your failure to set up a strongly policed frontier between the inner and outer worlds – wantonly cut yourselves off.'

He smiled, as though ironically citing an official view with which he did not necessarily agree. He continued to smile, somewhat dreamily now, as he said:

'Soon, I have no doubt, gently, imperceptibly, with none of the smoke and noise of revolution (for revolutions are always bred in the inner world), we shall see a withering away of the unwritten political constitution which was always held to be one of Britain's instinctual masterpieces. A parliament has become a time-wasting formality, as you know. We need only an executive and a civil service. A political college is already in process of formation, wherein the executives of the future will be trained. This executive will require, for the mystical purposes of continuity, a permanent head. If you're thinking it will be Bill the Symbolic Worker, you are, of course, mistaken. A monarchy suffices, an entity outside politics. The devotion of the British Worker to the British Royal Family is of long standing, and it expresses an instinctual sense of value of a nominal executive that is outside the sweaty world of the political professionals. Our fellow workers in America are already turning against the republican principle, seeing in the presidency a mere monstrous absolutism that is the ultimate fulfilment of the dirty struggle for political power. Who knows? – soon the Declaration of Independence may be repealed, and the English-speaking peoples of the world – or should I say the speakers of Workers' English? – reunited through a common purpose under a common head.

'But this is for the future, and I apologize, ladies and gentlemen, for a digression that is not to our immediate purpose. What is our immediate purpose? What aim do we seek to encompass during your stay – alas, enforced; would that it could have been voluntary – at Crawford Manor? Primarily, we wish you to feel in your hearts what you are perhaps ready enough to accept with your reason. We wish you to feel equality in your pores. The equality of the outer world, in which there is no privilege and where the very notion of the exceptional man or woman – the Hitler, the Bonaparte, the Genghiz Khan – is an abomination. What of the exceptional artist, you may say, of the scientist or genius, the thinker whose new vision threatens to burn up the old? Such will not be strangled at birth, I assure you, as the principle of egalitarianism gains

the strength which it still struggles to achieve. Art,
thought, research belong to the inner world, the private
sector of life. The exceptional genius thrusting into the
outer world – heesh is not wanted, but that does not mean
that heesh is not valued. But the value does not belong to
the world of the workers, and the value must seek its own
encouragement in that inner world which you, ladies and
gentlemen, sought to confuse with the greater one which
you thought to reject but which, you find, rejected you.'

He became suddenly stern and loud, and Bev knew that
he was probably mad. Mr Pettigrew cried:

'You have sinned. Sinned, yes. Sinned against equality,
sinned against fraternity – '

'But not against liberty.' Bev looked round, embarras-
sed, to see who had so rudely interrupted. He was
astonished to find that it was himself. There was a murmur in the audience, and the murmur grew. It was hard to
know who the murmur was against. But Mr Pettigrew at
once seized the word and drew all eyes and ears to his
now large-eyed and gesticulating person.

'Liberty,' shouted Mr Pettigrew. 'You do not even know
the meaning of the term. You have swallowed whole the
triple shibboleth of a misguided foreign revolution. You
have failed to see that two of its terms belong to the outer
world, but that the other has no meaning except in the
inner. Liberty – who denies you liberty? Liberty is a property of the private universe which you explore or not as
you please, the universe where even natural laws are sus-
pended if you wish it so. What has it to do with the world
of working and earning one's bread? You chose an impossible liberty, seeking it in the outer world, and you found
nothing but a prison.' There was a chill silence, in which
eyes were averted from Bev, as though even a look might
bring dangerous contagion. Mr Pettigrew, with frightening speed, relaxed, grinned boyishly, took off his glasses
and wiped them again on his tie. 'Liberty,' he said,
vague-eyed. 'It's use in Workers' English is the right one,
the only one. I have taken a bloody liberty in talking so
long this evening.' There was a slight gasp, chiefly from
the ladies, at the shocking intrusion of a colloquialism that
Mr Pettigrew's oratorical style had not seemed capable of
encompassing. 'I have played the dreary demagogue. It is
not, I assure you, my true forte. I hope we shall have

opportunities to meet while you are here and share for a
space our blessed inner worlds. Good night.' He said this
glassed again, sharp-eyed.

And off he went, to applause. Bev did not applaud.

11   Spurt of dissidence

There were a few rooms in Crawford Manor where inner
worlds could be visited. Some of these rooms had a bed in
them and could be locked from within. There did not seem
to be any bugging devices, visual or auditory. You were
welcome to take bloody liberties there during your leisure
periods. Bev had learnt, during a session on Workers' English with the very humorous and erudite Mr Quirk, that
the terms *leisure* and *pleasure*, though not etymologically
cognate, could be used interchangeably in WE, though in
practice the second word had swallowed the first. In
AWE, or American Workers' English, such assimilation
had not taken place, since the words had never rhymed in
America. Workers in Britain, anyway, talked of being at
pleasure during their pleasure hour, and that, since it was
current usage, must be regarded as correct. Bev was
pleasuring and being pleasured by a pleasant girl in her
thirties named Mavis Cotton. He had met her before in the
old days when she and he had been on a History Teaching
Course at Ambleside, and both had agreed that it was a
load of rubbish.

They lay back naked, sighing with satisfaction, on the
bed. Bev had to admit to himself that, in his five or six
bouts in this room with Mavis, he had known more sexual
satisfaction than in all his years of marriage to Ellen. They
had had a pleasant enough year together, though never
ecstatic, the whole world burning up, before Bessie was
born. After that birth, which had been a difficult one, she
had shied from his embraces. He had remained loyal but
frustrated. After all, he'd told himself, sex wasn't everything. Now, he saw, sex was a great deal. It was ironical
that he should have to make this discovery in a place dedicated to that Outer World of abstractions which denied
ecstasy. But, of course, no, not ironic: this paradise of the

nerves was free to all, nothing elitist about it. And yet –
wasn't there really perhaps a kind of Workers' Sex that
owed nothing to erotic education, self-betterment, sex
horny-handed, thrusting, bestial? Perhaps there would be
a lecture on that before the course ended. Mavis said:

'You was good. You did that proper.'

He looked at her, smiling and frowning. 'I never know
whether you're being facetious or not. With your WE, I
mean.'

'Oh, yes and no. Or, I suppose, neither do I. My father
spoke like that. A terrible man for aitchlessness. Who was
it said how easy it would be for the middle class to become
proletarianized? You have nothing to lose but your
aitches, he said.'

'George Orwell,' Bev said. 'My uncle fought with him in
Spain. God, fifty years back. Orwell died very unpleasantly at Pamplona or somewhere. Planning, so my uncle
said, a book about homage to Catalonia till the very day he
was shot. He spoke rather refined, my uncle said.'

'What are you going to do?' asked Mavis.

'What are *you* going to do? Have they convinced you
yet?'

Mavis said nothing. She twined a long hank of her black
silk hair in her shapely, rather rosy, fingers. Then, 'Yes
and no,' she said. 'I can see myself standing up there
lecturing on the Tolpuddle Martyrs and forgetting about
imperial expansion and Brunel and the 1851 Exhibition. I
can even hear myself doing it in WE. 'They was fighting
like for their rights, wasn't they, and they was not allowed
them rights.' Because I can go home then and play my
Bartók records and read Proust. The Inner World.'

'And when your Bartók records are worn out, who will
press new ones? Who'll play Bartók? The Inner needs the
Outer. Books have to be printed. I bet you had a long
search in the second-hand barrows looking for Proust. The
whole business is based on false premises. There's only
one world. If you can't fire some kid in one of your classes
with an enthusiasm for Gibbon, who's going to read him?'

'I can always bring in some aside about the fall of the
Roman Empire and read a paragraph of Gibbon and – '

'If you can find Gibbon around. And then you'll be had
up for bourgeois irrelevancies and watch it sister this is
your second like warning. Don't you see how it's going to

be, has to be? The universities are going to lose their sub-
sidies if they don't turn themselves into cats – '

'Into – ? Oh, CATs.'

'And a Centre of Advanced Technology isn't going to be
allowed to regard literature as a technology, even though
it is. Look at the authors already out of print and likely to
remain so. The levelling's going to reach the limit. Not
even technical brilliance in the performing arts is going to
be allowed. Them kids what sings and plays the guitar
does all right, don't they, earning millions though they
loses it all in tax, and they never had a bleeding lesson in
their bleeding puffs.'

'You do that very well. WE, I mean,' She rolled over
and lay half on top of him, her sweet warm breath and her
searching tongue-tip in his ear. 'And,' she said, 'the other
thing.' She looked at her wrist-watch, the only clothing
she had on. 'Oh, my God. It's 15.55. Seminars.' She leapt
off the bed and grabbed her one-piece garment – the siren
suit or uniform overall they had jocularly been issued with
on arrival, the quartermaster saying: 'Some of you poor
buggers looks a bit the worse for wear, here, a nice bit of
denim with the complimongs of the ouse.' Bev said:

'And if one doesn't go to one's seminar?'

'If yer don't go, ducks, yer gets beat up proper in a cellar
wiv very strong lights burning away on yer bleeding
body.' She hadn't quite got it yet: a whiff of refined vowel
spoiled her demotic, but she'd learn. Bev looked somewhat grimly at her, arms behind his head. She'd learn,
and she wasn't the only one. Some had learnt already.
That religious Scot, for instance, had been ably argued at
by a genuine theologian who'd persuaded him that the
twelve apostles were the first trade union, that Christ had
been martyrized for the principle of free organization, that
the Kingdom of Heaven meant a proletarian democracy.
There was one old man who had taught everybody something – a reformed dissident now on the staff of this centre
of rehabilitation. He had given a very moving talk in WE
on his sufferings, saying:

'I held out, brothers and sisters, to the bloody limit. And
I saw after six months of begging and tramping the roads
and sleeping beneath hedges and in the nick and out of it
that I was a bloody fool and a flaming idiot. I had a trade
and a good one – hydraulic-press checker – and here I was

not doing what I could earn good money for, and the money was getting better all the time, I could see that from odd bits of dirty newspaper I picked up here and there. I was wasting my life and, what was a bleeding sight worse, I was depriving others of what I could do, I was in a manner of speaking wasting the resources of the community. Forgive them long words, but they're the right words, brothers and sisters, and if you can think of better ones just let me know. I didn't believe in jumping to the whistle, but then I saw the light. I even heard like a voice out of the sky. 'It's your hand holding the whistle,' it seemed to say, 'It's your breath blowing it. There's no such thing as a solitary worker, you're all one big body. Horrible to think of an organ of the human body sort of deciding to go its own bleeding way. You want to raise a nice hot cupper to your lips and you're dying for it, being parched, and then your thumb goes into rebellion and says it won't help to lift it. Horrible, horrible.' Them was the words, or something as near like as make no bleeding difference. I saw it was not somebody else making me jump, it was me telling myself through the mouth of somebody I'd set up to do it for me. I had visions of workers marching together. I saw the power flaming from them like a flame like of fire. There'd been a time when the government had said: 'Haw haw, crush him, he's only a bloody workman, we've got the bastard in our power,' but now I saw it was all different. I saw that I had the power, and my mates with me, and I've never looked back since.'

Very moving, almost as moving as the films they'd been shown, very well made creatures of TUCFILM at Twickenham, historical films of the Struggle that made you want to cry out with rage. But nothing, neither film nor lecture nor group discussion, had yet dared to make the point that denied all history, centuries of religious and humanistic teachings alike: the right of man to loneliness, eccentricity, rebellion, genius; the superiority of man over men.

'Okay, love, I'll jump,' said Bev, and he donned his uniform with its TUC badge of a silver flywheel on a ground of shed workers' blood. He put on his issue slippers. The 16.00 hour bell shrilled. They kissed, they parted, she to her seminar, he to his.

'I know what is still in the minds of most of you,' said Mr Fowler to his group of twelve. They sat informally in what, in the days of its aristocratic ownership, had been the Blue Room. It was now distempered in buff and very plain, and even the old baroque cornices had been chipped off. 'You're seduced still by the traditional notion that to give one's total allegiance to a collective is to deny one's rights as a human being. You're holding out, a lot of you, against what you regard as the philosophy of the anthill.' Mr Fowler beamed, a beaming sort of man in these sessions though, strolling on the paths outside, he frowned much and muttered to himself, and concentrated the beam on Bev. 'You anti-anters have to provide an argument powerful enough to shake us collectivists, but none of you has yet done so. Am I not right, me old Bev?'

Bev shuddered at the facetious colloquialism, then growled briefly, then said: 'I want to approach this business from a perhaps illegitimate angle – '

'Bastardize all you will, Bev boy.'

'You, I mean you, Fowler. You're not a worker. I'd say you were a product of a middle-class home, father a clergyman perhaps, with a middle-class education – '

'My father,' said Mr Fowler, 'was an agnostic. A bank inspector, if you must know. As for my education – '

'Middle class,' said Bev. 'You've never practised a trade, am I right?'

'Teaching is a trade, as you know. Books are the tools of it. As for class, your term is outmoded. There are only employers and employees.'

'What I mean is – why,' asked Bev, 'do you put the generality in front of the individual? Why do you so passionately blazon this belief in the Syndicalist Society?'

'I've explained all that. Because it is the will of the majority and the aspirations of the majority that must count in the modern age, that the cult of minority power, interests, culture – '

'Of course I bloody well know all that,' cried Bev. 'What I want to know is this – what's in it for for you?'

'There is nothing in it for me except the happiness of seeing fulfilled – '

'Come off it, Fowler. You don't like the majority. You don't like beer, football pools, darts. A spell on a factory floor would give you neurasthenia. You don't give a monkey's for the worker's cause. What are you getting out of all this? For that matter, what is the great bloody Mr

Pettigrew getting out of it?'

'What am I getting out of it, Mr Jones?' It was Pettigrew's own voice. All turned. Pettigrew was sitting on a plain wooden chair by the door. He had made a sneaking entrance at some point in the session unacknowledged by Mr Fowler in smile, nod or bow. Bev, abashed, turned and stoutly said:

'Power.'

Mifflin the librarian and that other travelling companion of a fortnight back, the Midland youth who had whined about Christian martyrdom, both seemed to make 'That's torn it' gestures with their mouths. The rest of the group looked among themselves with smiling eyes of anticipation: this bugger's up for the chop, he is that. Pettigrew rose and came forward, nodding pleasantly at Fowler. He took one of the standard-pattern easy chairs and said:

'Of course. Power. So obvious one doesn't even bother to think about it. Why do people become shop stewards, union leaders, group chairmen? Because they want power. A more interesting question is: why do they want power? Can you answer that, Mr Jones?'

'Because,' said Bev, 'the exercise of power is the most intoxicating of narcotics. Sexual power, the power of wealth, the power which can grind to a stop the wheels of industry at a mere lifting of a finger, that can hold a whole nation dithering in fear, the power of the blackmailer – what does it matter what kind of power it is? It's always the same potent drug, desirable for its own sake. And it's usually a substitute for a more wholesome kind of fulfilment. A compensation for the failure of the creative urge, or for sexual debility, or because one's mother doesn't love one enough.'

'Because your mother doesn't love you enough,' said Pettigrew. 'Do get rid of that impersonal pronoun. It's the most tiresome vestige of Bourgeois English. Yes,' he then said, 'one kind of power instead of another. You've told us nothing new, Mr Jones. There has to be a dynamic. But the power invested in the leaders of the new community is, you must admit, not dedicated to human destruction. It's not Nazi or communist power. We have no concentration camps or extermination chambers. The power of the leaders of our collective is the power of the collective itself. It has never yet done anything that has not benefited that collective. The strike weapon, the most evident instrument of power, has, without exception at least in the last forty years, always succeeded in bettering the worker's lot. Can you deny that?'

'Yes,' said Bev, 'I can. The bettering has all too often been purely nominal. Wages shoot up and prices follow. The vicious spiral, as it used to be called. Small firms can't meet new wage demands or go smash because they're strike-bound and can't fulfil their orders. Okay, they're nationalized, there's a blood transfusion of public money. But where does that money really come from? From increased taxes the workers immediately strike against. It's not true capital, it's only paper money.'

'How old fashioned you are, me old Bev,' beamed Mr Fowler. 'Capital isn't money. Capital is resources, energy, the will to create. Money is nothing.'

'Interesting,' Bev beamed back. 'Money is nothing, and yet it's the only thing that the workers care about.'

'Substitute the word *consumption*,' said Pettigrew, 'and you've said all that has to be said about the Outer Life. Yes, the workers want to consume, they have a right to consume, and the Syndicalist State uses power to fulfil that right. They had little enough chance to consume during those glorious historical epochs you were prevented from stuffing the heads of the kids with, and sulked because you were stopped.'

'Consumption,' said Bev bitterly. 'And what consumption. Colour television and food without taste or nutriment, workers' rags that call themselves newspapers and substitute nudes for news, low comedians in working men's clubs, gimcrack furniture and refrigerators that break down because nobody cares about doing a decent job of work any more. Consumption, consumption and no pride in work, no creative ecstasy, no desire to make, build, improve. No art, no thought, no faith, no patriotism – '

'Me old Bev,' said Mr Fowler, 'you forget a very simple truth. That the techniques of modern manufacture do not allow for pleasure or pride in work. The working day is a purgatory you must be paid well for submitting to, paid well in money and amenity. The true day begins when the working day is over. Work is an evil necessity.'

'It was not that to me,' said Bev. 'I enjoyed my work. My

work as a teacher, I mean. My work as a rather better paid dropper of nuts on chocolate creams was a mere nothing, a sequence of simple bodily movements above which my mind soared in speculation, meditation, dream. But to educate young minds, to feed them – '

'To feed them rubbish,' said Pettigrew. 'Force-feed them with innutritious fibre or downright poison. Your chocolate creams were a more honest fodder, Mr Jones. Listen to me, sir.' That *sir* was like a promise of steel whips. 'You were wrong to enjoy your work. Even the Bible says that work is hell: "In the sweat of thy brow shalt thou earn bread." You are at your old business of confusing two worlds.'

'There's only one world,' cried Bev.

'One world is coming,' nodded Pettigrew, 'but not the one world you mean. Holistic syndicalism, the fulfilment of the ancient battle cry about workers of the world uniting. You mentioned patriotism, which means what it always meant – defending the property of a sector of the international bourgeoisie against an imagined enemy, for the only enemy of the worker was the ruling class that sent him off to fight against other workers. This is old stuff, Mr Jones. The age of war is over, along with the age of the blown-up national leaders. The age of the imposed mystical vision, the madness, the cynicism. Done, finished.'

'And now we have the age of dullness,' said Bev. 'I wonder how long it can last? Because it can't last for ever. There's something in man that craves the great vision, change, uncertainty, pain, excitement, colour. It's in Dante, isn't it? "Consider your origins. You were not made to live like beasts, but to follow virtue and knowledge." You've read Dante, I don't doubt. Read him and rejected him because he's nothing to say to the workers. *Homo laborans* replaces *Homo sapiens*. Caliban casts out Ariel.'

'Gentlemen,' said Pettigrew to the group, for there were no ladies in it, 'I'm glad you've had this chance to listen to the arguments of one kind of dissident. Conceivably, some of these arguments were once your own. We're coming to the end of this rehabilitation course. Next week, after a four-day break for the staff, the next one starts. During these last few days, I have the task of visiting your discussion groups or syndicates and putting straight ques-

tions: how are things with you now? Simple things are
required of you before you effect your re-entry into the
world of work. First, a choice of job. Our Employment
Officer, Miss Lorenz, is at your disposal with a list of vacancies. Second, the issue of a new union card, meaning a
reinstatement, a resumed citizenship of Tucland. Third
and last, a formal recantation of heresy – chiefly, I may
say, for our own propaganda purposes. A whole-hearted
acceptance of the closed shop principle and a rejection of
the delusion of right to unilateral action.'

'So,' said Bev, 'in effect you ask us to set up a new
morality in our hearts. A hospital burns down and the
firemen stand by waiting for their £20 rise. We hear the
dying screams and we say: This is right, this is in order,
first things first.'

'No,' cried Pettigrew with such force that the word
struck the opposed wall and came bouncing back. 'No and
again no,' more softly. 'You see the breakdown of a public
service and you regret that this should be so. You regret
the stupidity of the public employer that has allowed
things to get so far, that has refused to listen to the just
demands of the workers and has now forced them to use
the ultimate terrible weapon. You look beyond your
immediate vision to the reality.'

'To a man whose wife has perished in a burning building,' said Bev bitterly, 'such a mystical vision is hard to
attain.'

'And yet,' said Pettigrew, 'there have been moments,
and very recent moments too, when you have said to
yourself: I cannot altogether regret what happened.'

'What do you mean?' Bev felt his heart tumbling into his
belly and blood pumping up to his throat.

'You know what I mean.' Pettigrew looked at him steel-
ily. 'We here are entitled to know what inner worlds you
enter. After all, you are in our charge.' He turned to the
rest of the group. He said: 'Do any of you still have misgiv-
ings? If so, speak honestly.' Nobody answered because
they were preoccupied with the shock of seeing Bev leap
on to the great Mr Pettigrew and belabour him with his
fists. Pettigrew's glasses flew off and were heard to tinkle
tinily on the floor. He tried to get up from the chair where
Bev had him pinned, blinking and gasping. Fowler, not
now beaming, was on to Bev's back, disclosing a strength

none of the normally beamed at would have suspected.
Nobody came to assist Bev. Two men, metalworkers, once
very bloody-minded, came to assist Fowler.

'You damned traitors,' breathed Bev, while Pettigrew
looked with woe at his broken glasses and Fowler panted,
straightening his tie. A metalworker said:

'You're mad, mate. Fucking nutcake case, do you know
that?' Pettigrew said:

'Perhaps, Fowler, you'd get me one of my spare pairs.
In the left-hand drawer of the desk in the office.' Fowler
went. Pettigrew tried blearily to focus on Bev. 'Strangely
or not,' he said, 'this will not be held much against you.
It's a last spurt of dissidence. I think you're going to find
yourself cured. Group, dismiss. I'll see you all sometime
tomorrow.'

12   Clenched fist of the worker

Supper that evening was a solid worker's meal of cod
deep-fried in batter with chipped potatoes and a choice of
bottled sauces, spotted dick and custard to follow. Tea was
served, as usual, in half-kilo mugs. Everybody looked
strangely at Bev, not knowing whether to approve his belligerence or not, since none really liked Pettigrew though
they feared him; some seemed to be fearing the worst for
Bev, sucking their teeth thoughtfully at him as they
lighted up their penultimate issue fag of the day. Pettigrew was not present at what he facetiously called High
Table. Mavis said to Bev, as they entered the cinema
together after supper:

'How could he know?' Bev whistled a few bars of *I have
heard the mavis singing*. Mavis was quick. 'Don't be a
bloody idiot. I'm not a nark. Do you honestly think I go
round telling the staff who I sleep with.'

'How many do you sleep with?'

'That's none of your flaming business, Jones.'

'Sure you're not the Official Whore of Rehabilitation?'

She cracked him a damned flat-handed slap for that and
bounced off to sit with some of the girls. Bev, his cheek

tingling, sat alone but not neglected. There were many sad or wondering eyes on him before the lights dimmed. The curtains opened to show a wide bloody screen and a turning silver flywheel, with the first two measures of *Tucland the Brave* stereoing out in hunting-horn harmonies. TUC-FILM presented *The Fury of the Living*. The story was conventional but it was given painful force through the technique developed by Paramount's experimental workshop in the seventies, whereby the minute blackness between frames, normally filled in by continuity of vision, had been eliminated, and the images on the screen struck like raw actuality. The subject might have been chosen specially for Bev, since it was about a factory fire service going on strike in order to secure better equipment and working conditions, and the rest of the employees going out in sympathy. The dirty employers, who had planned its demolition anyway in a programme of improvement and expansion, set on fire their own warehouse, making sure first that the pretty young wife of Jack Latham, one of the strikers, was imprisoned in a washroom there. None believed this when told: a filthy employer's trick, no more. The strikers watched the warehouse burn, and then Jack Latham heard his wife screaming: 'Jack, Jack, save me, Jack,' and after that actually saw her arms and hair waving from the flames, but his mates held him back: a filthy trick, don't look, don't listen. So the warehouse burnt out, and the strike remained unbroken, and the workers had won. But in the charred ruins Jack found his wife's asbestos identity-disc and went wild with grief and attacked his own mates. And his mates admitted: yes, they had known. But a calmly wise elder, a veteran of the cause, put him right: the cause needs martyrs, the cause is sanctified by their blood or their black heavenward-soaring flinders. But why the innocent? Why should the innocent. . . .? Jack screeched from the four walls and the ceiling of the cinema. Bev went out.

Bev went out, a thing not previously known, and encountered two bruisers in official overalls. One of them said:

'Well, mate. Not satisfied with the entertainment provided?'

'I've seen it all before,' said Bev. 'Indeed, I've lived **through** it.' And he made off towards the dormitory,

'Indeed indeed,' said the other, a man with unusually close-set eyes and no lips, 'indeed.'

'Well, it adds to it,' the first said, barring Bev's way. 'We don't like what you did to Mr Pettigrew earlier on. None of us here does.'

'Who,' asked Bev, 'is *us*?'

'Mr Pettigrew,' said the second, 'is the boss.'

'There are no bosses any more,' said Bev. 'There are representatives, delegates, secretaries, chairmen. But no bosses.'

'For your type,' said the first, 'there has to be bosses. Boss language is all your type understands. This way.'

Bev was gloomily pleased that the organization was at last showing, as he had always suspected it would, the quiet face of violence. He was elbowed to a lift he had not previously seen used. It went down, as was to be expected. It stopped, and opened directly into a cellar that still held wine bins, though all now empty. There were a plain deal table and three chairs. There was strip-lighting, already on. Another man, not tough looking, was standing thoughtfully under the light, cleaning his nails with a match. 'Ah,' he said, looking up, without enthusiasm. 'This him?'

'Him, Charlie. What they call an educated taff. He's going to do something nice for Mr Pettigrew. It will bring tears of joy to Mr Pettigrew's eyes, it will that.'

'Ah, that,' said Charlie. He tucked his match away in the top pocket of his overalls and, from the broad and deep thigh pocket, brought out a folded piece of foolscap. 'It's here to be read. Then signed. But read first. Sit down, Taffy boy. Read it careful.'

Bev sat and read:

> I hereby acknowledge that, after a most useful course of rehabilitation at the Trades Union Congress Education Centre, Crawford Manor, East Sussex, I have been brought to a very clear understanding of the errors I formerly cherished concerning the aims and organization of British Syndicalism. I have no hesitation in recanting those errors herewith and wish it to be known, publicly if need be, that henceforth I will be a co-operative member of my union and an ardent supporter of the principles for which it, with its brother unions, stands.
>
> *Date:*   *Signed:*

Bev said: 'I'm not too happy about that verb at the end.

Mr Pettigrew's work?'

'It's nice and flowery,' said Charlie. 'It's a good piece of writing. Here's a pen here.' He held out a ballpoint. 'All you have to do is shove your moniker down. I'll put the date in.'

'Does this happen to everybody?' asked Bev. 'Does everybody have to come down here to sign? Or am I specially favoured?'

'Some comes here,' said Charlie, 'but not many. It looks like you're the only one on Course 23. It's good reports on the rest, but you seem to be a right bastard.'

'Did Mavis tell you that?' asked Bev.

'No names has to be mentioned. And if you're thinking this is Mr Pettigrew's idea, then you've got another think coming. Mr Pettigrew is above this cellar business. He grieves if anybody leaves here still a bloody-minded bastard, though them wouldn't be his words. He's innocent, Mr Pettigrew is, and has to be protected like from the rough side of life. So now you know what's to be done, Taff, and, if not, what has to happen, so let's get it over, shall we?'

They all nodded sadly as Bev tore up the document. The lipless man said: 'Charlie here has got plenty more of those.'

'Not all that number,' said Charlie. 'You'd better start, lads.'

They started. They were good at their work, which left no marks. Bev lay panting on the floor, trying to draw air in, and the air just wasn't available.

'Come on, lad,' said Charlie. 'All you have to do is sign. You can do what you like when you leave here, but for God's sake, lad, don't be more of a swine to Mr Pettigrew than you've been already.'

Bev found enough breath to say, '*Fuckyou*.'

'Dear dear dear,' said Charlie. 'Naughty words. Try again.'

'Did you bring the pliers, Bert?' asked the first tough. 'The dentist's ones? This geezer's got a fair number of pegs in his cakehole.'

'Left them upstairs,' said the one with no lips. 'Shall I get them?' To Bev he said: 'Always used those when I was in the police. Hurts more than just knocking them out and it shows less.'

'Later perhaps,' said the other. 'We'll see how we get on now.'

'Perhaps he'll sign,' said Charlie. 'Come on, Taff, be reasonable.

'*Bastardsfuckyou.*'

'Oh, all right then, ungrateful little swine.'

I can always recant the recantation, said Bev's brain clearly as he was kicked and thumped. I'll sign, but not just yet. I'll wait till they start the tooth-pulling. I can stand this, I can stand any amount of – The brain itself was astonished as its lights began to go out, having just time to say: 'No need to sign after all.' Then there was nothing.

13 A flaw in the system

Bev had been the only patient in the little sickbay; he had, indeed, been very nearly the only inmate of Crawford Manor. His course had ended, the reformed had gone off to the world of resumed work and consumption and syndicalist loyalty, the staff had taken their four-day break. But Bev had had a male nurse with a doctor's telephone number, and the male nurse had dished him up coarse meals made mostly of corned beef and onions, no invalid diet. But Bev was no longer really an invalid. Tomorrow, when the new course started, he would be free to go. But Mr Pettigrew did not wish him to go, not just yet. Mr Pettigrew did not take breaks. He worked all the time. He and Bev, Bev in an issue dressing-gown, had been together nearly all day for three days, either in the ward or the up-patients' tiny sitting-room. Bev wanted to know about the medical report, Mr Pettigrew wanted Bev to sign the document of recantation.

'I say again, Bev, that you were found in the grounds at night in a condition of syncope. The medical officer diagnosed slight anaemia. Our psychiatric consultant considers that the loss of consciousness might well have been caused by profound psychic tension, a struggle between selves, as it were. I incline to the latter view.'

'I was beaten up. I want that to go on the record.'

'You may have been. I can well understand that some of your er fellow-students might have wished to use violence against you. But to allege that violence might have been administered here, officially, is wholly monstrous. Violence is not a proletarian weapon. It is the monopoly of capitalism and totalitarianism. Besides, there were no marks on your body – except such marks as were obviously occasioned by your falling heavily on to a gravel path.'

'The lack of marks,' said Bev wearily, for the tenth time, 'is a sure sign of professional violence. But how can one man's truth prevail?'

'That is very nearly a sound aphorism,' said Mr Pettigrew. 'How can one man prevail in anything? Truth and virtue and the other values can only rest in the collective. Which brings me again to our unfinished business. I wish you to be manumitted, clean and reformed. Comprehensive School B15, Isle of Dogs, is only too anxious to have you. Your union card is ready. Sign, please please sign.'

'No,' said Bev.

'You know the consequences. The consequences have been presented to you very candidly.'

'I know,' very wearily. 'I'm an unreformed criminal. I can only survive by living the life of a criminal. And if I'm caught next time, there'll be no course of rehabilitation.'

'Next time,' said Mr Pettigrew gravely, 'it could be a matter of indefinite confinement. I'm not saying *will be*, but I *am* saying *c* – '

'I beg your pardon?' Bev interrupted him in large-eyed incredulity. 'You mean if I steal another bottle of gin – or try to; Christ, that's all I did last time: tried to – you mean I get a life sentence? I don't believe it. God, man, that's going back to the eighteenth century.'

'In the eighteenth century you could have been hanged for stealing a loaf, let alone a bottle of – '

'Gin was cheap then,' said Bev in the schoolmaster's way that not even impending death can kill. ' "Drunk for a penny, dead drunk for twopence, clean straw for nothing." '

'Hanging then was done without regret. We're not in the so-called Age of Enlightenment now.'

'We're certainly not. Universal darkness buries all.'

'You ought to know that the concept of penal servitude

has drastically changed in the last ten years. Prison with hard labour is not permitted by the TUC. Labour of any kind entails union representation. We cannot allow prisons to be sweatshops. Very well, there is only one kind of confinement available now.'

'You mean solitary? Solitary for life?'

'Oh no. The TUC would not permit any such fiendish punishment. May I put it this way – that the distinction between the place of penal detention and the mental home must, of necessity, progressively narrow. Which represents, in terms of the amenities of enforced confinement, an improvement. Mental homes don't become like prisons, I mean – it's the other way round. You can see that this had to happen.'

Bev looked at him with wide eyes of horror for at least five seconds. 'The bin? The asylum? Impossible, you have to establish insanity.'

'Would insanity, in your case, be so difficult to establish? You're recidivist, atavistic, a confirmed criminal, a danger to the community. You reject the sanity of work.'

'I reject,' said Bev in a small voice, 'the insanity that goes along with work in your syndicalist state. I'm entitled to my eccentric philosophy.'

'You admit the eccentricity? Yes, of course, you have to. The gap between eccentricity and insanity is easily bridged. Put away – think of it – with paranoids and schizophrenes and cases of general paralysis of the insane – that's how you'll be, Bev. Not indefinitely for punitive reasons, but because it's impossible to quantify the time in terms of a judicial sentence. *Indefinitely* meaning until somebody thinks it worth while to initiate the long bureaucratic process of approving your discharge on the grounds that adequate familial custody and care will be available. *Indefinitely* not in the sense of permanently but because there's no rational period of confinement shorter than an indefinite one. All a question of somebody caring. The State won't care. The TUC won't care. Why should it care about one who's thrust himself deliberately away from the protection of its maternal bosom? As for family – you have no family, Bev.'

'I have a daughter.'

'You have a daughter – Elizabeth or Bess or Bessie. She presents another problem. The State Institutions for Chil-

dren in Need of Care and Protection are, unfortunately,
overcrowded and, being desparate as to vacancies, they
must consult a strict table of priorities. There seems to
have been a mistake made in the documentation that
accompanied the admission of your daughter to SICINC G7
in Islington. You said, apparently, something about being
distraught over the death of your wife and unable to look
after your daughter. It was naturally understood that the
arrangement would be temporary. It was not appreciated
that you had decided to deunionize yourself and join the
beggars and vagrants and criminals. You are not one of
the legitimately unemployed. You have no claim on the
beneficent offices of the SICINC system. Your daughter
must leave. She can, of course, accompany you in your
derelict hopelessness, but to subject a child to that situation is a crime in itself. Sign, Bev. Join the comity of workers. Teach what you have to teach, draw your pay. Organize voluntary evening classes in the history of the Renaissance and the Reformation. Show sense. *Sign*.'

He had the document and the pen ready. The pen was
an attractive one, a stout ink-barrel of old-fashioned vul-
canite, the nib sturdy and gold and blackly moist.

'No,' said Bev.

Pettigrew kept his temper. 'Very well,' he said. ' "Between the stirrup and the ground – " You still have till
tomorrow. One more thing. The MO says you must watch
your heart. He wasn't too happy with what he heard.
You're not fit to cope with the stresses of the life of the
outcast. Tomorrow morning you may dress in whatever
clothes you possess and report to me in my office at nine. I
would pray, if prayer was in order, for some angel of good
sense to descend on you in the night.' He got up, smart in
his tweeds (for this was, after all, the country), and settled
his glasses and pushed back his tow lock before giving a
valedictory sad shake of the head. Bev said:

'As, in one capacity or the other, I'm to re-enter the
outside world, would it be possible for me to have news of
it? We've been sealed off for the last – '

'The strike of the communication media continues, and
rightly. You need no outside news. You have enough to
do this evening without reading rags or gawping at the
box. Think, man, think, think.' And he left.

Bev did not think. He merely mused on various possible

futures. He was quite certain that he would never give in. If the worst came to the worst, London afforded many spectacular opportunities for martyr's suicide. But how about poor Bessie?

He tossed much of the night but had one period of still sleep in which he dreamt, irrelevantly to his troubles, of angelic trumpets blowing over the city (of course, Pettigrew had put angels into his head) and then a voice crying: 'The kingdom is fulfilled.' Workmen in strange robes were hacking at barrels, and golden liquids gushed out to flow bubbling along the gutters. Banners with unreadable inscriptions flew from high buildings. There was a distant thunder of horsemen, and the thudding hooves came nearer though the riders remained invisible. 'They're coming,' cried Ellen, restored and whole, 'but for the sake of the All High don't let them get away with it.' Then the hooves were deafening. The sky, blood-red, turned primrose. Bev awoke sweating.

It seemed, from the light, to be about seven in the morning. He rose, bathed and shaved with the issue razor, then put on his old clothes and shoes. Carrying his ragged overcoat across his arm, he left the sickbay and walked the corridors and descended the stairs that led towards the eating-hall. He grieved distractedly at the low estate to which this eighteenth-century manor had fallen. What beauty of line and texture had been left in wall, pillar, curve of staircase had been wantonly rubbed out with buff distemper, posters, cheap syntex carpeting, a three-metre cut-out representation of Bill the Symbolic Worker. All that beauty, all those exquisite possessions of the tax-ruined Crawford family – gone, sold to Americans or Arabs. No room for beauty, for beauty was always for minorities. Pettigrew and his like were at least consistent: no vestige of the privileged past to be left, even though this could not but be a self-inflicted wound on those who, knowing what privilege meant, must also know that the spiritual and imaginative transports they had started to liquidate (all that nonsense about the Inner World!) were what human life was about. Perversion, masochism, martyrdom. Taste and intelligence vociferously denied by those who, possessing them, knew they were the ultimate value. Such men were fanatical. Such men were dangerous. Approaching the eating-hall, Bev knew in his tripes that he would be pursued to the limit. *Pursued by his own kind*.

Two tables were already full with early arrivals for the new rehabilitation course. As Bev filled his tray at the counter – tea, yoghurt, buttersub, toast white as leprosy – he saw Mr Boosey the conducting officer slurping his tea while waiting for three eggs to be freshly fried. Mr Boosey recognized him and grinned unpleasantly.

'Put you right, have they? A good boy now?'

'Sod off,' said Bev. 'Shove your gun in your fetid left armpit and squeeze the trigger, bastard.' Mr Boosey growled. Bev looked for a place and saw Mr Reynolds smiling up at him. Bev sat. Reynolds said:

'Yes, I thought this was what must have happened to you. It happens to everybody, I'm told, sooner or later. Are you converted?'

'No. What were you caught doing?'

'I stole a whole ham. I ate much of it too, with some of our old friends of the community. Then they came from the grocery store with the police and said: That is the man. *Ecce homo*. Will I find it amusing here?'

'A lot are converted,' Bev said. 'Be on your guard.'

'Drugs in the tea? Positive reinforcements? Torture?'

'*I* was tortured,' said Bev. Reynolds went pale as the yolk of his fried egg. 'But I leave here as I came.' Reynolds nodded and nodded. He said:

'You remember my little black friend, Trevor? Illiterate, or near, but very stubborn about human rights. Well, he joined this free army or whatever it's called. Came round flashing a bottle of *bought* gin and his first month's pay. A generous boy, happy as a king. Not a real army, man, he said. We ain't got no guns. A clever organization, I'd say. Not easily bannable. You can't even call what they wear a true uniform. Rather a smart suit really – green, belted, with a yellow enamel badge of rank on the lapel. Green for England, I suppose – '

'Yellow for Islam,' Bev said. 'You seem interested. Did you think of joining?'

'My dear boy, at my age? With my arthritis? How old are you, by the way?'

'Thirty-eight in February.'

'Consider it. They need instructors, they say, but in what God knows. Trades, I gather. Black Trevor used to be a builder's labourer. I'm in the Engineers, man, he says, proudly of course. It sounds better than being a class three hod-carrier or whatever he was. Perhaps they need history courses too. It was history you taught, wasn't it? Wait – ' He pulled from inside his ruined brown-bread-coloured suit a crumpled copy of the *Free Briton*. 'Everybody reads it,' he said. 'There's nothing else to read. I gather they put out radio and television programmes also. Formidable people. You'll find addresses and phone numbers in there somewhere. Not that the telephones are working at the moment, of course. The trains started just in time for our trip here. What a filthy mess it all is.'

'Have you,' asked Bev, 'any money?'

Reynolds looked at him sternly. 'Not here,' he said. 'Is it forbidden to go unescorted to the toilets?'

In the toilets Reynolds handed Bev three ten-pound notes. 'This is one little crime that went undiscovered. Not even the frisking police found this lot. They rarely look inside one's socks. As for a surgical stocking – I regret the crime in some ways. An old lady coming from the bank. Still, they've driven us to it, the swine. I'm sorry it's not more. It won't take you very far.'

It was with perky confidence that, jump on nine, Bev went to Mr Pettigrew's office. He wouldn't starve for a day or so. He would consider joining the Free Britons. He said, before Pettigrew uttered a word:

'No. I'm not signing.'

Pettigrew's little office was something like a presbyterial interview-room, though there was no crucifix on the wall and no musty smell of unwashed soutanes. Pettigrew said:

'A special dispensation is sometimes granted. You are more than welcome to take the course again. Miss Cotton would help you. She seems genuinely fond – '

'No,' said Bev.

'Well,' said Pettigrew, and he rose from his chair for the commination. 'I must deliver the secular equivalent of a curse. Everything possible has been done for you. On the bathroom scales this morning I noticed that I had lost several hectograms. My appetite is failing. I have never met such painful obduracy.'

'Am I entitled to a travel warrant?'

'Go and see Miss Lorenz, it's nothing to do with me.

Get your travel warrant and go. Never let me see your face
again. You're a flaw in the system, a blight. Death will
come for you soon, make no mistake about it. You've cut
yourself from the blood supply of the commonalty and
must fall off, a piece of stinking gangrenous flesh. I can
smell your putridity from here. Get out, you piece of
death.'

'You're mad, Pettigrew,' Bev said. 'You prophesy my
end, so let me prophesy yours and the end of the system
you and your kind have brought into being – '

'Get out. Now. At once. Or I'll have you thrown out – '

'You'll come up against reality, Pettigrew. The reality of
no more goods to consume, no more fuel to burn, no more
money to inflate. The reality of the recovered sanity of the
workers themselves, who know in their hearts that this
cannot go on. The reality of the invader whose insanity
will flood a sphere more fanatical than yours. If I'm to die,
I say: so be it. But you believe that death is really life – '

'Charlie,' called Pettigrew loudly. 'Phil, Arnold.' His cry
was a supererogatory act, for he had his finger pressed on
a button on his empty desk.

'Ah,' smiled Bev. 'The thugs are coming. I've finished,
Pettigrew. I'm off.'

'Finished, yes, yes, finished, finished, that's what you
are, finished and ended and done for.'

Bev left just as the thugs started coming in. Charlie
nodded at him without rancour. 'Still not signed?' he said.

'Not yet,' Bev said. 'Mr Pettigrew seems to need you. A
small fit of hysteria.' And he dashed off to get his travel
warrant.

He breathed deeply of the free January air as he left
Crawford Manor. He walked briskly and came to Batemans, Kipling's old house, now a cybernetic centre.
Somebody there had remembered the poet, for there was
a kind of wayside pulpit near the entrance to the grounds,
the text as follows:

OH IT'S TOMMY THIS, AN' TOMMY THAT, AN' TOMMY GO AWAY,
BUT IT'S THANK YOU, MR ATKINS, WHEN THE BAND BEGINS TO
PLAY.

Bev walked into Burwash village, needing a bus to get to
the station at Etchingham. There was no bus for another
three hours. He thumbed at passing cars, of which, the
price of gasoline being what it was, there were not many.

Eventually a green Spivak stopped. A gaunt man leaned out to say:

'Where?'

'Well, London.'

'Where in London?'

'Anywhere.' Bev realized that he didn't honestly know where. Islington would come into it, but not just yet.

'Hop in.'

'Thanks.'

The gaunt man drove with skill. His ethnic group was hard to place: Armenian? Greek? Some obscure people of northern India? But it was he who asked the questions.

'One of the dissidents they treat at the Manor?'

'Right. Still a dissident.'

'Trade? Profession?'

'Confectionery operative. Before that, schoolmaster.'

The man digested this. 'And you don't like things as they are,' he at last said. 'Well, you're not the only one. It's all got to change.' His accent also was hard to place. Sharp and patrician, but with a round foreign *o* that could come from anywhere. 'You'll see it soon, I think. Terrible change, terrible.'

'What's *your* trade?' asked Bev, 'or, of course, profession?'

'I'm with Bevis the Builders,' said the man. 'We specialize in the erection of mosques. I've built mosques all over the world. I built that one off the Via della Conciliazione in Rome. You know Rome?'

'Unfortunately, I've never been able to afford to travel.'

'Rome is not worth knowing. Not now. There you see what bankruptcy is really like. At present I'm engaged on the Great Smith Street contract.'

'Ah,' said Bev. 'The Masjid-ul-Haram.'

'You speak Arabic?'

'*La. Ma hiya jinsiyatuk?*'

The man chuckled. 'First you say no, then you ask me where I'm from. Call me Islamic, no more. Islam is a country, just as your Tucland is a country. Ideas and beliefs make countries. The big difference between Islam and the materialistic syndicalist states is the difference between God and a bottle of beer. Does that shock you?'

'Not at all.' Bev's dream was regurgitated in small gobbets.

'You shivered. Are you cold? Shall I turn up the heating?'

'No, no, thank you. You talked about terrible change. I was reacting belatedly.'

'I shudder too when I think of it,' said the man. 'But I do not shudder for myself. No no no, not for myself.' A light snow began to fall.

14 All earthly things above

The address was Number 41, Glebe Street, in Bev's own, or erstwhile, Chiswick. He checked it again with the last page of the *Free Briton* before ringing the bell. It was a very shabby terraced house with a neglected front garden and overflowing dustbin. A girl chewing something, frizzy auburn in a green suit with a yellow badge, opened for him. 'You'll have to wait in there,' she said, head-jerking towards a door to her right. But, clattering down the carpetless stairs, came a moustached man with papers in his hands, green trousers, white shirt. He looked foxily at Bev while he handed the papers to the girl, saying:

'Five of each there, Beryl. Good God, don't I know you?'

That was to Bev. Bev said: 'Wait. You did that last inspection. HMI. Your name's Forster.'

'Faulkner. Yes, indeed, I was one of His Majesty's Inspectorate. Welsh, aren't you, some Welsh name? You come for a job?'

'I came to see about the possibility of a commission of some kind. Jones is the name. Master of Arts, University of – '

'I'll get my jacket,' said Faulkner. 'Very fuggy in there. I'm due for a break. I've got a thirst I wouldn't sell for – Beryl, tell the Democrat-Major to carry on for a bit, will you? This gentleman and I will be at the Feathers.'

In the lounge-bar of the Feathers, Faulkner, whose yellow lapel badge was embossed with the black square of a major, drank off his gin and tonic thirstily and called for more. Bev ravaged a plate of cheese and chutney sand-

wiches and sipped at a double scotch. 'The price of it,' said
Faulkner. 'Still, it won't be for much longer.'

'You mean the price is going to go down?'

'I mean that there just won't be any,' said Faulkner.
'There'll be a hell of a row, but it has to happen. Never
mind, never mind, first things first.' He surveyed shabby
though clean-shaven Bev. He was natty, pretty, vulpine,
his polished black hair short and parted as with a ruler.
'You one of the naughty boys, then? All right, don't tell
me. I was had up for my hundred-page report on the state
of secondary level science teaching. If you don't like it, I
said – you know the rest. What sort of job are you after?'

'What sort of jobs are going?'

'Entries to commissioned rank are dealt with at the top.
That's the way his lordship wants it. I can't ring Al-
Dorchester, but he's certain to be there tomorrow. You can
go along with a note.'

'His lordship?'

'Oh, we call him that. The boss. Colonel-in-chief. Lawrence isn't his real name. He's not even Anglo-Irish, or
whatever T.E. was. The money's good. The money is very
very good.'

'Accommodation?'

'You married?'

'My wife was burned to death just before Christmas.
When the firemen were on strike. I have a daughter. Thirteen. Mentally retarded. A victim of one of the easy-birth
drugs. Look, could I have another one of these?' His
whisky glass shook in his hand.

'You certainly could.' He waved at the barman. 'A
pretty girl, is she?'

'In a blowsy way – oh God, I shouldn't say that about
my own daughter. Sexually precocious, of course. A telly
addict.'

'She sounds like any other girl of thirteen,' Faulkner
said. Then: 'When you go to Al-Dorchester, take her
along.'

'Why? Thanks.' He took his new double and squirted
soda in.

'They'll want to know everything there,' he said vaguely. 'I'll write you the note now.' He scribbled something
on a message pad, tore, folded, gave. Then he said: 'How
religious are you?'

'*Religious?* Does that matter?' Faulkner waited. 'Well, I was brought up Primitive Methodist. Dropped it, of course. I'm nothing now. God's abandoned the world.'

'Ah,' said Faulkner. 'Not everybody would say that. I'm Unitarian. It helps. His lordship will want to know. He'll inveigh against a society gone mad with materialism. He believes the only answer is a return to God. He'll want to know how you feel about that."

'Accommodation?' asked Bev again.

'The usual. No married patches, I'm afraid. But take that daughter of yours to Al-Dorchester. Ask for the Abu Bakar Suite. Where are you staying?'

'I've only just been let out of Crawford Manor. My rehabilitation course didn't work. But I've thirty pounds.'

'That won't take you far. We have a sort of miniature transit depot by Turnham Green station. Officers only. I can fix you up for the night if you like."

'You're kind.'

'No, just doing my job. We need good officers. Plenty of recruits for the lower levels. *Leading* an army is always the problem.'

'How much of an army is it? Thanks.' He had been given a third double scotch. Faulkner surveyed him coolly before answering. Then he said:

'Like the Salvation Army in a way. But we're not for derelicts. We're for energy and patriotism, skill and God. We're the alternative State. We have no arms. We've no desire to function outside the law. Not, that is, until the law puts itself beyond reason.'

'It's done that already,' Bev said with gloom.

'No. Use your imagination. Or just wait. I don't think you'll have to wait long. Events have a peculiar genius of their own. Whatever the mind imagines, the mind itself is primarily a boggling machine. Wait. One for the road?'

The transit depot had formerly been a small biscuit factory. Bev found several six-bed chambers, with very clean lavatories and a kitchen that provided bread and cheese and very strong tea. There was no officers' bar. Talking to Lieutenants Brown and Derrida, Captain Chakravorty and Acting Major Latimer, Bev discovered that they were waiting for postings to provincial barracks – Darlington, Bury St Edmunds, Durham and Preston. Chakravorty estimated that the strength of the Free Britons was now above 50 000 and growing, but it was, he said, sadly under-officered. The problem of placing arms caches worried Latimer. He was convinced that it would soon be necessary to be armed. He was recommending crash instruction in the use of automatic weapons, with dummy guns if need be. But they needed an arsenal network and they needed to be able to ensure the free passage of arms. 'We'll have to wait till G Day,' he said, 'but that's cutting it very fine.'

'G Day?' puzzled Bev. They looked at him as at one who was unforgivably ignorant, but then Derrida said:

'Of course, you're new, you can't know. General Strike Day. Ours as well as theirs. There's going to be terrible opposition.'

'And where will the arms come from?' asked Bev. They held back their laughs, but Chakravorty said:

'That's something you ought to know. There's no excuse for that kind of ignorance.' He said no more. He yawned genteelly and said it was time to turn in. He had to take a train at 05.15, picking up a Drains and Sewage detachment half an hour before.

Bev was up early enough. He had to get Bessie before the 08.15 virginibus took her to school. He rode the underground railway – a diminished service but not now on strike – from Turnham Green to the Bank, and then changed lines for Highbury and Islington. The Girls' Home was off Essex Road. He had bought a newspaper at Turnham Green, the media strike over, and found it full of blanks where the printers had not allowed certain items to be published. The front page news concerned the beginning of a construction workers' strike that day. There was a pugnacious photograph of Jack Burlap, the union leader, saying that sweet reason had failed and the twenty-hour week and the £20 rise reasonably requested had been brutally thrown out at a joint meeting of the National Productivity and National Wages Boards. They knew what was coming, brothers, and now here it is.

Bessie, waiting with her friends for the virginibus, chewing roundly on something, listening to raucous rock on a gipsy-looking girl's transistor radio, did not at first recognize her father. Then she said, 'Dad,' and embraced him lusciously. She was clean in a short blue skirt and a provocative red sweater, was much fined down in body except for her breasts. 'He was on the telly, my dad was,' she told her friends, 'The strike's over,' she told her father. 'It was terrible, wasn't it, Linda, having no telly. But tonight it's *Road Floozy*.' The gipsy girl was turning the selector. Talk came through an instant and another instant and another as she sought noise:

'Sheikh Abdulrahman said he was ... under no circumstances would the strike be permitted to ... Great Smith Street was scheduled for....' And then music, loud, crude, brash. Bev said:

'Put the news back on. It sounded important.'

'Up your fucking arse,' said the gipsy. 'Bus is coming, Bess.'

'You, Bess, are coming with me,' said Bev. 'Get packed.' Bessie howled. Her friends climbed aboard, miming sexual assault on the driver, who wearily said, 'Stop that lot now.' Bessie sought to follow them. Bessie's friends got off to rend Bev with their nails. Bev said:

'A day out. Lunch. Cinema.'

'It's *Road Floozy* tonight.'

'I'm talking about *today*.'

'So I don't have to pack, do I?'

'I suppose not.' Bev and the driver exchanged a nod of large frustration. 'We'll get you things, whatever one means by things.'

'Lipstick? Manegloss?'

'Come on,' said Bev. He still had, after his tube-fare, twenty-five pounds in his pocket. He took her to a Crumpsall's Yumbox and watched her eat sausages with her fingers. She told him about her life at the Girls' Home, which meant mostly what television programmes she had seen. The strike had been terrible, strikes shouldn't be Allowed by Law, but Miss Bottrell had put on film shows. And they didn't have a wide-screen telly there, anyway, which was a fucking cheat, and there was only one set, and there had been scratching and hair-tugging and gouging about what they should all look at. But it would be all right tonight, they all wanted to see *Road Floozy*. She did not seem to remember her mother; she was vague about her old address; her father she remembered because he had been on the telly. She spoke of Red Azel and Dirty Nell and Black Liz and the night they had got a boy into Dorm B and thrown his clothes out of the window and made him do things to them, but he couldn't do much and it wasn't as good as the telly. Bev sighed.

He gave her lunch at the Pig-in-a-Blanket on Tottenham Court Road and watched her eat sausages with her fingers. She ate two helpings of Cream Corn Heaven with Old Piggy's Chocsauce. Bev had enough cash left to take her to the one o'clock showing of *Sex Planet* at the Dominion, and she wanted to see it round again, but he said:

'No. We're having tea now,' knowing that they weren't unless it was going to be stood them, 'at one of the finest hotels in the world. And don't ask if they have telly there, because they do.' He counted up his deckers. They could afford to ride to Green Park. From there they must walk. By the tube station the *Evening Standard* was being sold. A headline said: MOSQUE SCABS THREAT. Bev couldn't afford a copy.

High above Al-Dorchester on Park Lane a yellow flag flew, with the name of the establishment in beautiful Arabic script, and floodlights flooded it with light. Bev and Bessie went through the swing-doors. The vestibule was full of Arabs, some in robes, others in badly cut Western suitings. In the long lounge tea was being taken. Bessie said:

'Look at them lovely fancies.' Weary British waiters pincered cream horns and éclairs on to the plates of disdainful male Arabs. Bev said:

'Sit down there.' And he shoved her into a canary-coloured armchair while he went to the desk to ask about Colonel Lawrence. Colonel Lawrence was expected at any moment, he was told. He went back to Bessie. Bessie complained:

'You said we was going to have tea. I want some of them cakes.'

'Be quiet child. I haven't enough money.'

'You promised.' She beat on his chest with a sturdy fist. Some tea-taking Arabs looked amused. One man, in snowy robes and corded headpiece, gazed through dark glasses long and with no discernible expression. He said something to a big-eared young man in an atrocious brown suit. The young man nodded and came over to Bev. He said:

'His Highness says you join him for tea.'

'Well – ' Bev was doubtful. Bessie said:

'His Highness?'

'He says you join him for tea.'

'Then tell his Highness ta,' said Bessie, and she pulled Bev vigorously up from his chair. They went over. Bev inclined to His Highness.

'Sit,' said His Highness. 'Sit.' There was a clapping of hands. Two waiters appeared with silver teapots and fancy cakes. Bessie couldn't wait for the pastry-tongs. She grabbed. His Highness smiled with reluctant indulgence. He spoke long Arabic with many throat-clearings and glottal checks to a fat man in a navy blue double breasted of which the bosom sagged sadly. The fat man said, nodding:

'*Gamil, gamil. Harusun?*'

'What precisely is – ?' Bev began, and then he was aware of a stirring in the lobby. Somebody important had arrived.

'Al Orens,' said His Highness. Bev said, rising:

'Excuse me. An appointment. I – '

'You leave her,' said the fat man. 'She eat. She be safe.' As an earnest of this he clapped his hands for waiters. Bev now saw Colonel Lawrence for the first time. He was immensely tall, had a Mediterranean nose and a northern pallor, was dressed in a green suit with discreet yellow piping on the lapels, wore a black cloak. He had an entourage of five or six, white, brown, black. To an aide of an aubergine colour he spoke rapid Arabic. He bowed to the Arab tea-takers with deferential grimness, making for the lifts. He carried a riding-crop. Bev went, pulled out his note of introduction, addressed the aide:

'Sent by Major Faulkner – '

'Okay, you come up. Long wait maybe, maybe not. Many things going on now. You take next elevator.' Too tall for the ascending box, Colonel Lawrence seemed to bow towards Bev. The door closed. Bessie was on her, surely, seventh éclair. His Highness encouraged her gently to eat. Bev took the next lift.

The room where he was made to wait was a sumptuous lounge half-transformed into an office. Office? More like a map-room, war-room, operations-room. Two girls in green, one of whom greeted Bev with, 'Hi,' were dealing with, respectively, a telex machine and a typewriter whose carriage moved the wrong way (of course: Arabic). A map of the United Kingdom was on one wall, on another a map of Greater London. There were flags stuck on these maps. In the Westminster area was a black lozenge with the moon of Islam in the middle. Of course, the new mosque. The typing girl, very English rose and yet a great clatterer of Arabic script, got up and took a Coca Cola from a drinks-fridge. She offered one silently to Bev. Bev was thirsty.

He was standing with a black bottle stupidly in his hand when Colonel Lawrence came in. The eyes that looked down on him were speckled and flashed irregularly and disconcertingly. 'There is little time,' the voice was a reedy tenor, the accent vaguely Scottish, 'for formalities. Things are beginning. I have a strong recommendation from Major Major – '

'Falk er ner,' said the aubergine aide.

'You are, I gather, highly literate. Have you had journalistic experience?'

'I edited the university magazine for a year. But listen, sir, I would like – '

'You would like to know terms of engagement etcetera etcetera. There is no time, I say. This is the evening of the double strike. We need full eye-witness information ready for press by at latest 22.00. We wish you to go to Great Smith Street.'

'I fear, I'm afraid – '

'Afraid? Ah, I see. Give him money, Redzwan. Give him, ah, one of our anonymous raincoats. Take a taxi. Take a notebook and a pencil. You seem, if I may say so, to have nothing. Soon, I promise you, if you are obedient and faithful, you shall have everything.' Colonel Lawrence, aide following, strode back to the neighbouring room. Bev frowned and swigged his coke. The typing girl, without looking up, said:

'He's like that.'

Bessie was still stuffing, but more slowly. 'Oad Oozie,' she said. The entire Arab company watched benevolently. 'Telly,' she said. Bev said:

'I have to go. Work. For Colonel Lawr – '

'She be safe.'

Bessie, drugged with goo, looked up at her father and did not seem to recognize him. The white raincoat perhaps. The oversize bowler hat that was really a light-weight steel helmet. Bev went to the door and the Cockney doorman whistled him a taxi. Bev gave him a five-pound note. Sophisticated by Islamic prodigality, the doorman scowled. Bev rode off through the winter evening. There was not much traffic. The price of petrol, the cost of cars. Hyde Park Corner. Grosvenor Place. Victoria Street. The taxi-driver sang some bitter recitative to himself. The corner of Great Smith Street, Westminster Abbey just ahead. Of course, the great mosque must challenge the ancient temple of the people of the scriptures, British branch. Bev heard the noise of crowds. He gave the driver a ten-pound note and told him to keep the change. 'Ain't no bleedin' change.' Bev gave him a twicer. 'Ta, mate.' And there it was facing him: the start of the great confrontation.

The crowd was angry and was hardly to be held back by an unhappy police cordon. Mounted constables clacked up and down. There was much light. Huge generating trucks fed huge brutes of floodlamps. By the light of these men worked. How many? A hundred? More? Two sky-high cranes were gravely busy, their gantries gyrating, their cabled grabs placing great blocks of masonry with delicate care. A brace of concrete-mixers ground and growled. Workmen in aluminium bonnets climbed ladders and descended them. An electric hoist took up a whole brickie gang to a boardwalk. The crowd of strikers yelled filth at the scabs. A loudspeaker truck rolled into Great Smith Street and a voice hurled and echoed:

'The building of the mosque must proceed. It is not a supermarket or a high-rise apartment block. It is a temple dedicated to God. To God, the God of the Jews and Christians and Muslims alike, the one true God of whom Abraham and Jesus and Mohammed were the prophets. I say again, the work must proceed. The wage offered is twenty pounds above the new rate sought by the Builders' Union. Be free, be free Britons, do the work you can do. We need your skill, your energy, your devotion.' A television team drank in the strikers' response: fists of anger, stroked bristled chins of indecision. The voice of Jack Burlap countered. Jack Burlap himself was there, on top of a truck, a loud-hailer to his face like an oxygen mask.

'Don't listen to the swine, brothers. It's the old capitalist trick. No guarantee, no contract, no security, no right to withdraw labour. You blackleg bastards up there, listen to

the voice of reason. Get off that filthy job, you're playing
into the bastards' hands. You're done for, you've given up
your freedom, they can kick you off the job when they
want to. It's wog money, it's dirty Arab oil. You're
finished, brothers, you stupid swine, you've given up
your buggering birthright.'

'You hear the voice of reason?' cried the loudspeaker
van. 'The voice of intolerance, rather, of racism and
chauvinism. You Muslims, you hear yourselves called
dirty wogs. You Jews and Christians, will you allow your
brothers in God to be reviled and spat upon? Be free,
throw off your chains, honest godly work awaits you.'

A huddle of strikers tried to overturn the loudspeaker
van. The police held them off. Jack Burlap addressed
them:

'Now then, you police, do your duty. Don't turn against
your comrades. You know the law, and I don't mean the
law of the courts and the statutes. I mean the law of
labour. You're workers too. Join your brothers. What's
happening here is fragrant infringement. Don't let it happen – '

He was drowned by an unearthly blast of music. Eyes
and open mouths sought its source. Loudspeakers, but
where? A thousand mixed voices, a Berliozian orchestra,
brass bands added:

> I vow to thee, my country,
> All earthly things above –
> Entire and whole and perfect,
> The service of my love. . . .

A police sergeant on a prancing mare reined in the better
to hear what was coming through on his walkie-talkie. He
put down the instrument and nodded at a waiting constable. The constable blew a whistle thrice shrilly. Everybody out. The police were on strike. Jack Burlap seemed to
halleluiah against the music, as though at a personal
triumph. Perhaps union leaders were now interchange-
able, inevitable result of holistic syndicalism. The cordons
broke. Odd policemen removed helmets to wipe brows.
The mounted cantered off.

> The love that asks no questions,
> The love that stands the test,
> That lays on the altar
> The dearest and the best. . . .

The strikers howled or deeply moaned. They moved in on the holy building site. The music stopped in mid-minim. And then –

A platoon of men in green suits, lieutenant and leader of thirty ahead, marched down Great Smith Street at a light infantry pace. A brace of outriding motor-cycles grunted and spluttered. Another platoon followed. The police, shambling off, did not interfere. The green men carried no arms. In files they fought their way through to the making of new cordons. They were, Bev now noticed, all green-gauntleted. The right hand that had to strike out at occasional strikers seemed unusually heavy. It cracked dully on jaws. One hit a skull whose owner dithered and went clumsily down to be trampled on. Knuckledusters, of course. Bev felt sick. Another green platoon came from round the corner, this time doubling. The two cranes kept gravely to their lifting, one, setting down the other. Concrete heaved like simmering porridge. The builders went on building.

15   An admirer of Englishwomen

'NOT armed,' said Colonel Lawrence. 'That is important.'

'I say armed,' said Bev. 'Arms aren't necessarily guns. Your troops used violence.'

'A hard word,' said Colonel Lawrence. 'Try and see this thing in proportion. Ah.' His telephone rang.

'Impossible,' Bev said. The colonel widened his nostrils in a sort of triumph. He picked up the receiver. He listened. He smiled. He said:

'Your shorthand man? Good. Mr Jones will dictate.' To Bev he said: 'We've certain lines open. They will stay open. Our newspaper is to have eight pages tomorrow. Come, to work.' Bev improvised fluently from his notes. He had never expected to be a pressman. It was easy, money for jam.

'That,' said Colonel Lawrence, 'is contrary to my instructions. He had listened keenly to Bev's dictation. '*Not* armed. Never mind. Major Campion will know what to do.' He said thanks into the handset and then replaced it.

'Censorship, eh?' Bev said. 'The not so *Free Briton*.'

'Mr Jones,' said Colonel Lawrence, 'we will discuss later the true nature of freedom. And, in respect of yourself, the freely assumed constraints of army discipline. The *Mr*, by the way, means acting full lieutenant. For the moment, can you be trusted to write the editorial? Phone it through, Major Campion will make such adjustments as are needed. He knows my style. I must go out now.' He shook his aide Redzwan, dozing in a chair. Redzwan came up fighting. 'I must inspect the stricken city.' He went over to the window and looked out on a black London. There was light here in Al-Dorchester, though. It was dim and fluctuating, but it would get better: they were at work in the cellar adjusting the generators. 'The situation you know – before dawn the strike will be general. The first British General Strike since 1926. Point out the great difference between then and now. Now there are no communications, no law and order. In 1926 there was at least an army that kept its oath of loyalty and a non-syndicalized police force. Ours is now the only organization capable of maintaining minimal services. Say that when the TUC leaders see sense they will be more than welcome to the hospitality of these columns – '

'You mean that, Colonel? Your organization thrives on a TUC that doesn't see sense. You want this strike to end? Remember, you or your Islamic masters started it.'

'*Your* organization, *your* masters. Tomorrow we must see about your formally taking the oath of obedience.' The telephone rang. Redzwan picked up the receiver. His jaw dropped. He handed it to Colonel Lawrence with great staring eyes on him. Colonel Lawrence said: 'Yes?' His face too lengthened. '*Allah ta'ala*,' he prayed. 'Yes. Yes. I agree.' He hung up and looked tragically at Bev. 'Tungku Nik Hassan has been assassinated,' he announced.

'Tungku – ?'

'Malay. From Brunei. Head of the Pan-Islamic Commission in the Haymarket. There are mobs of striking workers with nothing to do but attack various buildings flying the flag of the star and the crescent. This was inevitable, I suppose. I just did not think it would start so soon. Say something in the editorial about the deplorable racism and bigotry and, indeed, atheism that have become associated with – '

'Wait,' Bev said. 'How was he killed?'

'He was struck on the head with a length of lead piping. The Tungku courageously ventured into the mob, trying to make them see reason. He was an eloquent man, his English always of the most persuasive. Put it in about his virtues – ' The Colonel's nostrils were wide.

'You smell a special danger, don't you?' Bev said. 'Britain is now wide open to the punitive invader. The services are on strike. NATO will dither, the constituent countries worrying about their oil supplies. Are the Arabs coming?'

'The Arabs are here, Mr Jones.' Colonel Lawrence made his eyes project something fearsome on to the map of Greater London on the wall. 'Retaliation, Mr Jones. Do you think the Holy War ended in the Middle Ages?'

'Look, Colonel sir. What exactly are you after? A free Britain or an Islamic Britain? I have to know. You've appointed me as your provisional mouthpiece.'

'The only way out of Britain's troubles, Mr Jones, is a return to responsibility, loyalty, religion. A return to God. And who will show us God now? The Christians? Christianity was abolished by the Second Vatican Council. The Jews? They worship a bloody tribal deity. I was slow in coming to Islam, Mr Jones. Twenty years as one of His Majesty of Saudi Arabia's military advisers, and all the time I kept, as was my right, to my father's Presbyterianism. Then I saw how Islam contained everything and yet was as simple and sharp and bright as a sword. I had dreamt of no Islamic revolution in Britain but rather of a slow conversion, helped by an Islamic infiltration expressed in terms of Islamic wealth and moral influence. Slow, slow. The working man's beer grows weaker, since so many of the breweries are in pseudonymous Arab hands. One cannot impose prohibition with a sudden stupid Volstead Act. Pork is swiftly pricing itself out of the market. But sometimes the North African blood that is my dear dead mother's cries out for fast action, while the Scottish side of me counsels care, *festina lente*. We will talk more of these matters tomorrow. But for now I fear the swooping of the sword.' He turned his eyes, alive with rivet-sparks, away from Bev and on to Redzwan. 'The striken city,' he said. 'Come.'

Alone, for the two girls were snatching sleep on camp

beds somewhere, Bev leaned back in his chair and yawned, arms behind his head, trying to think out the opening of his editorial. There was a knock and the door opened. A slim Arab entered, a Savile Row suit of quiet grey on, gold wristwatch, cufflinks, Gucci loafers. 'Mr Jones?' he said, in a very fair British upper-class accent.

'I don't think I've had the pleasure – '

The Arab sat down gracefully on a hard chair. 'My name is Abdul Khadir,' he said. 'His Highness's personal secretary. Which Highness, you will want to know. The answer is: His Highness Sheikh Jamaluddin Shafar ibn Al-Marhum Al-Hadji Yusuf Ali Saifuddin. You had the honour earlier of taking tea with him, so he tells me. The question I ask now is: does she possess a passport?'

Bev stared. 'Who? Why? What are you talking about? Oh my God. I'd forgotten clean about her. Where is she now?'

'Sleeping. Happily, I think. Alone, I must add. She watched the television programmes. The strike did not begin until well after the termination of a particular programme she had expressed much desire to view. She viewed it. She ate much. I think I can say she sleeps happily. His Highness leaves tomorrow – ah, I see it is already tomorrow. As she will be a member of His Highness's entourage, perhaps there will be no need of a passport. Still, His Highness has this democratic concern with the obeying of regulations.'

'You mean,' Bev said. 'I just don't,' he said. 'I don't think I. She has no passport, no. She's never had a passport. Please,' he said, 'explain.'

'I must first explain about His Highness. He is at present Chairman of IOU. It is a rotating chair, as you will know.'

Bev's brain swam. 'IOU?'

'The Islamic Oil Union. In Arabic, of course, the initials are different. His Highness's territories, as you will know, comprise – '

'Spare me. A hot territory, with oil and Allah. Muezzins and yashmaks. No need to tell me precisely where he sits on his revolving chair and watches the mineral fatness gush. Somewhere in Islam let us say.'

'Somewhere in Islam will do very well. Of course, the chair does not literally rotate.'

'And what does His Highness require of my daughter?

God knows, she has little enough to give.'

'Concubinage for a probationary period. And then marriage. His Highness already possesses four wives, which number represents the statutory allowance. Probationary concubinage until the marital vacancy is arranged. Do you object to the term?'

'What does Bessie say about it?'

'Besi has no objection. She does not know the word. Besi has, anyway, no option but to obey her father. I may say she thinks already very highly of His, ah, Highness. She has never before, she gives us to understand, seen such a capacity for bestowal. She is yet to encounter his library of videotapes in Ghadan. Western television programmes are very popular in His Highness's gynaeceum. His Highness travels widely throughout Islam. Also throughout the infidel world. His tastes are enlightened. But he is mostly in Islam. He pays frequent visits to London.'

'You seem to regard London as part of Islam.'

'It is the commercial capital of Islam, Mr Jones. I have a document in preparation for you to sign. It is being engrossed at the moment, in English and in Arabic. We could meet perhaps for breakfast here tomorrow. Here, of course, there is no strike. This is regarded as Islamic territory.'

'Is there anything for me in all this?' Bev asked coarsely.

'Satisfaction,' said Abdul Khadir, 'that your daughter is well provided for. I do not think your England is a good place to bring up a daughter. Unless, that is, the father has much wealth. Money? You require payment? You consider your daughter an object for sale? May I remind you that you have not been asked to provide a dowry.'

'You said something about concubinage. Aren't concubines bought and sold?'

'*Probationary* concubinage. It is not uncommon in Britain, and here there is no talk at all of money. But you may take it as certain that there will be marriage. His Highness has a great regard for Englishwomen.'

'She's only a child.'

'She is thirteen years old, Mr Jones.'

Bev sighed and then felt a qualified elation cautiously approaching. He was free, by God or Allah. He had now for shouldering only the burden of himself. He said:

'If the bar were still open we could drink on it.'

'The American Bar here has been long abolished, Mr Jones. Alcohol, in our faith, is *haram*. On the other hand, I have an adequately stocked drinks cabinet in my suite downstairs. If you would care to – '

'Thank you,' said Bev. 'On second thoughts, no. I have work to do. In the name of Allah and a Free Britain.'

'We will meet at breakfast, then. Your delightful daughter is looking forward to breakfast, she tells us. She has a great fondness for the *naknik* – no, that is the Hebrew name. *Sougou* is the right word.'

'*Sou* – ?'

'Sausage. It is common among Western children. She will not be allowed to have pork ones, of course, but she will hardly notice the difference. She did not notice it tonight.'

16   Strike diary

G1

Near the Cherry Blossom Boot Polish Factory, Chiswick, I got the first physical impact of strikers' enmity towards Islam. Three Bentleys going to Heathrow, flying Muslim flag. Sheikh in middle one, me and Bessie in third, father and daughter saying farewell. We stopped to let two loudspeaker vans go down Devonshire Road. Ten or so strikers threw stones at us, shouting wog bastards, up Allah's arse and so on. Our offside rear window starred and, from the noise, bodywork dented. Bessie open-mouthed with joy as though seized by scruff and thrust bodily into TV scene of violence. I expected we'd shrug it off, go on to Heathrow, but HH did not shrug it off. He was out of the car, giving Arabic orders. Two chauffeurs, Pakistanis probably victims of East End paki-bashers, dragged two Nimr automatic repeaters from trunk of Car 2. Clicked their weapons to ready and waited for signal to fire. I tumbled out of car yelling No no no no for God's sake, got into fireline. Stonethrowers ran like bloody hell, one Paki ran a few yards and spluttered shot at them, got one in leg, other in chest. One dead certainly. HH shrugged, dark glasses on, cigarette in Dunhill holder. Guns stowed, continued to Heathrow, leaving 1 dead 1 wounded. Bessie said it was like Grimm's Law or some such bloody TV nonsense, then wondered if she'd be in time to see Pornman that night, very vague indeed as to where she was going.

Heathrow Terminal 3, Islamic corner where nobody on strike. We whizzed straight on to tarmac. Sheikh's Nisr jet waiting, fuel nozzle to breast. Giant jets everywhere becalmed, no control tower staff, no customs, passport formalities. Whole airborne army could land here without opposition. Felt tremor of fear. Two Arab Wizzahs were there, mechanics peering into their innards, wooden crates being unloaded. Major Latimer, man met at Turnham Green, posting to Preston cancelled, was there with swagger stick and two trucks. Weapons he said – Okottas, Ghadibs, Vihainens, also British Mark IV Angries. Real army now, he said. If bastards want trouble bastards can have bloody trouble. Wind whipped up Bessie's skirt to arse level. Latimer went click click in soldier's vulgarity. My daughter, I said. Sorry old boy, nice piece of goods, daughter or not. I said ila allaqaa to HH, my prospective son-in-law, kissed poor or lucky Bessie. She said: I'm hungry, dad. They'll serve elevenses when you're aboard, Bessie. But I'm hungry NOOOOOOW! Last words Bessie spoke to me. Went back townwards in Bentley No. 3, starred and dented.

Strike absolutely and totally bloody general. Went round getting news. Rain, mud, piled refuse, squalor of streets growing. Women crowding and scratching to get into supermarket, Free Britons trying to control. Strangely, some of the strikers help. Hope there. Bloody ideological nonsense from top of unions must fail sometime, workers basically decent, must see sense. Later saw windows smashed of liquor store not by strikers but by Free Britons, coming out loaded with booze. Free Briton NCOs tried to make them see sense, barked orders, got the usual Up yours Jack and so on, then put on knuckledusters, waded in. Very nasty, very necessary. At Great Smith Street work on mosque goes on, but workers on mosque obviously unhappy at being marched to and from shifts by platoons protecting them from angry mobs. How long can this go on? File news, write editorial, cautious, no

word about being armed or the necessity of violence. I
have wads of cash in pocket worth little at moment. Loaf
of bread £5. Bit of chuck steak £9.50. A Free British bakery
is being set up in, appropriately, Bread Street. Have own
bedroom Al-Dorchester.

G2

Ill-printed bulletin going the rounds with facsimile signa-
tures of appropriate ministers of the crown, saying that
builders' demands have been met – 20 hour week, £20 rise.
That is to get that particular bit of unrest out of the way.
Great Mr Pettigrew himself turns up at Gt S. Street to
harangue from loudspeaker van mosque workers. Join
your brothers, leave this illegal workforce, back into
union, your action paralysing whole country. Some of
mosque workers scratch heads, doubtful, unhappy, but
NCO foremen shout and prod them back to labour. Which
is worse – obeying NCOs, WOs, officers or jumping at
shop-steward's whistle? Pay better in Free Britons? Yes,
notice posted on worksite of £25 rise in soldier's pay.
Half-hearted cheers.

Food supplies remain a problem, though not in well-
stocked Al-Dorchester, in front of which now barbed wire
and sentries armed with Chanzir 45s. Col. Lawrence says
all ammunition blank, but I do not believe. He wants me to
take oath of obedience, come properly under military
discipline, but I say no time, too much to do. A certain
Syed Omar, mufti for Central London, comes into office to
deliver statement to be published in *Free Briton*. Col. L
translates for me. Gist: must be clearly understood that
mosque erection is holy work not subject to secular laws or
covenants, that the site may be British soil in geo or topo-
graphical sense but in deeper or spiritual sense this is
Islam, holy ground, promise made to the whole Islamic
world that Great Mosque of London, chief Muslim temple
of all of West, would be opened with great ceremony on
first day of Shawwal. Promise must be kept, strikes and
industrial disputes generally most frivolous, let British
people and their governors clearly understand that Islamic
leaders will stand no bloody nonsense or holy words to
that effect.

Car of Syed Omar pelted with stones and rubbish on his
way home from Al-Dorchester. Small irregular patrols

going the rounds of the town, armed with pistols, staves, coshes, anything, all Muslims, Pakistanis, even Northern Chinese, Anglo-Saxon converts to faith, women too, no Arabs, nothing to do with Free Britons, protecting Muslim shops, residences, mosques of course. An infantry detachment from Lockheed Barracks, against instructions of army shop-stewards, marched round East End, with auto weapons taken from armoury broken into, tried goodheartedly to organize distribution of flour supplies for communal street baking. Candles, when obtainable, cost £10 each. Much breaking-up of property – furniture, shop fronts etc – to light street fires. Frozen mud everywhere today, people slipping and cursing. Free British sentry slipped outside Al-Dorchester on to arse, gun went off accidentally, mortally wounded woman who turned out to be Lady Belcher, wife of TUC peer. Hell of a row. Tanks reported rumbling through streets of Birmingham. More arms certainly coming in at Heathrow and other airports. Cannot get much news from provinces except of riot, killing, gaspipe leaks, explosions, water supplies frozen. Hot argument with Col. L about his lying about sentry blank ammo. He says: I hate violence but you can see situation. You can see also no compromise possible re mosque. I say end of strike in your hands and those of your bosses, whoever or wherever they are. Call off blackleg Free Briton labour, let unionized labour take over. He says: So this your view, eh? You've changed, by Allah. Not really, I say, have always believed in a minimum of protective unionization, am, after all, a historian, but object to rigidity. He says: once for all, no possibility of compromise, Islamic leaders will not accept unionized labour, the British union leaders must be made to see reason. See reason in nozzle of gun, I say. Don't like this situation one bit, I say.

Curious event in Piccadilly. Devlin's son, model for Bill the Symbolic Worker, turned up by Eros statue dressed as in poster and recognized as such, very very drunk, stripped off naked despite cold and indulged in homosexual cavortings, saying Bugger the Workers, Workers, come and be buggered. Posters of Bill the Symbolic Worker all over town being defaced, great pricks and dirty words spraygunned on. Woman I met in street sobbed at me and said you must help, I have to get to Darlington, have no

money, terrible things happening in Darlington they tell
me, married daughter there, very worried. I gave her my
travel warrant issued at Crawford Manor, blank but
signed, and she nearly grovelled in gratitude. How
ridiculous really. No northbound trains running beyond
Leamington, manned by Free British engineers. Warrant
probably useless anyway. But anything with royal coat of
arms on, as warrant has, being issued by State Rail
Authority, is a talisman of sanity and stability. Some day
she may be able to use it, poor woman.

Remembered Kumina boys – so long ago it seems – telling me of UU or Underground University. Saw one in
action today in broken and totally looted supermarket,
Latin literature being taught to gang of attentive toughs.
Striking sec. school teachers come along to protest at
blackleg education, scholastic scabs etc, and UU students
show how violence, not gratuit though, necessary to protect human right to be taught Virgil and Horace. Gesta
sanguinaria (?).

G3

It is quite certain that feeble government no longer in existence. Mr Sheen, Prime Minister, was heard yesterday on
Free Brit radio asking both sides to see sense, Islamic
authorities to temper fanaticism, TUC for that matter to
temp. fan. Today story came through very rapidly that he
had resigned and that King had done nothing about asking anybody else to form new government. Makes no difference. Proves conclusively that we have never had a
govt in Tucland except for going through motions of delay-
ing enactments demanded by TUC. Constitutional situation interesting, though. Has monarch right to leave country govtless? Traditionally he must ask some member of
majority party, usually recommended by retiring PM, to
take over Cabinet, reshuffle, form new Cab. Will next
stage be deposition of King and promotion of Mr Pettigrew as (Temporary?) Head of State? End of Constitution?

Increasing demand in streets, esp outside Gt Smith St
mosque site and United Arab Embassy, for Arabs to leave
Britain. Get rid of bloody wogs etc. Race riots on small
scale, perhaps to grow greater. Free Britons openly using
arms. Story of tanks in Birmingham proved false. They

were small World War II Bren carriers. Food growing short at Al-Dorchester.

Persistent rumours from East Coast of Arab planes, or at least planes with star and sickle moon glinting in winter sunlight, trying to land but NATO forces buzzing them off. Too fantastic to be true. Bombers? Troop carriers? I will believe nothing of this nonsense.

G4

Hunger, chaos, thawed mud everywhere, uncollected debris, water pipes bursting, unofficial warnings of tainted water supplies, gas explosions. Unrest among Free Britons. Today being pay day, pay parades lined up punctually at FB centres at 09.00 hours. Moratorium on pay declared. No cash available. Violence. Arab leader spoke Oxford English at conference in Al-Dorchester ballroom (Sheikh Isa Ta'ala? Name seemed to be in doubt) about awareness of unpopularity of Arabs and Muslims generally in angry strikebound Britain, but Islam had known hostility throughout its long existence and there was no intention of withdrawal of Arab presence. Much Arab money tied up in British property. The Sheikh, statutory dark glasses on, cigarette in Dunhill holder lighted by brown-suited aide, seemed uneasy. I gained impression from Free Briton higher-ups, other Arabs, anonymous men who might have been from TUC or MPs or higher civil servants, that there had been serious discussion of kind of Pan-Islamic take-over under Sultan or Kalif or President, in accordance with instructions of The Prophet to plant the flag of the faithful in the land of the infidel. Feared opposition from USA cartels with substantial, if dwindling, financial interests in Britain. Much talk of CIE, which I did not understand. Found out later that the letters stand for Channel Islands Experiment. Cannot believe. Cannot at all believe what I was told.

Apparently a French-speaking Algerian force collected in Avignon and Orange, backed by money from Saudi Arabia, took over the islands of Alderney and Sark some months back. Muzzled press and radio, no news leaking to either French or British mainland. Enforcement of Islamic law, closing of bars, splitting of beer and liquor casks in streets, golden fluids singing down the gutter, banning of pork and other pig products, conversion of main churches into mosques, conversion of Jesus Christ into Nabi Isa, penultimate great prophet but no more. Much hostility on part of Channel Island citizens, blood chasing golden liquor down gutters. So – my dream! General conclusion that experiment was a failure, that enforced conversion impracticable. French government persuaded seignories of Sark and Alderney to hush up incident, embarrassing to French. How little we know, God help us, how little we are told. It seems unlikely, anyway, that there is going to be an imposition of Islam here. Festina lente.

G5

A very nasty incident today and a very unpleasant row with Col. L. Five or six mosque workers wanted to pack the job in. They hated being marched to and from barracks and being yelled at, cursed, and threatened with violence. They wanted to re-enter the ranks of the unionized construction workers and quit the Free Britons. They were marched off under heavy guard and not seen again. I wanted to know what had happened to them. Col. L knew but would not tell me. Disciplinary action necessary against the defaulters of any army, he said. What kind of disciplinary action has been taken? I wanted to know and still do. Not important, he said. They have been punished. Mutiny totally impermissible. Shot, have they been shot? No, of course not, we do not shoot our own people. But these, I said, are not your own people, these are just people in it for the pay. Tell me, I want to know. You have no right to know. It's time you took that oath of allegiance. Tell me, I said, and to hell with your bloody oath. Do not swear at me, Lieutenant Jones, and so on.

I decided I would quietly walk out.

I can join the looters. I can join the dead. I can teach history in one of the UUs. There is great confusion now, a blurring of the conflict, an indistinctness of frontier. Free Britons mingle with the strikers (having first discarded their uniforms and put on looted mufti) to restore a bit of human decency. Many of the strikers want to go back to work. There is a strong collective desire for a nice piece of meat, a quiet bottle of beer, an evening with the TV. Union speakers on top of trucks (fewer now, there being no petrol around) are howled down. But, of course, they are also cheered. The mosque workers work surlily. They are supervised by NCOs who carry pistols but use coshes. The illness has to be resolved. How?

17 His Majesty

The thirteenth night of the General Strike was the night of the big fires. Those who believed that these had been started by the Sons of the Prophet were disabused by the spectacle of the bright destruction of the tall thin building in the Strand (a building so slim and sharp-apexed that the Arabs themselves called it the Mibrad Azafir or 'nail file') devoted to Islamic popular culture. Many, indeed, could see clearly now why the Free Britons were backed by Arab money: it was primarily so that, in desperate times like these, Arab property could be protected or salvaged by a body that resided outside the syndicalist covenant. The fire services did not, of course, break the strike but they rendered their equipment available to such as wished to fight fires, though they grumbled about this being a bloody liberty. The Free Britons were driven to fire-fighting almost literally at bayonet point. But, in the middle of the night when the fires were at their brightest, cash suddenly reappeared from sources unknown and pay parades were held in the streets. Some of this money unfortunately went up in flames, but for all that the fire fighters fought fires from now on more willingly, though not with a more notable expertise.

It was the Irish Republican Army at work, of course. But was it that same band of eternally and illogically disaffected who sent over the bombing planes? The fires of the night of G13 had evidently been laid by hand, but, at 02.35 the night following, the fires that ravaged the dock area and even set blazing some of the idle freighters on the Thames had an aerial provenance. There had been in history, so said the experts, only one Irish airman (the one celebrated by W. B. Yeats in a famous poem); the IRA was essentially a land force; where would they find the money to buy or borrow bombing planes?

Puzzled and perturbed, Londoners followed an invisible and inaudible bell-wether to Trafalgar Square on the morning of G15. This was the traditional forum where grief and worry could find expression, resentments could be aired, words of reassurance spoken by one leader or another. Four docile couchant lions brooded and, high in air, the one-eyed, one-armed (and, as the vulgar had it, one-arsed) hero of a great sea battle seemed to drink of air that today was like chilled Pouilly Fumé. Bev stood on the periphery of the vast muttering ragged bruised, convalescent – could one, he wondered, say convalescent – crowd. Jam-packed and grumblingly patient. Hopeful, though, of something. On the plinth of the pillar there was as yet nobody. But, of course, nobody officially knew anything. There had been strong rumours of a meeting here, but rumours are only noise. The loudspeakers trumpeted dumbly to the corners of the square. What a target, thought Bev, for a phalanx of day bombers. But the sky was clear and empty. Bev saw Mr Pettigrew in the crowd, along with burly union leaders. What stopped them from getting up there and starting a fluent harangue about something? But everybody waited. The air was full of pigeons, comically bombing with putty-coloured faeces or vainly seeking low-level landings. There were ironical cheers when someone got one with an airgun, deadly accurate. There were also growls about leaving the poor bloody birds alone. Then there was a rustle, a growing hum of expectancy, incredulity. Vehicles were coming along the Mall. The more agile of the waiting Londoners leapt on to the plinth to get a look. 'It's the King!' somebody yelled. Everybody laughed, nobody believed it. And then some believed, and soon everybody, and cheers began. Some rude children near Bev began to sing:

> 'God save our gracious cat
> Rub his belly in bacon fat
> God save our'

The royal Rolls-Royce, with the Royal Standard flying, gently nosed into the square, with behind it a plain van. The plain van opened up first, and overalled technicians with the monogram CIIIR jumped out. Why weren't the buggers on strike like every other bugger? Royal servants, not allowed. Up for the chop if they did. Leads and cables

snaked. The royal car opened and His Majesty King
Charles III got out. Lean moustached men in good subfusc
suits escorted him to the plinth. A microphone was placed
in his woolly gloved hand. He wore a tight blue Melton
overcoat of vaguely naval cut. There were cheers and
countercheers. The King grinned. His ears were pink with
cold. He said, and all listened:

'What I'm doing right now is against the law, I suppose,
but it strikes me that we've all been a bit against the law
lately. What I mean is I've no constitutional right to stand
here and speak. I mean, the monarch's only supposed to
be a kind of figurehead and only say what his government
tells him to say. The trouble is, we don't seem to have a
government at the moment. Any of you seen a government about lately? I looked under the bed this morning,
but whatever it was I found there, it wasn't a government.'

He shouldn't do that, thought Bev, he shouldn't play for
laughs. But he's getting the laughs. When will we bloody
British learn to take things seriously?

'As there's no government,' said the King, 'and as I'm
constitutionally a sort of head of the State, I thought I'd
better come along and say a few words. I mean, nobody's
working at the moment, you can all spare the time to
listen. Not that I'm going to say much. One thing I have to
say, though, is that Sir Malcolm McTaggart, the royal
physician, is a bloody blackleg. He broke the strike this
morning against the orders of the shop stewards of the
British Medical Association. I asked him to. Had to. You
see, my wife, the Queen that is, is just starting to give. I
mean, any minute now we're going to have an addition to
the family. I think we might call him Bill.'

There was an affectionate uproar. A little chinny man
with glasses on, just in front of Bev, yelled:

'Another bloody mouth to feed.'

'What I want to say is this,' said the King, 'and thanks
very much for that er loyal expression of er you know
what I mean, is this. That this bloody nonsense pardon my
French has gone on long enough. I think it's time we all
went back to work.' Cheers and jeers. 'And I'm not just
politely asking the Navy and Army and Air Force to go
back, I'm *telling* them. If they don't want the King to be
their commander-in-chief, then they'd better stop calling

themselves the Royal this and that and the other. Right,
let's see them jump to it. Because if they don't jump to it
it's going to be a bit late to do the job they're paid to do,
which is defending the country. I mean, look at what happened last night and the night before. The whole damned
country's wide open for anybody who wants to walk in.
We're not mugs at Buck House, you know, not all of us.
Some of us know what's going on. For instance, there's
this business of a number of big battle wagons prowling
the oceans round our shores, and they don't belong to the
Sons of the Prophet, oh dear me no. There's an aircraft
carrier been spotted just off Cromarty, and the Arabs don't
go in for that sort of hardware. You all know who these
things belong to. No, not the IRA, not them. And don't
think our pals the Americans are going to flush them out
in accordance with their North Atlantic Treaty Organization commitments. There are a lot of big American business concerns in that particular country, and that means a
lot of hard Yank cash. It's a country they don't want to
start a shooting match with. Too useful. It's one of the few
countries in the world where the workers don't go on
strike.'

Boos, cheers, laughter. The King said:

'Anyway, I want to see the boys in blue and khaki jumping to it and shouting *Sah* and getting on with the job. We
all know there's a little army been flitting about, and with
our own army we don't have any need for private armies,
thank you very much. So this organization is disbanded as
from this moment on, and anybody who belongs to it and
has weapons and ammunition had better start handing it
all in to the nearest police station. Which means we want
to see our brave bobbies back on the beat as from the
moment I step down from this pedestal here. As for the
work that's been going on in Great Smith Street, seat of
the old Colonial Office and now site of the new mosque,
that's strictly a union job as from now on. I had dinner last
night with one or two of our Arab pals. It was a whole
sheep and they gave me the eye, which they consider a
great delicacy. Delicious, well, no, not really. I put it in my
pocket when they weren't looking, still got it here somewhere – never mind. The point is that a mosque may be a
sacred place and all that, but when it's just bricks and
mortar it's no different from a supermarket or a public

urinal – bigger, of course. When it's finished it can be as holy as they like. As for now – sorry, chaps, I said, but you see what happens when we start making exceptions to the rule. They saw the point all right, decent chaps really, and they're going to let us carry on doing things our own way. I know there've been some hard words said lately and a few blows, but apologies have been offered and accepted on both sides. If you don't believe me about us having our own way, just take a shufti at Great Smith Street and you'll find things nice and normal, with nobody doing a stroke.

'We've got to stop all this nastiness between the different races, you know. I shouldn't really have to tell you that. I mean, the future peace of the world depends on everybody respecting everybody else's colour and creed and what have you. I mean, race means very little really. When I think of the racial mix of my own family my head starts to spin. Scottish and German and Greek and God knows what else. There'll be Israeli and Arab before it's finished – if, that is, it's allowed to carry on and produce constitutional heads of State and so on. But that's up to you. Everything's up to you. That's what they mean by that big word democracy.

'So I think everything ought to be okay now. Tonight, so they tell me, the telly will be starting again. Of course, not according to what's printed in the *TV Guide* or whatever it is – I never buy it, I just switch on and take what's going – I go to sleep, anyway – anyway BBC1 is doing *Gone With The Wind*, uncut, and that sounds like a nice way of filling in an evening. Of course, we need a bit of electricity, but I don't doubt we'll have that by lunch-time. That's about all, I think. I suppose I'm going to be for the chop now, though God knows who from, since we haven't got a government yet. Ah well, never mind – '

One of the moustached thin men passed up a message. The King's face became suffused with boyish joy as he listened. Then he told his subjects:

'It's happened. I'm a father. A fine lad. Mother and infant both doing well. God bless you all.' He waved his woolly gloved hand and got down from the plinth. His chauffeur held the car door open ready for him. The car pushed gently through the crowd. The crowd sang fervently as the National Anthem began to pulse from the loudspeakers:

> 'Send him victorious
> Appy an glorious
> Long to rine orious
> Gawd sive ve – '

They sang with perfect WRP (TV) – Workers' Received Pronunciation (Thamesside Variety). Then they all got down to thinking of the possibility of going back to work.

18   His Majesty's pleasure

'Jones,' said old Ashthorn, presiding, as previously, in Number 3 Court, 'you've been up before me already at least once – '

'At most once,' corrected Bev.

The clerk of the court, loud and insolent, bawled:

'Watch your tongue, Jones.'

The assistant magistrate, a plain flat-chested woman with a drab hat on, though not the same woman as on the previous occasion, whispered something to old Ashthorn, who sourly nodded. He said: 'You still do not seem to have pondered sufficiently the errors of ah ah your ways. I have before me a record of recalcitrance and ah recidivism and ah what's this word?'

'Atavism probably,' Bev said. 'I recognize the hand of the great Mr Pettigrew.'

Old Ashthorn humphed and puffed and then said: 'You have been given every opportunity, every. You remain what it says ah here. What have you to say for yourself this time?'

The clerk of the court bawled:

'Come on, Jones, we've a lot of work to get through.'

'Yes, of course, that strike of court officers has left you with a nasty backlog. Felicitations, by the way, on your latest salary award. Sorry. Well, then, I'd like to express satisfaction that this time I'm up for achieved theft instead of, as before, merely theft attempted but unaccomplished. Boodle's Gin, your honour, is a fine cordial and I enjoyed it. I wish also to say that I do not accept the jurisdiction of this court. The British judicature in all its branches has become the mere legal instrument of State Syndicalism. Let me add – '

'All that is down here too,' said old Ashthorn. 'And it is all ah ah irrelevant, not to say impertinent.'

'Very well, then, I protest against the sentence you are now compelled to impose – '

'You know nothing, sir, of the sentence till the sentence has been delivered. You have said enough, I think.' The assistant magistrate whispered to him. 'Yes, I quite agree,' said old Ashthorn. 'More than enough. The sentence of this court is that you be detained in a state institution for as long as His Majesty's pleasure shall determine.'

'I knew the sentence,' said Bev, 'before you uttered it. I protest.'

'Take him down,' bawled the clerk of the court to Bev's police attendant.

He had not done too badly really, thought Bev as he travelled north in a closed van, a white-coated orderly beside him, a conducting officer in grey next to the driver. It was spring now, very nearly Shakespeare's birthday, and he had lived free, though dirty, for nearly the whole of a hardish winter. He had not given in to the swine. As for now, was he really beaten? Hardly, since he remained unsyndicalized despite all their entreaties and bludgeonings. He could live freely in the large periphery of his brain. He knew precisely what was going to happen to him.

'Here it is,' said the orderly. 'SI-5, Purfleet Castle as was. Hear them birds sing, see that lovely green and them daffodils,' for the van door was now open. 'Consider yourself bleeding lucky to be here and not in the bleeding jug.'

'Anybody's free to enter,' said Bev, 'so long as they see sense.'

'Shut your fag-hole,' said the conducting officer. 'Get out there and get in.'

Bev was handed over by the white-coated orderly to a couple of men in cleaner white coats. They had clipboards and the frowns of the overworked. Bev was sent in for a physical check-up.

'Go on, bend down proper. We've got to see right up. That's more like it.'

Undernourished, underweight, physical tone poor, right lung somewhat spotted, heart to be watched, teeth dreadful, in dire need of a bath.

A clean Bev in an institutional dressing-gown had his mind gone over by a Dr Schimmel and a Dr Kilburn, the latter a woman, washed-out blonde, thin and sharp. He tried to get the matrix tests wrong, but his wrongness was so consistent as to be adjudged right. Dr Schimmel said:

'What's the matter with you, man? You could live a sane healthy productive life if you wanted to.'

'I know. But that would mean approving of an insane morbid slothful State philosophy.'

'That's undemocratic. Insanity is defined as a rejection of the majority ethos. You proclaim insanity in words and actions.' Both doctors frowned over the thick dossier that had accompanied Bev on his journey.

'What are you going to do to me?' asked Bev. They did not answer. Bev said: 'Look, I can't see where I've gone wrong. I was brought up under a system of government that was regarded as the triumph of centuries of instinctual sanity. I see the world changed. Am I obliged to change with it?' Both looked at him in quiet satisfaction, as though the asking of that question was a kind of capsule confirmation of his insanity. Dr Kilburn said:

'You're part of it. Your error is in supposing that the human observer can be separated from the things observed. Your aberration, to use a charitable term, is that you resist change.'

'I won't resist the change that brings the world back to sanity. To an acceptance of justice and the wholesomeness of spiritual and aesthetic ideals.'

'Yes?' said Dr Schimmel encouragingly.

'Consider,' said Bev, 'the British Constitution. I believe that the people should be represented, as they have been for centuries. All we have now is an upper house legislature crammed with TUC life peers. The House of Commons is withering away. The monarch, as head of the executive, presides over a cabinet made up of alumni of the TUC Political College. The elective principle has disappeared.'

'The people,' said Dr Schimmel, 'elect their union representatives. Isn't that fair enough?'

'No,' said Bev, 'for life is more than what nowadays

passes for work. More than a fair wage and a dwindling selection of ill-made useless consumer goods to spend it on. Life is beauty, truth, spiritual endeavour, ideals, eccentricity – '

'Ah,' said both doctors.

Bev felt very tired. 'It won't do, it won't, it won't, it won't.' And then: 'Forget it. It's like addressing a couple of brick walls. Do what has to be done. I'm in your hands.'

Don't let them get away with it. The man who slept in the next bed, formerly a professional signwriter, made a beautiful job of inscribing those words in Gothic letters (upper and lower case) on a panel cut from a shirt-box lid (institutional shirts, grey, medium, 10). This had, with permission from the wardmaster, been affixed with tacks to the wall above Bev's bedside locker. Nobody enquired as to what the words signified: they were taken as an emblem of Bev's derangement.

The food was plain and adequate. There were football or cricket matches in the ample grounds. There was even a library made up of books that had escaped liquidation in the State taking over of ancient aristocratic country seats. Volumes of seventeenth-century sermons, Thomson's *The Seasons*, Pope, Cowper, *The Rights of Man*, John Milton, nothing later than about 1789.

Don't let them get away with it. Don't let who get away with what?

They rarely bothered with news of the outside world. Mr Thresher, who had been a television news reader given, in his later (literally) days, to ribald asides on the items he retailed, kept his hand pathetically in by announcing in the day-room public occurrences that might or might not be fictitious:

'British inflation is running at the rate of fifty-five per cent per annum. This was stated unofficially by Dr Erlanger, World Bank economic adviser, at a conference in Chicago of United States economists. The figure was neither denied nor confirmed by the Tucland authorities.' Or:

'The National Union of Comprehensive School Students has reached an amicable settlement with the National Union of Teachers as regards the relegation of school-teachers to an advisory capacity in the conduct of State education. The help of the teachers in devising school syllabuses of a more realistic content than has hitherto prevailed will be gladly accepted, said Ted Soames, National Secretary of NUCST, at a press conference, but students will consider themselves under no obligation to implement the advice given – '

'Ah, shut it,' Mr Cauldwell, a boilermaker, would shout, looking up from his game of checkers with Mr Toomey, a ruined cobbler.

' – Among projected school courses at the secondary level may be mentioned sex drill, porn hard and soft, strip-cartoon teaching of trade union history – '

'Shut it, or I'll bleeding bash you.'

But Mr Cauldwell was frightened of Mr Ricordi, a thin frail man who had run a bookshop and was believed to have the Evil Eye. Mr Ricordi would turn it on him, and Mr Cauldwell would gulp and go back to his slow game. Or:

'The Islamicization of the Isle of Man, or Gazira-ul-Ragul, has, thanks to the fervour of Nabi Mohamed Saleh bin Abdullah, formerly Joseph Briggs, been effected with comparative smoothness. Protests at the imposition on the community of total abstinence from alcoholic liquors were to be expected, but scientific demonstrations of the absence of alcohol in Manx beer, the stimulant-depressant LMP having been long substituted for it, convinced the community that no real hardship was being imposed.'

'Shut it shut it, or you'll get my fucking fist in your fucking face,' Mr Ricordi having gone out for a moment. *Don't let them get away with it.*

They wouldn't get away with it, not indefinitely. They couldn't. You can't take without at the same time giving. Bev was prepared to get out there and fight again, preach, get his own army together. Was this a sign of dementia? The only way he could get out was to have his family claim him. That meant Bessie. He got a letter to Bessie, sending it through the London agents of the Arab ruler who was his son-in-law, potential or actual, or else merely the man who had debauched, and was perhaps intermittently still debauching, his daughter. Six months later he got a postcard, its glossy picture showing camels and street beggars: 'der dad i am alrit ere tely very gud i am ok luv besi.' The next letter he wrote received the following reply:

Dear Sir,

I am directed to inform you that no one of the name of Elizabeth (Bessie) Jones is resident in any of His Highness's establishments. Conceivably you are mistaken as to either the name or the address, perhaps both.

Yours very truly. . . .

From the Astana, Ghadan, the 12th day of the month Shaaban, in the year of the Hijrah, 1364.

Mr Coombes, a Jehovah's Witness, tried to escape. He was powerfully reminded that he was undergoing an indefinite period of penal servitude. The perimeter wires were electrified. The institution had its own generators; there was no hope of their being rendered harmless through a strike. Mr Coombes, a tough man in his late fifties, was badly burnt. One of the medical officers told him he was lucky he had a strong heart. There were also big dogs which Bev could hear howling sometimes in the night. Presumably the supervision of the inmates could be left to these animals if the human staff were to go on strike. Dogs had, as yet, no union. Anyway, the human staff had it cushy and showed no desire to withdraw what was euphemistically termed their labour.

The long days that grew into months and years were enlivened by the deaths of the older inmates and, very occasionally, the entrusting of some of them to the care of their families: farewell tea parties, with an extra cake each. New inmates brought news of the outside world; the news did not greatly interest such veterans as Bev. One day none other than Colonel Lawrence appeared. He had been convicted of manslaughter. Discharged from his army, he had found work as a State interpreter, under his real name of Charles Ross. Frustrated for one reason or another, he had broken a habit of abstinence that had lasted a quarter of a century, and, drunk in a pub, had quarrelled with a Persian. He had not intended to kill the Persian, he said; the skull of his victim had, at the autopsy, been shown to be preternaturally fragile. Anyway, here he was.

The Persians, he said, were going to go to war with the Arabs. The Islamic union had been broken. The Iranians were Aryan and the Arabs Semitic, and blood was thicker than a Koranic *surah*. The Shah, whom the Americans had long considered to be the only reliable magnate of the

Middle East, was well armed with what the Pentagon called a nuclear capability. The Arabs, who had never been
favoured customers of the American armourers, would be
at the mercy of Iran. Iran would take over all the oilfields
of the Middle East. The Arabs, aware of American partial-
ity to Iran, were withdrawing their megadollars from the
American banks. There was bank panic in the United
States, with little depositors lining up for cash and finding
their local banks declaring a moratorium. The Federal
Reserve was printing too much money, desirous of quel-
ling the panic by increasing – in fact, doubling – the cash
flow. Too much cash in the United States. Twice the
amount of cash chasing the same quantity of consumer
goods. Stores closing down, their shelves emptied, an
awareness among the economically literate that inflation
was spreading like a southern Californian fire. Other cur-
rencies responding to dollar inflation. The sterling situation unbelievable. Bankruptcy on its way. The end of syndicalism? At least three and a half million unemployed in
Tucland. Nothing much heard of Mr Pettigrew these days.
Deposed? Assassinated? A burly man called Big Tim Hol-
loway heard much in the land, ranting about workers'
unity and the wicked capitalists.

Bev had taken to teaching history to a small interested
group, giving a lesson on Elizabethan England every
afternoon in one of the day-rooms. Later he gave a course
on England in the seventeenth century. It seemed reasonable to push on to the end, all from a memory that grew
ever more defective. He seemed, even to himself, to be
dealing with the history of another planet. But he and his
students escaped daily to this unreal past, as to a fuggy
room from a biting wind. The First World War, recovery,
Wall Street crash, rearmament, the rise of totalitarianism.
The Second World War and after. History dangerously
began to approach the present. The present could not be
summarized, explained, even well understood. A great
river seemed inexplicably to be dissipating itself into a vast
number of muddy little streams and creeks. One afternoon
he sat hopelessly in front of his class – Mr Tyburn, Mr
Gresham, Mr Hooker, Mr Merlin, Mr Lyly, others. He
said:

'Shall we start again? Shall we go back to the rise of
capitalism and try once more to trace the cracks in the

structure, to discover where everything began to go wrong?' Mr Hooker said:

'I think we've had enough.'

Bev nodded and nodded. After supper that night he went out into the grounds. That heart was weak, watch that heart. He stumbled through the unknown pasque-grass to that part of the electrified perimeter that was framed by two knotty apple trees. Those trees had given sour crabs for a long time. They would survive a while, and that was a small comfort. The moon, defiled by politics, its poetry long drowned in the Sea of Storms, had but recently risen. Bev addressed to it certain meaningless words.

But, of course, they all got away with it; they always would. History was a record of the long slow trek from Eden towards the land of Nod, with nothing but the deserts of injustice on the way. Nod. Nod off. Sleep. He nodded a farewell to the moon. Then he bared his flesh-less breast to the terrible pain of the electrified fence, puzzling an instant about why you had to resign from the union of the living in order to join the strike of the dead. He then felt his heart jump out of his mouth and tumble among the windfalls.

A note on Worker's English

Worker's English represents the rationalization of a general pattern of proletarian language, formulated by Dr R. Stafford and Dr A.S. McNab, of the Ministry of Education, during the 1970s, and made compulsory as a subject and as a medium of instruction in State schools, under the provisions of the Democratization of Language Act, 1981. The basis of the language is the urban workers' speech of the Home Counties, with a few additions from the industrial Midlands and North-West, but with very few elements of rural dialect. The primary aim of Drs Stafford and McNab was less the imposition, under political or syndicalist pressure, of the language of the dominant social class on the rest of the community than the adaptation of an existing form of English to the fulfilment of a traditional language planner's aspiration – namely, the development of a rational kind of language, in which grammar should be simplified to the maximum and vocabulary should achieve the limitations appropriate to a non-humanistic highly industrialised society. What appeared, in fact, to be the implementation of part of a political programme was actually a social achievement with no political bias, with the two philologists concerned activated by a scientific desire for the reduction of entities and only secondary ambitions in the fields of class domination and pedagogic economy.

The simplification of such elements of inflection as parts of verbs, declension of pronouns, irregularities of pluralization in nouns could, it was admitted, be pushed a great deal further than the forms actually formulated in *A Grammar of Workers' English* (His Majesty's Stationery Office, 1980), but it was recognized that certain traditional irregularities had been long condoned by considerations of prosody, apart from the fact that the British working class, itself a development out of the Anglo-Saxon serf class, accepts the patterns of vowel-gradation, characteristically Teutonic, at a deep level, whose genetic, as opposed to cultural, provenance has still to be sufficiently examined. Thus, there seemed no necessity to rationalize *man/men*, *woman/women*, *mouse/mice* etc., into pluralizing patterns on the *cat/cats*, *dog/dogs*, *box/boxes* formula, though, in later developments, there may be some attempt to make such rationalization an optional, and even creditable, feature of Workers' English.

That a considerable economy has been effected in verb conjugation may be seen chiefly in the invariable negative form *ain't*, which serves to negate the present tense of both *to be* and *to have*:

```
He ain't there = He isn't there
He ain't been there = He hasn't been there
```

The preterite of *to be* takes the invariable form *was* (*I was* etc, but also *we was* etc), though the present tense remains, at present, identical with that of the verb in Bourgeois English (BE). In strong verbs, preterite and past participle are usually the same in form – as in *I done it; I ain't done it* – though the choice of form from the two available in BE follows a seemingly arbitrary procedure:

I seen it; I've seen it	(BE past part.)
I done it; I've done it	(BE past part.)
I ate it; I've ate it	(BE pret.)
I swum; I've swum	(BE past part.)
I forgot; he's forgot	(BE pret.)
I wrote; he's wrote	(BE pret.)
I fell; it's fell	(BE pret.)
I drunk it; I've drunk it	(BE past part.)

Considerations of syllabic economy seem to determine the preference for the shorter of the two forms available (*wrote*, not *written*; *forgot*, not *forgotten*), but there is no ready explanation of *seen* for *saw* and *done* for *did* in the demotic tradition embodied in WE. It should be noted also that there has never been, in that tradition, any impulse to level strong verbs under weak forms (*I eat; I eated* etc); the ablaut transformation – as also in certain nouns – is rooted deeply in the language of the workers, and the rational weakening of strong verbs, desirable to the regularizing philologist, would find no acceptance among WE speakers, who would consider such formations as 'childish'.

The verb *get* – not always considered elegant in bourgeois education, so that *rise* has been preferred to *get up* and *enter* to *get in* – is regarded as a useful form in WE and its increased use in verbal phrases may, it is hoped, enable a vast number of verbs to be eliminated from the language. Indeed, it is believed that, with the exception of such verbs as *to be* and *to have*, practically all existing verbs can be replaced by a *get*-phrase. Thus:

    drink = get some drink down
    eat = get grub in your guts
    live = get some living done
    eliminate = get rid (shot) of
    fuck off = get the fuck out of here
    sleep = get your head (swede, loaf) down
    read = get some reading done; get your head into a book; get a bit of
        bookwork into your fat lazy swede, etc.

Admittedly, it may be necessary to employ a verbal noun or gerund in a *get* phrase, but the indicative mood of the great majority of verbs can, in time, be rendered supererogatory.

Pronouns in the demotic English of industrial regions have rarely shown a willingness to imitate the invariables of rural dialects, (*give un to I; he do hate she*, etc.), and only the levelling of the demonstrative adjective *those* under the form of the demonstrative pronoun *them* and the occasional use of *us* for *me* – as in *give us one of them bottles there* – may be adduced as indicative of a need for rationalization in this area. An attempt, in early pedagogic experiments with WE, to replace *she* and *her* with the invariable Lancashire *oo* (from Anglo-Saxon *heo*) was greeted, even in Lancashire industrial towns, with strong resistance.

Before considering the semantics of WE, a word may be said about its phonetics. It is felt that no legislation from the State's philologists is required as regards pronunciation, whose regional variants are accepted as unlikely to impair the unity of WE. Only one traditional BE phoneme has been omitted from the consonantal inventory, this being the aspirate, and the typographical signal of its absence – the apostrophe – is regarded as a regrettable relic of an age when Bourgeois English posed as a standard to which other varieties (rural, industrial and colonial) aspired. The following sentences are considered orthographically correct:

> Enry Erbert Iggins, being ot and in a hurry, ad to ang is at up in the all.
> E's a orrible unk of atefulness.

On the other hand, the aspirate is to be retained as an emphasizer, only initially however, in such statements as, 'I said, eat up my dinner, not heat it up' (the meaning here being diametrically opposed to the meaning conveyed by a speaker of BE when uttering this sentence). This means that the presence of an emphatic aspirate has absolutely no etymological or lexical significance, being a purely prosodic device:

> The law is a hass.
> You're a hugly great hidiot.

Coincidentally, of course, emphatic aspiration may match phonemic usage in BE, but the statement, 'You're horrible,' in WE represents no return to BE pseudo-gentility of utterance. The phoneme *ng* in verbal-noun terminations having been traditionally replaced in demotic, as well as rural genteel, usage by *n*, this usage is now formulated as regular. The fricatives found initially in *thin* and *then* are to be regarded, considering their absence in the phonemic inventories of most metropolitan speakers, as optional in speech, being replaced by *f* and *v* respectively, though the digraph is retained in writing and printing.

We come now to the question of vocabulary and that principle of economy of lexis which, instinctually consulted in traditional demotic, is to be more deliberately and rationally applied to the development of WE as a living and progressive language. Generally speaking, the speaker or writer of WE is expected to possess a trade vocabulary, wherein amplitude and exactness may constitute factors of efficiency and safety (thus, the generic *thing* or *wotsit* or *oojah* or *gadget* will not serve in the designation of parts of a machine which have opposed functions), and a social vocabulary whose elements are of mainly Teutonic origin and serve to denote physical and emotional states and processes. WE is not concerned with the abstractions of philosophy or even science, though, for rhetorical purposes, an arbitrary sub-lexis of polysyllables of Latin or even Greek origin is available, whose lexicographical definition is regarded as otiose. Examples of such terms are *verification, obstropulosity, fornicator, supercodology*:

> I ask you in all bleeding verification whether or not you think it's bloody fair.

> I've had enough of his bloody obstropulosity and I'm bleeding well going to do the bastard.

> That fucking fornicator got his hands in my coat pocket when I'd got my eyes on the dartboard.

> Don't get working on any of that supercodology when I'm around, mate, or you'll get a bunch of fives in the fag-hole.

(Here in deference to the BE reader's habits, traditional orthography is used.)

Generally speaking, statements in WE are expected to be of a tautologous nature, thus fulfilling the essential phatic nature of speech; as modern linguistics teaches us, non-tautologous statements are either lies or meaningless:

> I like a nice pint when I've done my work, because a nice pint's bloody nice, mate.

> The working class is all right, because they're a very nice class of people.

> I love that girl, I can't hardly keep my hands off of her.

> They want to get rid of that new left-half, because he's no bleeding good.

(It will be noticed that qualifiers of emphasis formerly regarded as obscene have full lexical status in WE.)

As an example of the expressive capacities of WE, a rendering of the opening of a well-known speech in Shakespeare's *Hamlet* may here be appended:

> To get on with bloody life or not to, that's what it's all about really. Is it more good to get pains in your fuckin loaf worryin about it or to get stuck into what's getting you worried and get it out of the way and seen off? To snuff it is only like getting your head down, and then you get rid of the lot, anyway that's how we'd like to have it. . . .

The passage from the Declaration of Independence which Orwell regarded as untranslatable into Newspeak yields easily enough to WE, though its meaning is somewhat modified:

> This is true, and there's no arguing the toss over it, that everybody's got the same rights to belong to a union, to live for ever, to do what the hell he wants to do, and watch TV, get drunk, sleep with a woman, and smoke. It's the job of governments to let the unions give union members what they want, and if the governments do not do what the unions want, then they have to get kicked out.

Epilogue: an interview

Do you really think this is going to happen?

A question to be answered by waiting a few years. It's always foolish to write a fictional prophecy that your readers are very soon going to be able to check. Take it that I merely melodramatize certain tendencies. In Britain, the unions are certainly growing stronger and more intolerant. But by the unions I probably merely mean the more belligerent union leaders. I leave out of account too, as Orwell did more spectacularly, the good sense and humanity of the average worker.

I'm an American, and it seems to me absurd that the USA could ever become Unhappy Syndicalized America. American society will never be tyrannized by the unions.

Probably not. I was extrapolating certain experiences of my own in the field of American show business. The tyranny of the musicians' union, for instance, on Broadway. It's hard to prophesy the future of the United States. That cacotopia of Sinclair Lewis's, *It Can't Happen Here*, still seems to me to be the most plausible projection, though it was written in the thirties. At least it shows how a tyranny can come about through the American democratic process, with a president American as apple pie, as they say – a kind of cracker-barrel Will Rogers type appealing to the philistine anti-intellectual core of the American electorate. Core? More than the core, the whole fruit except for the thin skin of liberalism. My old pappy used to say: Son, there ain't no good books except the Good Book. Time these long-haired interlettes got their come-uppance, and so on. And so book-burning, shooting of radical schoolmasters, censorship of progressive newspapers. Every repressive act justified out of the Old Testament and excused jokingly in good spittoon style.

I think we're past the naïveté of letting mere novelists do the prophesying. They're fantasists, they don't really examine trends. The futures they present couldn't possibly have their beginnings in the present we know.

True. Novelists have given up writing future fiction. They leave that to the think-tank people. What fantasy-writers like to do nowadays is to imagine a past when history took a turning different from the one it did take, and then create an alternative present based on that past. Keith Robert's *Pavane*, for example, and Kingsley Amis's *The Alteration* both posit that the Christian Reformation never got to the Anglo-Saxons, with the result in both of the killing of the empirical spirit, which means the death of science. And so a modern world without electricity and a powerful theocracy ruling it from Rome. Amusing, stimulating, but a time-game. Prophecy is no longer the province of the fictional imagination, as I say, as you say. The question is: are the futurologists of MIT and elsewhere doing the prophetic job any better?

It's not a question of prophecy. Professor Toffler tells us that the future's already here, in the sense that a technology and a way of life are being imposed on us that belong neither to the past nor the present. A lot of people, he says, are in a state of shock at what they regard as things alien to the present. When your thinking and feeling and, above all, your nervous system reject certain innovations, then the future's arrived and what you have to do is to catch up with it. The symptoms of rejection are hysteria or apathy or both. People drug themselves out of the present which is really the future, or else exile themselves into pre-industrial cultures. Violence, madness, neuroses of all kinds abound. We don't define the future in temporal terms, but in terms of the new stimulus that overstimulates to dementia. The future's a solid body we've never seen before — something dumped on the shore for the wary natives to sniff at and run away from. Then they come back, see what it is, accept. The future has become the present. Then we await the next new solid bodies, with the inevitable syndrome of temporary rejection.

But what we fear from the future is not new solid bodies but war and tyranny.

Which function by means of solid bodies. Is there going to be a tyranny in the United States — not a tyranny of the syndicates, like the British one, but a good old-fashioned Orwellian Big Brother?

If it happens, it will happen through war.

Is there going to be a war – not the little contained wars of which we have, on average, two a year, but a really big Second-World-War-type war?

Your compatriots Doctors Kahn and Wiener, of that Hudson Institute which was looking after the year 2000 for us, give us a table which shows how limited and total wars tend to form into a time pattern. An alternation of eras devoted to the two kinds of war, like this:

1000–1550 limited war – feudal, dynastic
1550–1648 total war – religious
1648–1789 limited war – colonial, dynastic
1789–1815 total war – revolutionary nationalist
1815–1914 limited war – colonial, commercial
1914–1945 total war – nationalist, ideological

And since 1945 we've had thirty-odd years of limited wars conducted for various, often spurious, reasons – territorial, anticolonial, ideological, what you will. If history really follows a pattern of alternation, we can't have an indefinite period of limited wars. We have to break out on a world scale once more sometime. Consider that thirty years is the longest period the modern world has had without a global war. Perhaps our economic troubles, the inexplicable yoking of recession and inflation for instance, stem from the fact that we don't know how to run a peace economy. War economy is different—we have precedents. I've dreamed of a Malthusian world war conducted with conventional weapons—one that can only break out when the world's planners realize that the global food supply is not going to feed the global population. Instead of famine and riot we have a pretence of nationalist war whose true aim is to kill off millions, or billions, of the world's population. I even wrote a book in which Enspun fights Chinspun –

What are those, for God's sake?

The English Speaking Union and the Chinese Speaking Union. The third great power is Ruspun, and you know what that is. Actually, the war is made up of local extermination sessions called battles, in which men fight women.

A real sex war. And then the cadavers are carted off to be processed into canned food. The recent bout of enforced cannibalism in the Andes proves that human flesh is both edible and nourishing, despite the new dietetic taboos which condemn it as so much poison. The processed human flesh is sold in supermarkets and called Munch or Mensch or something. People will eat anything these days.

Seriously, though.

In a way I was, am, being serious. That kind of war would be a just war and a useful one. But the world will have to wait till the year 3000 to see it. As for the new world war that's waiting in the womb of time, a healthily developed foetus, who can say what will spark it, how destructive it will be? We've already played at this war in film and fiction, indicating that there's a part of us that desperately wants it. What nonsense writers and film-makers talk when they say that their terrible visions are meant as a warning. Warning nothing. It's sheer wish fulfilment. War, somebody said, is a culture pattern. It's a legitimate mode of cultural transmission, though the culture transmitted is usually not the one we expect –

How?

To take a trivial example, popular Latin American song and dance flooded North America and Europe in the forties and after because of the need of the United States to make Latin America a 'good neighbour' – we know how much sympathy for the Nazis there was in the Argentine, for instance. This meant that we all had to see *The Three Caballeros* and Carmen Miranda, dance congas and sambas, sing *Brazil* and *Boa Noite*. To be less trivial, Americanization of both Japan and Germany could best come about by defeating them and confining their post-war industrial production to pacific commodities. Soviet Russia transmitted her brand of Marxist control to Eastern Europe. War is the speediest way of transmitting a culture, just as meat-eating is the speediest way of ingesting protein. It used to be possible to see war as an economic mode of exogamy on a large scale – transmit your seed and produce lively new mixes, avoid the weary incest of perpetual endogamy which is the dull fruit of peace. The greatest war picture of all depicts the Rape of the Sabines. War uses international politics as a mere pretext for fulfilling a deep need in man, which he's scared of admitting because he doesn't like to relate the enhancement of life to the meting out of death.

The Third World War?

It could start anywhere. It will pose as an ideological war. It will use conventional weapons. It will end in a truce with a million men and women dead but the great cities untouched. Flesh is cheap and is growing cheaper all the time. Great cities contain valuable artefacts, which cost dear and had better not be bombed. Computers for example. We've read so many scenarios about the next war; you don't want another. What interests me is how a species of totalitarianism could come about in the United States through uneasiness about the enemy at the gates. A communist revolution in Mexico, helped by the Chinese, might set America dithering, looking for spies, deploying her immense cybernetic and electronic resources to keep citizens under surveillance. The enhanced power of the presidency, the temporary dissolution of Congress. Censorship. Dissident voices silenced. And all in the name of security. No war is necessary, only the threat of war and, in good Orwellian style, the notion of an enemy, actual or potential, can be the device for justifying tyranny. Orwell was right there. War is the necessary background to State repression. War as a landscape or weather or wallpaper. The causes don't matter, the enemy can be anybody. When we think of a future world war, we get quickly bored with working out the causative details, since these could literally be anything. India drops a bomb on Pakistan. An East German coup breaks down the Berlin Wall. Canada resents American capital and American military installations and tells the US to get the hell out. You remember how H. G. Wells made the Second World War start? He wrote a book in the middle thirties called *The Shape of Things to Come*, a history of the future and mostly, as it had to be, absurd. But he had the war start in 1940 on the Polish Corridor, which was astonishingly accurate. A Polish Jew is eating a hazelnut, and a bit lodges in a back hollow tooth. He tries to get the fragment out with his finger, and a young Nazi interprets the grimace as a jeer at his uniform. He fires a shot. The Jew dies. The war starts. That the causes of war are so vague, that the priming incident is so trivial—don't we have here a proof that we want war for the sake of war?

I was born in 1951, but I had a vivid dream the other night about the First World War. Not about battles. I was in a London restaurant and there was a calendar on the wall showing the month to be February and the year 1918. The place was crowded, and I was sitting drinking tea, very weak tea, at a table where two ladies were talking. They were dressed in the style of the time as I've seen it in films and photographs—the décor of the dream was amazingly accurate. One of the ladies said something like, 'Oh, when will this terrible war be over?' Of course I knew exactly when. I very nearly said: '11 November this year,' but held myself back just in time. That isn't the point of the dream, though. The point is that I felt the period. I could smell the under-arm odour of the ladies, the dust on the floor. The light bulb seemed to belong to that period and no other. When I consider the future, I don't care much about the generalities – the type of government and so on. I want something more existential, the quality of quotidian living – Do you understand me?

I understand you very well. If dreams can't do it for you, novelists and poets ought at least to attempt it. Here we are in this room in this flat in London. The year is 1978. I've worked in this room since 1960, and it hasn't changed much. The desk and chair are the same, also the carpet, which was tattered enough, God knows, when I first laid it down. It should be possible to hang on to this furniture, if not this typewriter, until the year 2000. Unless there's a wholly destructive fire, or unless the town planners pull down this block of flats, there's a sort of guarantee that things in this room will remain as they are. I, of course, may be dead, but these dead things will outlive me. So, you see, we're already in the future. We leave this room and go into other rooms. How much else will be the same? The television set, I'm pretty sure, will have been replaced many times over by 2000.

I saw a photograph of President Carter and his First Lady watching television. They were looking at three programmes at the same time. It struck me that that would be the pattern of future viewing. In the United States, certainly with so many channels, it seems a pity to confine yourself to one. We'll learn the gift of multiple viewing. And listening. This will be a definitive change in our modality of response to a stimulus –

But there'll be no change in our assumption that the domestic TV screen will be the chief source of entertainment and information. The death of big-screen cinema, and the substitution of big-screen television. More and more newspapers closing down. Stereoscopic vision? Expensive, for a long time. That's going to be the trouble with a great number of innovations – price. I don't see money going very far. I don't see a real grip on inflation, even by the end of the century. Unless a new Maynard Keynes comes along. I think that governments are going to make the price of drink and tobacco prohibitive, to save us from ourselves, but that they're going to permit the free sale of harmless stimulants and depressants. Something like Aldous Huxley's soma –

What do you see on your wide screen?

Old movies. Two or three at a time, as you suggest – why not? *Casablanca* and *Emile Zola* and something silent, like Fritz Lang's *Metropolis*. New movies lacking in overt violence, but candid as to the sexual act, which will be presented to the limit. Arguments in the press, and on talk shows, about the difference between the erotic and the pornographic. Also news. Industrial unrest, inflation, pump-priming (that means our total war may be coming). Kidnapping and skyjacking by dissident groups. Micro-bombs of immense destructiveness placed in public buildings. More thorough frisking at airports and at cinema entrances and on railroad stations – indeed, everywhere: restrictions on human dignity in the name of human safety. New oil strikes, but the bulk of the oil in the hands of the Arabs. More and more Islamic propaganda. Islamic religion taught in schools as a condition for getting oil. The work of finding a fuel substitute goes on. Gasoline very expensive. Jet travel on super Concordes, swift but damnably expensive. Life mostly work and television.

And outside the house where you sit watching it?

Old buildings coming down, more and more high-rises. All cities looking the same, though lacking the raffish glamour of old Manhattan. Not many people in the streets at night, what with uncontrollable violence from the young. Women in trousers and men in kilts – not all, of course. Yves St Laurent makes kilts cheap and popular, arguing that men are not anatomically fitted for pants, though women are.

And what will 2000 smell and taste like?

The air *has* to be cleaner. It's a sign of grace on the part of America that America is aware of pollution, whereas so much of Europe, Italy for instance, pollutes without knowing or caring. England got a terrible shock in 1951, when smog killed off not only human bronchitics but prize exhibits at the Smithfield Cattle Show – cows and bulls worth far more than mere human beings. This mustn't happen again, so London was made into a smokeless zone. London air is breathable now, which it wasn't in the time of Dickens, and fish are returning to the Thames. When we're shocked sufficiently, then we're prepared to act. The air of the future will smell of nothing. Alas, food will increasingly taste of nothing, except additives. The steady decline of the taste of food, which I've marked since boyhood (I *remember* what the food of the twenties tasted like), goes on. The human body will become a better-cared-for instrument, but it will be less dedicated to pleasure than the syphilitic body of the Renaissance. Even the pleasure of sex has diminished, since there's so much of it available. Sex to me, as a young man, was unattainable caviar. Now it's hamburger steak and children of ten are allowed to eat it. The permissive age will last through 2000, and films and magazines will work hard at devising new variations on the basic copulatory theme. There's a limit, I should think. There's a law of diminishing returns. Abortion will be cheap and easy. A gloriously apt correlation between the disposability of the foetus and the availability of sex, since both proclaim the cheapness of human flesh.

Religion?

The Christian ecumenical movement will have reached its limit, meaning that Catholicism will have turned into Protestantism and Protestantism into agnosticism. The young will still be after the bizarre and mystical, with new cults and impossible Moon-type leaders. But Islam will not have lost any of its rigour. G. K. Chesterton published a novel called *The Flying Inn* at the beginning of this century, in which he fantastically depicted an England flying the star and crescent, with drink forbidden and two men and a dog rolling a barrel of rum round the roads, in constant danger from the Muslim police, trying to keep the memory of liquor alive. I see a distinct possibility of the fulfilment of the vision, say about 2100. Supernature abhors a supervacuum. With the death of institutional Christianity will come the spread of Islam.

I'd say that universal communism is a greater likelihood.

Isn't the term communism a vague verbal counter, all overtones and no fundamental note, in the minds of most Americans? History may, not much later than 2000, prove that the Marxist sequence was wrong. He thought revolution would come in the highly industrialized countries, with the workers turning against the capitalist oppressor. The answer to capitalist oppression has been syndicalism, not revolution. Revolution comes about in the underdeveloped countries, and it may be that the historical sequence is poverty, communism, capitalism. Take your choice of tyrannies – you're free to. I prefer the mild tyranny of the consumer philosophy. The underdeveloped nations have no choice. Communism is what happens to Lower Slobovia, not the United States.

Orwell says that Newspeak is fundamental to Ingsoc, that Newspeak in a sense is Ingsoc. Isn't it possible that the way language is developing, or deteriorating, we're preparing our minds for an incapacity to make rational choices, leaving them empty to be filled by some dictatorial philosophy?

There's a huge fissure in language. On the one hand, you have the rigidities of science and technology, where terms or words or symbols mean precisely what they say, on the other you have increasing vagueness, an oscillation between total inarticulacy and polysyllabic high-sounding gibberish. In American English you have a distressingly schizoid yoking of slang and jargon, like, 'Right, now let's zero in on the nitty-gritty of the implied parameters of the ontological, shit what's the word, right, yah, constatation.' I notice a tendency to pure verbalization, especially in public utterances, which we always expect to be lying or evasive. I mean, a statement can *sound* as if it had a meaning, so long as there's a coherent syntactical structure. The words have just got to be organized into a pattern of some kind, but it doesn't matter what the words mean.

Example?

Well, a newsman asks a president or a cabinet minister if there's going to be a war, and the reply is something like, 'There are various parameters of feasibility, all of which merit serious examination in the context of the implications of your question, Joe. The overall pattern of strike capability on both sides of the hypothetical global dichotomy is in process of detailed scrutiny, and the temporal element involved cannot, of course, be yet quantified with any certainty. Does that answer your question, Joe?' And Joe has to say, 'Thank you, sir.' Apart from what we can call the Language of Professional Evasion, there's an increasing tendency in ordinary communication to use technical language which has not been clearly understood. Things like 'a meaningful relationship,' which ought to mean a love affair, and 'you're overreacting,' which probably means: you're being damnably and unneccessary rude. Then there are all the acronyms, which a lot of people use without being able to reconstitute into the component antilogarithms – God, now I'm doing it. I mean, SALT and MASH and CHAOS.

What's CHAOS?

Council of the Hagiarchy of Anathematists of Onanistic Sex.

What will the English language be like in, say, the year 3000?

As sound? As semantemes and morphemes? Let's consider sound first. Remember there are many forms of English, all with equally respectable ancestries, but it seems that, on both sides of the Atlantic, we're accepting a kind of educated norm – newsreader's English, call it. It's not all that different in London from what it is in New York. New York English is conservative as to its sounds; it's closer to Pilgrim Father English, or Shakespearean English. London English has moved on a bit, bringing in the long *a* of *baaaath*, for example, and making *home* sound like *hèume*. Now, I always say that if Chaucer knew about the inherent instability of long vowels, he'd be able, in 1400, to predict what speech would be like in 2000. He'd know, for instance, that *mouse*, which he pronounced like the French *mousse*, would end up like the German *Maus*. What I mean is, it's possible to make rough prophecies about phonological change in English. You can't, by the way, necessarily hold change back by fixing language through film and tape and cassette. Spoken language tends to go its own way. I'll make one prediction about vowel sounds in the year 3000 – they'll all tend to move towards the middle of the mouth, approaching the sound we make at the end of *lava* or the beginning of *apart*. Consonants haven't changed much since the year 1000, and I don't think there'll be much change a thousand years ahead, but vowels will sound more and more like each other. *Light* and *loud* will be differentiated mainly by the final consonants. All this must sound frivolous, but you want to get the *feel* of the future –

How about language as meaning?

Have you noticed one curious, and rather endearing, thing about *Nineteen Eighty-Four* – the penchant for rural metaphors or similes that Orwell passes on to his characters? O'Brien talks of taking the child from the mother as we take an egg from the hen. The three superstates are spoken of as leaning on each other to keep each other upright, like three stooks in a hayfield. Winston and Julia have no doubt that the bird they heard singing was a thrush. There's too much country knowledge in this story of the ultimate urban culture. What's happening with our language already, and is going to happen far more, is the steady elimination of rural particularities, so that *elm* and *oak* and *sycamore* will have no very clear meaning, and all trees will be summed up as *tree*. Birds will be *bird*. Flowers will be *flower*. Language will become more and more abstract in its vocabulary, and its speakers will occasionally erupt against this in more and more ingenious obscenities, but obscenities too will be very generic. There'll be a large everyday technical vocabulary to replace the old natural one – words for the parts of a refrigerator, a tape deck and so on. But language will be cut off from its roots in basic physical experience. Language of the brain rather than of the body.

How about words like love, honour, duty, God, fidelity, treason, hate, infamy?

It is going to be extremely difficult, in the absence of a traditional system of moral values, to give words like that any precise meaning. There's a vague emotional connotation attached to each, but little more. It's here that the danger lies. Any dictatorial regime can take hold of these words, exploit the emotional response they excite, but provide its own definitions. 'God is the supreme being. I am the supreme being. Therefore I am God.' Yeah, man, but you ain't, you know, like spiritual. 'What do you mean by spiritual?' You tell me, man. 'With pleasure.'

Koestler says that we can only get rid of national enmities based on international misunderstanding by having a world language. Is that possible?

We already have a world auxiliary – English. It's the

language of commerce and air traffic, for instance. Ogden and Richards made, in the thirties, a reduced form of English, limited to about 850 words, called Basic. The British Government bought the rights to it, and it was in that that Orwell saw the possibility of language clear and simple and orthodox imposed on the people by the State. There can be an agreed imposition of a kind of Basic in all the countries of the world – a second language taught compulsorily in schools. But that can never be allowed to *replace* the first language.

Can governments tell us what words to use and what not to use – as with Newspeak?

They're certainly telling us what words we may *not* use. And it's not the governments so much as the pressure groups working on the governments. I don't doubt that, in Britain, there'll be a Restriction of Language Act. Certain racist terms, like *kike* and *sheeny* and *wog* and *wop* and, most terrible of all, *nigger*, are already taboo, as the four-letter obscenities used to be, and the next step is to make them illegal. The Gay Liberation movement – which ought to be prevented, by law if need be, from limiting a fine old word to a coy, giggly, totally inaccurate and quite arbitrary signification – will demand that terms like *poofter, fag, pansy* and so on be made illegal. Even your bowl of pansies on the dining-room table may be against the law, unless you call them geraniums. And then there are the forces of Women's Liberation, which demand a reorientation of generic pronouns, so that *he* and *his* cannot be used for either sex, and for that matter the generic term *man* – which in German corresponds to the pronoun *one* – must be replaced by some fabricated monstrosity like *manwoman* or, better, *womanman*. The Rights of Womanman. Already *chairman* has become *chairperson*, and there has been a response from accoucheurs, who want *midwife* turned to *midperson*. Now the Women's Lib philologists are probably working on *tallboy, carboy, chessman* and, conceivably, *talisman*. We're moving in the direction of increasing restrictions on speech as well as action, but few of these spring from a Big Brother kind of lust for centralized control. They derive from what, I suppose, must be termed a democratic situation.

We have an anomaly before us, then – pressurizable governments aware of their weakness, and yet increasing loss of liberty?

The governments of the West – and this may apply soon to the governments of the Soviet bloc – are less concerned about political orthodoxy than with people paying their taxes. Fiscal tyranny is not the worst tyranny you can get, but it's nasty enough, and it's going to get worse.

It only applies to people with money, and the great majority of the world's inhabitants earn too little to be taxed. Hadn't we better cease thinking narrowly about the future of the West – whether or not there's going to be more freedom or less – and concentrate on the future of the planet?

It's too much. As Voltaire said, we must cultivate our own Hesperides.

Hesperides?

Gardens of the West. Progress won't come through dilution, everybody being poor together.

Are you pessimistic about man, or manwoman?

Man has survived the first thirty-three years of the Era of the Bomb. He'll survive whatever new horrors are in store for him. He's remarkably ingenious.

And if he doesn't survive?

There remains Life. You remember the words of Lilith at the end of Shaw's *Back to Methuselah*? I do:

> 'Of Life only is there no end; and though of its million starry mansions many are empty and many still unbuilt, and though its vast domain is as yet unbearably desert, my seed shall one day fill it and master its matter to its uttermost confines. And for what may be beyond, the eyesight of Lilith is too short. It is enough that there *is* a beyond.'

That's what I believe in – mind, free mind, trying to understand itself as well as the world without, and to hell with the little men who try to stop free enquiry and the State is all that matters and no one has a right to hear Beethoven while the Third World starves.

You're under arrest.

I beg your pardon?

You're under arrest.

You're joking. Yes, joking. I knew somehow you were joking.

But for a moment you thought I was serious.

Yes, I did. God help me, I did. You think even the right to free speech may be a lulling device of Big Brother? You think he's really watching us? That he'll emerge as the persona of some great industrial combine, an international octopus, just when we least expect him?

We have to be on our guard.

I'll accept that.

Monaco 1978